D1744301

Civil Rights and the Environment in African-American Literature, 1895–1941

Environmental Cultures Series

Series Editors:
Greg Garrard, University of British Columbia, Canada
Richard Kerridge, Bath Spa University

Editorial Board:
Frances Bellarsi, Université Libre de Bruxelles, Belgium
Mandy Bloomfield, Plymouth University, UK
Lily Chen, Shanghai Normal University, China
Christa Grewe-Volpp, University of Mannheim, Germany
Stephanie LeMenager, University of Oregon, USA
Timothy Morton, Rice University, USA
Pablo Mukherjee, University of Warwick, UK

Bloomsbury's *Environmental Cultures* series makes available to students and scholars at all levels the latest cutting-edge research on the diverse ways in which culture has responded to the age of environmental crisis. Publishing ambitious and innovative literary ecocriticism that crosses disciplines, national boundaries, and media, books in the series explore and test the challenges of ecocriticism to conventional forms of cultural study.

Titles available:
Bodies of Water, Astrida Neimanis
Cities and Wetlands, Rod Giblett
Climate Crisis and the 21st-Century British Novel, Astrid Bracke
Ecocriticism and Italy, Serenella Iovino
Literature as Cultural Ecology, Hubert Zapf
Nerd Ecology, Anthony Lioi
The New Nature Writing, Jos Smith
The New Poetics of Climate Change, Matthew Griffiths
This Contentious Storm, Jennifer Mae Hamilton

Forthcoming Titles:
Colonialism, Culture, Whales, Graham Huggan
Eco-Digital Art, Lisa FitzGerald
Romantic Ecologies in Postcolonial Perspective, Kate Rigby

Civil Rights and the Environment in African-American Literature, 1895–1941

John Claborn

Bloomsbury Academic
An imprint of Bloomsbury Publishing Plc

B L O O M S B U R Y

LONDON · OXFORD · NEW YORK · NEW DELHI · SYDNEY

Bloomsbury Academic

An imprint of Bloomsbury Publishing Plc

50 Bedford Square
London
WC1B 3DP
UK

1385 Broadway
New York
NY 10018
USA

www.bloomsbury.com

BLOOMSBURY and the Diana logo are trademarks of Bloomsbury Publishing Plc

First published 2018

© John Claborn, 2018

John Claborn has asserted his right under the Copyright, Designs and
Patents Act, 1988, to be identified as Author of this work.

All rights reserved. No part of this publication may be reproduced or
transmitted in any form or by any means, electronic or mechanical,
including photocopying, recording, or any information storage or retrieval
system, without prior permission in writing from the publishers.

No responsibility for loss caused to any individual or organization acting on
or refraining from action as a result of the material in this publication can be
accepted by Bloomsbury or the author.

British Library Cataloguing-in-Publication Data
A catalogue record for this book is available from the British Library.

ISBN: HB: 978-1-3500-0942-4
ePDF: 978-1-3500-0944-8
eBook: 978-1-3500-0943-1

Library of Congress Cataloging-in-Publication Data
Names: Claborn, John author.
Title: Civil rights and the environment in African-American literature,
1895–1941 / John Claborn.
Description: London ; New York : Bloomsbury Academic, 2017. |
Series: Environmental cultures ; 11 | Includes bibliographical
references and index.
Identifiers: LCCN 2017024324 | ISBN 9781350009424 (hardback) |
ISBN 9781350009431 (epub)
Subjects: LCSH: American literature–African American authors–History
and criticism. | Ecology in literature. | Environmentalism in literature. |
Civil rights in literature. | American literature–20th century–History
and criticism. | American literature–19th century–History and criticism.
Classification: LCC PS153.N5 C485 2017 | DDC 810.9/896073009041–dc23
LC record available at https://lccn.loc.gov/2017024324

Cover design: Burge Agency
Cover image © Shutterstock

Series: Environmental Cultures

Typeset by Newgen Knowledge Works Pvt. Ltd., Chennai, India.
Printed and bound in Great Britain

To find out more about our authors and books visit www.bloomsbury.com.
Here you will find extracts, author interviews, details of forthcoming events
and the option to sign up for our newsletters.

Contents

Acknowledgments

Many friends, mentors, and fellow travelers have helped turn a dim idea about race and nature into a brighter beam. This book is the product of some off-hand remarks about ecocriticism and African-American literature in William J. Maxwell's spring 2007 graduate seminar. Over the years, this project grew out of my dissertation, "Ecology of the Color Line: Race and Nature in American Literature." Many thanks go to my doctoral committee and especially my codirectors, William J. Maxwell and Michael Rothberg. Michael Rothberg has been generous with his counsel, friendship, and almost superhuman ability to provide timely feedback on all my writing. Both have been reliable and conscientious editors, mentors, and friends. Spencer Schaffner and Stephanie Foote offered invaluable advice and feedback during the process. I also want to thank Debra Hawhee and Mark C. Thompson for their crucial input at the beginning stages of this project.

The Universities of Illinois and Louisville have kept me employed during precarious times. My activist friends in the Graduate Employees' Organization and the Non-Tenured Faculty Coalition: knowing that they were fighting indefatigably to improve working conditions for teachers and scholars in higher education kept me resilient through this project. I also want to thank a number of friends, critics, and coworkers: Michael Burns, Ann Hubert, Marilyn Holguin, Mia McIver, Dave Morris, Christy Scheuer, Nicole Seymour, Michael Simeone, and Katherine Skwarczek. Special thanks go to John Reuland, who has been an intellectual soulmate of sorts since we started a Derrida reading group together in 2005; and also to Christopher Simeone, who has played a vital role in my survival, figuratively and literally.

Greg Garrard, one of the editors of the Environmental Cultures series, has consistently been a supporter of my work. In 2011, I had a debate with Greg in *ISLE* over the value of Heidegger for ecocriticism. Since then, Greg has spotlighted my work in his *YWCCT* review of the *MFS* article version of Chapter 5 and in his edited collection, *The Oxford Handbook of Ecocriticism*.

I am filled with gratitude for Greg's faith in me and his generous spirit. I also want to thank Richard Kerridge, the other editor of the Environmental Cultures series. Four anonymous reviewers for Bloomsbury Academic provided invaluable feedback during the revision process. Anne Raine from the University of Ottawa has also offered a generous critique of Chapter 5.

For support more indirect, I go to my family. For their love and kindness, I thank my stepparents, Bob Engel and Belinda Claborn, as well as my sister and brother-in-law, Jennifer and Matt Holler. I thank my grandparents, Al and Theresa Ferrero, for teaching me the value of education. I thank my father, Tim Claborn, whose intellectual curiosity has always been a model for me. I thank my resilient mother, Alyse Engel, who taught me a love for reading at an early age. This book is dedicated to my parents.

Introduction

In the shadow of 1919's "Red Summer" of nationwide race riots, the president of the National Association for the Advancement of Colored People (NAACP), Walter White, published *Thirty Years of Lynching in the United States* (1919). In Georgia, White reports, a black sharecropper killed a white farmer, sparking a week of white mob violence directed toward black men and women. This form of terrorism—part of what W. E. B. Du Bois dubbed the "lynching industry"—ended with an estimated ten people lynched and pushed about five hundred black southerners to flee the town of Valdosta (White 26–7). When she read White's account of the ritual lynching of a pregnant black woman, Harlem Renaissance poet Anne Spencer[1] wrote "White Things" (1923). This protest poem condenses the histories of slavery, colonialism, and lynching into two stanzas of twenty lines. Its repetition of "things" reinforces the power of a metaphysics of whiteness to turn the world into objects to be dominated:[2]

> Most things are colorful things—the sky, earth, and sea.
>   Black men are most men; but the white are free!
>   White things are rare things; so rare, so rare
>   They stole from out a silvered world—somewhere.
>   Finding earth-plains fair plains, save greenly grassed,   5
>   They strewed white feathers of cowardice, as they passed;
>   The golden stars with lances fine,
>   The hills all red and darkened pine,
>   They blanched with their wand of power;
>   And turned the blood in a ruby rose   10
>   To a poor white poppy-flower.

This stanza plays on inversions and reversals. The opening lines identify nature with a multitudinous sea of colors. Nature is integrated color, and white instead of black is *absence* of color. Spencer also displays her pan-African sensibility, as she provocatively casts people of color in the *majority* of the world's population, while whites are the "so rare, so rare" minority. Rare suggests both the sense of rarity as in few *and* the sense of rarity as distilled, rarefied material that has lost all attributes and all color. Descending from what is probably the cold climate of northern Europe—the "silvered world"—they conquer the natural resources and enslave the human labor of Africa and the Americas. "Silvered" also suggests the invention of silver currencies that helped beget the market processes of abstraction and dehumanization. They scorch the earth, bleaching and blanching the color out of the "hills all red," the land "greenly grassed," and the pines "darkened." White imperialism seeks to wipe the world of all color, of all racial difference. The pagan and phallic "wand of power" suggests advanced weaponry and technology—tools that "white things" use to conquer.

So far, Spencer retells with a wink the "Aryan" myth of whiteness—of the white race as an ancient race, as eternal as human civilization. But as Du Bois wrote in "The Souls of White Folk," whiteness is a "modern discovery," an invention of the nineteenth century. The Aryan myth of the first stanza is a modern confabulation. The second and final stanza of "White Things" slingshots around this myth by moving to more historical and geographical specificity. Now taking place during the historical moment of the Jim Crow South, the poem paints ritual lynching as a sinister dance of death:

> They pyred a race of black, black men,
> And burned them to ashen white; then,
> Laughing, a young one claimed a skull,
> For the skull of a black is white, not dull,   15
>   But a glistening awful thing
>   Made, it seems, for this ghoul to swing
> In the face of God with all his might,
> And swear by the hell that sired him:
>   "Man-maker, make white!"   20

While the poem ends by narrowing its scope to a specific time and region, it still emphasizes the large scale of black masses; an entire race, and not just a single black body, is "pyred" (l. 12). Both the white perpetrator and the black victim are dehumanized through this oxidation of the black body rarefied as whiteness, a white skeleton. The white kid is a "young one," nameless, and the victim merely a "skull," a white thing of death (l. 14). Both are further dehumanized when the skull become as "awful thing" and the white youth is a "ghoul" (l. 17). Turning the white supremacist Christian beliefs of the Ku Klux Klan on their heads, the speaker states that "hell" rather than heaven "sired" the white boy in a way that further animalizes whiteness. In the poem's Promethean final line, the white will to dominate becomes so consumed with hubris that it satanically barks orders at God—the "Man-maker"—to change the world white.

What makes "White Things" so rich for an understanding of civil rights and the environment is its movement from the universal to the particular, or the mythic to the historic: the "Aryan" mythology of the opening lines culminate in a concrete historical event: the lynching of southern African-Americans and in this particular case, Mary Turner. The insatiable white will to explore and exploit is also a will to death. Spencer may have also been influenced by Du Bois's "The Souls of White Folk" essay in *Darkwater*, where he associates whiteness with empire, writing sarcastically that "whiteness is the ownership of the earth forever and ever, Amen!" (1920: 22). The poem also moves from the white will to explore, exploit, and dominate, to the death drive, hinting at a psychology of whiteness. Freud published *Beyond the Pleasure Principle* in 1920, where he hypothesized that the death drive and the will to dominate are intertwined in the human organism's wish "to die only in its own fashion" (47). In Spencer's poem, the destructive impulse of whiteness recoils on itself, becomes self-destructive in its satanic rebellion against "colorful things" and creation. White European imperialism, or the will to master the world, is in the end only a master of death.

When Du Bois famously prophesized in *The Souls of Black Folk* that the "problem of the Twentieth Century is the problem of the color-line," he meant the problem of white domination of the world, of all the "colorful things" human and nonhuman to be exploited (1903: 3). By the 1920s, we can imagine Du Bois emphasizing the ecological dimension of the color-line problem. The 1920s were a theater of environmental catastrophes that especially affected southern black folk: the 1926 and 1928 Florida hurricanes, the boll weevil epidemic, the 1927 flood, and the expansion of industrialization in places such as coal-rich western Pennsylvania. Given these events, it must have become clear to Du Bois that intertwined racial and ecological crises were emerging problems of the twentieth century. In Du Boisian spirit, three questions motivate this project:

- In what ways do these two problems—the color line and environments— intersect in the era of Jim Crow and conservation?[3]
- What kinds of tropes and modes of representation did African-American writers develop in response to environmental events and crises? How did they develop these in relation to discourses of mainstream environmentalism and scientific ecology?
- What does this attention to environments tell us about the literature and politics of the civil rights movement during the Jim Crow era?

In pursuit of these questions, this book explores how the color line and the ecological line—the line that runs between humans and their environment— parallel, intersect, and veer apart by soldering African-American writing to the histories of the environment (especially the Southern environment), the conservation movement, and the rise of scientific ecology. *Civil Rights and the Environment* contributes to our understanding of how the politics of civil rights and the environment converged in the black literary imagination. "White Things" offers only one such example of this convergence.

Throughout *Civil Rights and the Environment*, I have avoided imposing an artificial unity on this literary history of civil rights and the environment—to not draw a straight line from a past black environmental imagination to the present's environmental justice movement. I have also avoided simply translating problematics in the African-American tradition (e.g., the racial uplift debates) into an ecocritical idiom. Since black intellectuals and writers in the early twentieth century were not centrally concerned with developing views on environmental causes such as wilderness preservation, their engagements with environment, ecology, and nature were focalized through civil rights. As a result, their engagements were more indirect and informal, and thus politically and aesthetically *plural* than the relatively coherent views within the early civil rights movement. This pluralism is why looking at civil rights and environment together does not yield a straightforward narrative arc.

This necessarily fragmented narrative notwithstanding, *Civil Rights and the Environment* reimagines many literary genres and critical disputes traditionally focalized through problematics of race and politics: the Washington–Du Bois debates on racial uplift, New Negro aesthetics, the Great Migration narrative, and black political radicalism. It further challenges the tendency to treat immediate and long-term ecological crisis as an equal-opportunity force when, in fact, it is unequal in its wreck and ruin. The writings of black intellectuals such as Washington and Du Bois offer a way of understanding the role of *difference* in the experience of ecological degradation. Intersecting racial and ecological problems erupted along the color line—and these problems form a hitherto unrecognized and yet constitutive element of our thinking about race, culture, and politics in twentieth-century America. The following sections outline the argument and methods of *Civil Rights and the Environment*.

Toward an African-American Ecocriticism

There are two limitations in the existing work of ecocritical and African-Americanist scholars that I want to redress in this book. The first is a tendency to reduce nature and environments in African-American literature to rhetorical tropes and figurations. For example, Melvin K. Dixon's *Ride Out the Wilderness: Geography and Identity in Afro-American Literature* treats nature and environment as signifying processes without much material and historical substance of their own (1987). Dixon examines spatial and nature metaphors of mountaintop, wilderness, and underground; these metaphors shape a "topography" for an African-American quest for selfhood; they invent "alternative landscapes where black culture can flourish apart from any marginal, prescribed 'place'" (1987: 2). Likewise, foundational texts in African-American literary theory such as Henry Louis Gates's *The Signifying Monkey* maintain a poststructuralist distance from "nature" or "environment" as categories (1988). Gates identifies and elaborates various patterns of "tropological revision" in the black vernacular tradition: the speakerly text, the talking book, and Signifyin(g) in general (1988: xxv). However, he does offer a glimpse of theoretical and historical points of contact between the environmental and the literary. Gates's study reflects a concern with the world as text, with the intertextuality of all texts, and an understanding of "reality" as a discursive construct. While Gates's analysis of animal metaphors and swamp tropes do fall within the purview of ecocriticism, they are discussed purely as processes of signification. In both Dixon and Gates, there is no concern with natural environments as such.

Similarly, Barbara Foley's *Spectres of 1919: Class and Nation in the Making of the New Negro* analyzes the prevalence of metaphors of rootedness, soil, and trees in the writing of the Harlem Renaissance (2003). Foley argues for the importance of 1919 as a year that marked turbulence in the United States and unleashed revolutionary energies. Much of this energy manifested itself in the race riots that tore asunder many American cities. Similar to Gates in the *Signifying Monkey*, Foley is "centrally concerned with questions of discourse and trope"—questions that encompass the social (but not environmental) history of these tropes during this period. The various nature tropes in New Negro writing, or "organic tropes" as Foley calls them, buttress a strategy of "metonymic nationalism," in which black intellectuals and artists of the New Negro aesthetic sought to deploy their status as a "black nation" as representative of the *American* nation (2003: 160). This strategy failed, Foley argues, because these organic tropes ended up reinforcing the racial essentialism of white supremacy that African-Americans tried to counteract (2003: 162). The "hyper-materiality of the organic trope," Foley argues, "functions metonymically to naturalize identity as a function of place, thereby largely occluding both historical and structural understandings of the 'roots' of racism" (2003: 237). In contrast, *Civil Rights and the Environment* reframes the use of organic tropes in this period by looking at them not merely as tropes for a black nationalism, but as evidence of black writers engaging, critiquing, and appropriating the politics and rhetoric of the conservation movement and scientific ecology.

Many ecocritics engaging with minority literatures have rejected this reduction to representation already, which brings me to the second limitation in the scholarship. Because of the violent histories of slavery and racism, African-American writing often expresses a traumatic and tragic relation to the natural environment—and this tragic relation has been overemphasized by ecocritics at the expense of more positive valuations of nature in African-American literature. Paul Outka's *Race and Nature from Transcendentalism to the Harlem Renaissance* exemplifies this tendency (2008). Outka formulates his study of the race–nature nexus in a colorful chiasmus: "by trying to see green in black and white, we might eventually come to see black and white in green" (9). Outka succeeds in theorizing the interconnection of race and nature by arguing that, where conventional (white) nature writing experiences sublimity, African-American writing registers trauma. Outka's white sublime / black trauma narrative, however, can be complicated with attention to cases where African-American writers do experience and represent the natural sublime. For example, this book's readings of Washington's *Working with the Hands*, Du Bois's "Criteria of Negro Art," and Effie Lee Newsome's poems published in *The Crisis* reveal more positive relations between African-Americans and the natural environment.[4]

Another problem with the tragic view is that it can potentially impose normative judgments about the "right" kind of relation one should have to nature. Kimberly K. Smith's *African American Environmental Thought: Foundations* sketches out a genealogy of the environmental justice movement that emphasizes mostly negative relations African-Americans have to nature (2007). She tells the story of how black intellectuals and writers positioned themselves in relation to the environment, from southern black folk culture arising out of plantation life to the Harlem Renaissance of the 1920s. Throughout her book, Smith uncovers traditions of black agrarianism as well as African-American challenges to scientific racism, environmental determinism, and primitivism. Even given these positive engagements with nature, however, Smith contends that for "black writers working in this tradition, America—not just the political community but the physical terrain—is a land cursed by injustice and in need of redemption" (2007: 8). Here, she slips into a normative environmentalist position, claiming that black writers' experiences of racism have "distorted" their relation to the land (2007: 6). Political and economic oppression, she continues, can "impair one's capacity to interact appropriately with the natural world" (2007: 12). In this model, African-American cultural history is measured against environmentalist standards and found wanting, when the critical relation between the two should be dialectical. From the point of view of a Marxian ecology (which I elaborate on soon), all forms of labor are alienated from nature under the capitalist mode of production.

Related to this tragic narrative of African-American engagements with the environment is the tendency to see the black environmental imagination as independent from the histories of white-dominated discourses about conservation and ecology, as Kimberly N. Ruffin does in *Black on Earth: African American Ecoliterary Traditions*. Her book weaves together a tradition of black environmental thought in nineteenth- and twentieth-century literature, focusing on mythic and spiritual understandings of nature. Like Smith, Ruffin argues that African-Americans have been alienated from nature by racial oppression, and that they experience "environmental othering" when restricted from fully accessing nature (2010: 4). Ruffin identifies an "ecological paradox" for African-Americans: they must shoulder the ecological "burden" of naturalized racism, while at the same time cultivating an ecological "beauty" that arises out of resistance to this burden (2010: 2–3). This "ecological burden-and-beauty paradox holds within it the articulation of a wide range of African-American eco-experience in one dynamic story" (2010: 16). Yet this black environmental imagination does not engage with the history of conservation or developments in scientific ecology; it exists as its own tradition, seemingly in a parallel universe. Contrary to my emphasis on environmental history, Ruffin speaks of a unified and ahistorical black ecoliterary imagination.

Environmental History, Environmental Justice, and Eco-historicism

The tension between Smith and Ruffin is a symptom of the disciplinary tension between environmental history and ecocriticism. For the ecocritic, Smith's account of African-American environmental history could benefit from close textual analysis of African-American writing. For the environmental historian, Ruffin's close readings of various cultural texts could benefit from a richer account of historical context. This tension between history and aesthetics (or, for literary critics, close textual analysis) is also there in the distance between African-American literary criticism and ecocriticism. Foley, for example, employs a Marxist historicism in *Specters of 1919*, in which African-American literary production of the early 1920s reflect the racialized class struggle and revolutionary fervor of those years. Just as a merger between environmental history and ecocriticism would be fruitful, so too would a synthesis of African-American literary criticism's historicist emphasis with ecocriticism's attention to ecological aesthetics and the environmental imagination.

This tension between history and close textual analysis has in many ways started to become reconciled through environmental justice criticism, which is inspired by the environmental justice movement. This movement originated in the South and has given ecocritics race-conscious ways of reading environmental literature. The South is where, according to sociologist and activist Robert D. Bullard, "marked ecological disparities exist between black and white communities" (1990: 14). Environmental justice grew out of protests organized by civil rights leaders against the high distribution of pollution and waste in traditionally low-income areas populated by people of color. The governments and industries responsible target disempowered communities in instances of what activists call "environmental racism" (McGurty 1997: 302). Environmental racism and discrimination refers to the "disparate treatment of a group or community based on race, class, or some other distinguishing characteristic" (Bullard 1990: 7).

It has thus become axiomatic among environmental justice critics that early US environmentalist movements were not always friendly to nonwhites. The environmental justice movement has also accused mainstream environmental organizations such as the Sierra Club and Audubon Society of indifference to problems facing the urban poor, while showing an elitist concern for wilderness preservation and the national parks—spaces difficult for inner-city, low-income African-Americans to access. The national parks also played a role in the postbellum wars against Native Americans: when Yellowstone National Park was established in 1872, the region's Native American inhabitants were forcibly removed by the US Army. Some early-twentieth-century conservationists—and even progressives such as Theodore Roosevelt—had sympathies for white supremacy and subscribed to scientific racism. The movement's—and the criticism it influences—historical recontextualization of environmentalism is invaluable to an ecocritical approach to African-American literature.

With its attention to historical recontextualization and close textual analysis, environmental justice criticism offers common ground for environmental history and ecocriticism. In an overview of the environmental humanities field, Bergthaller et al. claim that "environmental justice has acted, and continues to act, as a unifying principle for the two fields as multidisciplinary intellectual projects" (2014: 271). Such a multidisciplinary synthesis has been dubbed "eco-historicism" by scholars in the environmental humanities. Gillen Wood defines eco-historicist methodology as the reclamation of "historicist practice for the environmental critic, but with an emphasis on archive-rich historical reconstruction and discourse analysis" (2011: 527). In the context of *Civil Rights and the Environment*, the boll weevil epidemic or the industrial environment of western Pennsylvania in the early-twentieth century provide two such examples of a historical episode of ecological significance that I reconstruct. Eco-historicism is also multidisciplinary, stirring a callaloo of literary and cultural criticism and history with environmental history and related environmental sciences. Environmental humanities scholars such as Carolyn Finney, influenced by environmental justice criticism, have shown a greater attention to cultural texts and aesthetics. In her *Black Faces, White Spaces: Reimagining the Relationship of African Americans to the Great Outdoors* (2014), Finney's eco-historicist approach draws on multiple disciplines: environmental history, environmental science, ecocriticism, cultural studies, and geography.

Eco-historicism is an especially apt—and I would argue, essential—method for ecocritics' interpretations of African-American literature. For African-American writers, people are essentially historical creatures. Poets such as Langston Hughes, Claude McKay, and Anne Spencer try to come to terms with the traumas of slavery and Jim Crow. Others tried to invent a past, to create new myths for African-Americans. In "White Man's Guilt," James Baldwin describes white America's repression of its enslaving and genocidal past; trapped by that past, white Americans can never understand their need for hate and violence. Malcolm X's name stood for a lost past. In *The Fire Next Time*, Baldwin writes about the need for African- Americans to accept and overcome their past, to turn it into something useful so that they can face the future. History haunts all African-American writing, and no interpretation, including ecocritical interpretations, can ignore the call to historicize.

In the spirit of environmental justice criticism and recent articulations of eco-historicism, *Civil Rights and the Environment* employs an eco-historical method in each chapter. The interdisciplinary dimension of eco-historicism is reflected, for example, in my readings of Booker T. Washington's *Working with the Hands* (1904) and Zora Neale Hurston's *Their Eyes Were Watching God* (1937). These texts are historicized within not only just their sociocultural context, but also the slow time of environmental history; each text is treated as the discursive terrain on which two intertwining histories play out. For example, Booker T. Washington's 1895 Atlanta Exposition address, *Up from Slavery* (1901), and *Working with the Hands* (1904) display a regionalist's love for the southern environment, while also criticizing the cotton monocultures and sharecropping economy that depleted the soil, exacerbated plagues such as the boll weevil, and prevented subsistence farming. William Attaway's 1941 Great Migration novel *Blood on the Forge* portrays the plight of sharecroppers in Kentucky and steel mill workers in western Pennsylvania.

Through a series of eco-historical readings, I want to show that an emergent sense of environmental justice was there from the beginning of the civil rights movement after the failure of Reconstruction in 1877 (the year the last federal troops withdrew from former Confederate states). From Du Bois's concept of "double environments," to Hurston's writing about swamps, to *The Crisis* giving voice to conservationist concerns, civil rights has always already been environmental. This history matters not only because it complicates the history of civil rights and environmentalism, but also because it articulates the full, interconnected scope of civil rights and environmental struggles today.

Marxian Ecology and Intersectional Ecocriticism

In *Civil Rights and the Environment*, I supplement this eco-historical method with a Marxian and intersectional understanding of ecology and environments. I accept the Marxian-ecological critique of capitalism developed by such thinkers as Cedric Robinson, Gayatri Spivak, Lance Newman, Chris Williams, and John Bellamy Foster. A Marxian ecology places emphasis on the "natural"—the ecological and ontological—dimension of Marx's materialism, or what Kenneth Burke calls the "*total* economy of the planet" (1937: 157). An ecological rereading of Marx demonstrates that *Capital* does not elaborate a labor theory of value, but rather critiques Adam Smith's and David Ricardo's labor theories of value for *not being materialist enough*.

Though the terms were not readily available to him, Marx hints at some-thing like an ecological theory of value ("ecology" was coined in 1866 by Marx's contemporary, biologist Ernst Haeckel). In a key passage from *Capital* volume one, Marx speaks directly to the context of agriculture in the United States and describes capitalist forms of ecological violence:

> [Capitalist production] disturbs the metabolic interaction between man and the earth, i.e. it prevents the return to the soil of its constituent ele-ments consumed by man in the form of food and clothing; hence it hinders the operation of the eternal natural condition for the lasting fertility of the soil ... [A]ll progress in capitalist agriculture is a progress in the art, not only of robbing the worker, but of robbing the soil; all progress in increasing the fertility of the soil for a given time is a progress towards ruining the more long-lasting sources of that fertility. The more a country proceeds from large-scale industry as the background of its development, as in the case of the United States, the more rapid is this process of destruction. Capitalist production, therefore, only develops the techniques and the degree of com-bination of the social process of production by simultaneously undermining the original sources of all wealth—the soil and the worker. (1867: 637–8)

In theorizing the dual capitalist exploitation of the worker and the earth, Marx reveals their solidarity as the "original sources of all wealth," as produc-tive forces stifled by a metabolic rift. This rift cuts off the circulation of regen-erative material flows—the products of consumption—back into nature and relegates them to mere waste. In *Marx's Ecology*, Foster recuperates Marx's use of the concept of "metabolism" to express the material exchange between humans and nature (2000). Foster claims that Marx understands labor meta-bolically, as, in Marx's words, "a process between man and nature, a process by which man, through his own actions, mediates, regulates and controls the metabolism between himself and nature" (1867: 283).

Capitalism has a material limit: the total economy of the planet's ecosys-tems. All value ultimately derives from these ecosystems, including human labor-power, which relies on metabolic cycles to fuel it and survive.[5] Marxian critiques differ from other forms of environmental critique such as deep ecology because they recognize that systemic social and economic change is necessary to overcome the global ecological crisis; they refuse the ideology of half-measures such as "sustainable growth" that preserve capitalism. An eco-Marxism would uncover the homology between human and ecological exploitation, or as Newman puts it: the "same forces that generate exploitation and oppression, generate ecological damage" (2002: 21).

A Marxian ecology sees climate change primarily as a product of the capitalist mode of production and its constant need to expand, produce, and consume. The "Anthropocene" is too general; the "Capitalocene" is more befitting. While humans throughout their history have had environmental impacts, it took the capitalist mode of production to bring about ozone depletion, global warming, ocean acidification, deforestation, and human-made earthquakes (to name a few exemplars of the Capitalocene). A Marxian eco-historicism shares an affinity with Marxist historicism. While Marxist historicism may see history as the unfolding of capitalism and class struggle, a Marxian eco-historicism sees history through the zoetrope of the Capitalocene.

Examples abound of how Marxian ecology can reanimate the importance of ecology for African-American literary history. A Marxian view does not automatically have to see mystification and ideology when the problem of "nature" arises. Slavery and the exploitation of natural resources were central to the development of capitalism in its early stage of "primitive accumulation" (see *Capital* vol. 1). In his *Black Marxism* (discussed in greater detail in Chapter 1), Robinson incorporates the role of nature in his intersectional analysis of race and class, and his genealogy of the black radical tradition ([1983] 2000).[6] Swampy and wild terrains become relevant in Robinson's accounts of black resistance to slavery in the forms of marronage and agrarian rebellions. "To reconstitute the community," Robinson writes, "Black radicals took to the bush, to the mountains, to the interior" ([1983] 2000: 310). Maroons in the sixteenth and seventeenth centuries fled to the wilderness and formed their own communities, which sometimes became a significant threat to the white plantation system, as in the case of the Haitian Revolution ([1983] 2000: 130). The intersection of race, labor, and environments become particularly pertinent to my analyses of Washington's *Working with the Hands* (Chapter 1), Hurston's *Mules and Men* and *Their Eyes Were Watching God* (Chapter 4), and Attaway's *Blood on the Forge* (Chapter 5).

Intersectional or "integrated" approaches to literature augment my use of Marxian ecology, especially in my readings of Hurston and Attaway. Intersectional analysis has come into ecocriticism via ecofeminism and before that, black feminist criticism. The Combahee River Collective Statement is the source from which most scholars agree that the concept of intersectional or "integrated analysis" originated[7] (1977: 210). The statement focuses on black women's experience vis-à-vis "interlocking" systems of racial, economic, and heteronormative oppression (1977: 210). On the surface, these systems appear unrelated and may at first manifest themselves in black women as disjointed subjectivity, aptly characterized as "feelings of craziness" (1977: 211). But through the recognition of the underlying synthesis of these oppressive systems, identity politics can emerge as a counterforce to "combat the manifold and simultaneous oppressions that all women of color face" (1977: 210). Identity here is not a preexisting essence. Rather, identities are forged out of their historical, structural, and (for the ecocritic) environmental embeddedness. It is when one becomes conscious of these interlocking oppressions that identity becomes a politics.

The challenge for integrated analysis[8] is to go beyond establishing mere correlations among these intermeshed systems of oppression and instead to unearth points of causation, homology, and overdetermination. The premise of overdetermination—that the systematic oppression of historically and environmentally embedded groups and identities has multiple causes and origins—is crucial. At the same time, the goal of integrated analysis is not to treat all categories of analysis equally or to create an artificial totality (e.g., in this book I have placed greater stress on race and environment over gender, class, disability, and other identity categories). There is also the fallacy of totalization: that an analysis can never be "intersectional" (in the misleading sense of "total") enough because it leaves out a category or categories. But this fallacy carries with it the assumption that all categories of analysis are roughly equal. Instead, the overdetermination of interlocking systems of oppression is uneven: the lines of intersection do not form symmetrical angles when it comes to concrete power-structures and situated identities. While intersectional analysis is more complete than atomized analyses of race or class, it also necessarily remains an incomplete striving.[9]

Chapter Outline

Civil Rights and the Environment in African-American Literature, 1895–1941 begins by reframing the Washington–Du Bois rift within the contexts of environmental history and the conservation movement. Chapter 1, "Up from Nature: Racial Uplift and Ecological Agencies in Booker T. Washington's Autobiographies," argues that just as Washington's second autobiography, *Working with the Hands*, is double-voiced to address both white and black readers, so too does it speak within the dual temporalities of the post-Reconstruction New South and the *longue durée* of southern environmental history. This historical parallax reveals the text's covert promotion of eco-logical agencies—forms of resistance akin to that of colonial-era maroon communities—as occurring off the public grid and within the plantation zone. *Working with the Hands* narrates these forms of ecological agencies in two ways: first, by scientifically detailing practices of soil conservation designed to restore sustainability (and profitability) to the soil; and second, by representing the plantation zone as a black-dominated space reconstructed through agricultural labor. By using environmental history to reframe Washington's autobiographies, I reveal these texts to be more visionary than critics have believed.

Chapter 2, "W. E. B. Du Bois at the Grand Canyon: Nature, History, and Race in *Darkwater*," focuses on how Du Bois works with and against the emerging conservation and wilderness preservation movements of the early twentieth century. My reading of *Darkwater*'s chapter "Of Beauty and Death" examines Du Bois's juxtaposition of visits to national parks such as the Grand Canyon with his anecdotes about life under Jim Crow, bringing double con-sciousness to bear on the history of conservation. Through the use of mon-tage and other modernist techniques, he invokes Colonel Charles Young—the highest-ranking black military officer at the time and acting superintendent of Sequoia National Park in 1903—and casts him as the embodiment of the interfused histories of Jim Crow and conservation. For Du Bois, the national parks become an environmental correlative for integration and racial plural-ism, while also being constructs of modernity.

Moving beyond Du Bois and Washington, the next three chapters shift attention to avian, industrial, and swamp ecologies. Chapter 3, "*The Crisis*, the Politics of Nature, and the Harlem Renaissance: Effie Lee Newsome's Eco-poetics," examines Newsome, an overlooked but fascinating Harlem Renaissance poet who wrote scientifically about birds. Newsome wrote on top-ics unusual—even *radical*—for African-Americans at the time: birdwatching, entomology, ethology, and other forms of amateur nature study. I make a broader argument about the NAACP's *The Crisis* and its unexpected engagement with conservation, natural sciences, and other environmental themes, especially during the 1920s Harlem Renaissance. What Barbara Foley would see as a misleading "organic trope"—the yoking of nature imagery to black nationalism—I see as Newsome's and *The Crisis*'s attempt to critique scientific racism and to substitute conservationist politics as a buoyant alternative to and productive escapism from the burdens of the color-line problem.

Connecting the Harlem Renaissance to the 1930s, Chapter 4, "Sawmills and Swamps: Ecological Collectives in Zora Neale Hurston's *Mules and Men* and *Their Eyes Were Watching God*," analyzes representations of swamps in modern African-American literature, particularly in Hurston's ethnographic and fictional figurations. Drawing on work in environmental history, I argue that for Hurston the swamp is not only an ambivalent site of resistance and exploitation, but also a site for imagining multiethnic, interspecies, and ecological collectives. The tales in *Mules and Men* render into comic form the trauma of slavery and Jim Crow along with the southern environment itself, with its floods, boll weevil epidemics, and wild spaces. This ecological collective is even more evident in *Their Eyes Were Watching God*, when Janie and Tea Cake live "down on the muck" of the Florida Everglades with Seminoles and migrant workers. It is only when the hurricane strikes and this collective is invaded by white capitalist forms of forced labor and biopolitical regulation that it is disrupted; racial segregation is restored in the hurricane's aftermath, showing that cycles of environmental inequities complicate Hurston's vision.

"From Black Marxism to Industrial Ecosystem: Racial and Ecological Crisis in William Attaway's *Blood on the Forge*," Chapter 5, helps reimagine the relation of African-American and working-class fiction to ecology. Typically framed as a black Marxist allegory or a Great Migration novel, *Blood on the Forge* complicates and radicalizes both by focalizing them through the ecological problems of the 1930s. The chapter situates the novel alongside a materialist paradigm shift in scientific ecology marked by A. G. Tansley's introduction of the "ecosystem" concept. Attaway refracts the polluted Pittsburgh of 1919 through this shift, in the process linking ecological degradation to racial conflict, sexual violence, and exploitive labor policies. Finally, I argue that the character Smothers anticipates conservationist Aldo

Leopold's "land ethic," though with a black Marxist twist, in ways that echo and signify on the ecological agencies found in Washington's *Working with the Hands*. Through readings of James Baldwin and Ta-Nehisi Coates, the book's Conclusion explores what this convergence of civil rights and environments means for the twenty-first century.

On My Use of Terms: Ecology, Environment, and Nature

In the last two decades, work in ecocriticism, the environmental humanities, and new materialism has led to new theories of nature, ecology, and environment. Following work in philosophy and critical theory that analyzes and questions the concept of nature—Steven Vogel's *Against Nature* (1996), Bruno Latour's *The Politics of Nature* (2004), and Timothy Morton's *Hyperobjects: Philosophy and Ecology after the End of the World* (2013)—this project treats "nature" as a discursive category similar to the way that poststructuralists do. However, this focus on discourse does not mean that nature can be reduced to a mere signifier; this avoidance of reductionism is evident from my extensive use of environmental history.

I use the concept of environment in a general sense to designate built and natural environments. By contrast, my use of "ecology" is more specific and complex. Similar to my understanding of nature, I see ecology—and the sciences that lead to its formation—not as a transcendent worldview but rather an amorphous science with historical ties to specific institutions and the various forms of power they embody. I heed Dana Phillips's warning about the shiftiness of "ecology" as a science and "ecology" as a philosophical point of view (2003: 44). Thus, I distinguish between "ecology" as a perspective that encompasses the human and the nonhuman (usually qualifying it as "ecological perspective," or "ecological agency") and "ecology" as a science, which I usually designate as "scientific ecology." Scientific ecology, as Bruno Latour reminds us, is a scientific discourse that has "no direct access to nature as such; it is a '-logy' like all scientific disciplines" (2004: 4). Ecology deals with problems of representation: the science has developed an ever-shifting body of representational scientific concepts, including "community," "succession," "climax state," "ecosystem," and "ecotope." Thus, "nature" and "ecology" both gesture at the boundaries of signification, but our understanding of the environment is mediated by representation and interpretation.

To quickly illustrate these distinctions: in my first chapter on Booker T. Washington, I distinguish between scientific ecology (i.e., Tuskegee's emphasis on agricultural science) and ecology in its more general sense to refer to the integrated dynamics of the human and nonhuman. I use the term "environment" to refer to the local environment of the Tuskegee Institute, as well as the larger southern region. Washington writes a lot about "nature," so I treat it in multiple ways: as rhetorical strategy, as an ideological historical construct, and as a key element of Washington's political philosophy.

Up from Nature

Racial Uplift and Ecological Agencies in Booker T. Washington's Autobiographies

Nature Draws No Color Line

In 1902, Booker T. Washington delivered "Getting Down to Mother Earth," one of his weekly addresses to the Tuskegee Institute's students and faculty. When he sat down to write it, he may have had in mind his recent 1901 visit to the White House, where he became the first African- American to dine with a US president. Though a progressive, President Theodore Roosevelt subscribed to fashionable social Darwinist and white supremacist ideologies that invoked nature to justify racial hierarchies.[1] In his address, however, Washington turns white supremacy and social Darwinism on their heads, making what in 1902 would have been an outrageous assertion had there been southern whites present to hear it: "remember that when we get down to the fundamental principles of truth, nature draws no color line" (343). With this rhetorical strategy, not only does nature refuse to naturalize race, but it also acts as the fulcrum for lifting the second generation of southern ex-slaves out of poverty. In a compressed form, "Getting Down to Mother Earth" articulates nature's role in Washington's economic approach to racial uplift—a role more fully developed in two of his autobiographies, *Up from Slavery* (1901) and *Working with the Hands* (1904).

When we rethink Washington's politics from an ecological perspective, we find a figure more dynamic than the sycophantic boogeyman he became to the radical Du Bois. Letting Washington's rhetoric perform on the stage of southern environmental history forces us to look beyond the immediate historical context of the Civil War and Reconstruction. Monique Allewaert offers such a rethinking of black history with her argument about colonial-era slave rebellions in her book, *Ariel's Ecology: Plantations, Personhood, and Colonialism in the American Tropics*. Allewaert elaborates the concept of the "plantation zone," defined as a type of space that is "tropical (or subtropical) and whose political structures are shaped by the plantation form" (2013: 30). She goes on to describe the modes of being unique to this space:

> The entanglements that proliferated in the plantation zone disabled taxon-omies distinguishing the human from the animal from the vegetable from the atmospheric, revealing an assemblage of interpenetrating forces that I call an ecology ... At precisely the moment citizen-subjects were emerging in metropolitan centers, the plantation zone gave rise to an ecological prac-tice closely linked to *marronage*, a process through which human agents found ways to interact with nonhuman forces and in so doing resisted the order of the plantation. (2013: 30–1)

This rethinking of personhood and ontology begins to map an alternate his-tory of slave revolt that reimagines ecological forms of agency grounded in a space removed from the public sphere. Maroon settlements and their mate-rial culture anticipate twentieth-century forms of black radicalism.

To be sure, interpolating *Working with the Hands* into this radical tradi-tion does not make Washington a black revolutionary akin to Gabriel Prosser or Denmark Vesey. On one level, Washington's work reproduces discourses of the capitalist and anthropocentric domination of nature. But it is also true that this discursive mode:

1. resonates within the deep temporal context of environmental history and thus can be interpreted as symptomatic of this history through a method of eco-historicism;
2. is complicated in Washington's case because of the ambiguity produced by his masking and equivocation; and
3. should be differentiated from Theodore Roosevelt's or Andrew Carnegie's white capitalist mode of domination and placed within the context of other minoritarian discourses of empowerment for marginalized groups.

His politics were at once resistive and conformist: the purported successes of educated black laborers were also the economic successes of northern industrialists who financed Tuskegee and, indirectly, the political successes of white southerners. By Washington's death in 1915, it became clear that political change would not piggyback on economic change: while precarious livings were made, so was Jim Crow.

From an ecological angle, *Up from Slavery* and *Working with the Hands* gain a doubled perspective on the problem of racial uplift: consciously, a politics that prioritizes economic advancement over civil rights; unconsciously, a politics that evokes ecological agencies. The forms of ecological agency found in these texts consist of several qualities derived and modified from the radical tradition of marronage:

- a militarized, black-dominated space
- intimate knowledge of local ecologies (plants, soil chemistry, etc.)
- recognition of the role of "natural agencies" in farming (Washington 1904: 165)
- a focus on experimental farming that leads to what we today call sustainability
- a redemptive, georgic vision of self-determined black labor
- a materialist project of environmental (rather than political) reconstruction of plantation zones in response to the failure of post–Civil War Reconstruction.

The relation between these ecological agencies and marronage sometimes surfaces in the autobiographies, but more often it is only partly conscious or displaced, veiled in the text's eco-unconscious. By eco-unconscious, I mean both the historical–ecological subtext of the work, and the conditions of environmental history that make its production possible. Applied to *Working with the Hands*, this concept of the eco-unconscious opens the possibility for the text's descent from the tradition of marronage, while at the same time preserving the differences between that history and more conventional understandings of Washington's political and rhetorical strategies. This chapter first sketches out traditional and ecocritical critiques of Washington before reframing his literary production within the alternative history of colonial-era ecology, marronage, and slave rebellion. I then analyze *Working with the Hands* and its evocation of ecological agencies: soil conservation, experimental farming, environmental reconstruction, and the georgic mode.

The Washington–Du Bois Debates and Ecocriticism

Since *Working with the Hands* is unfamiliar to most literary critics (its last printing prior to 2015 was in 1969), I offer a brief overview before giving an ecocritical account of the Washington–Du Bois debates. It may have been ghostwritten by the white journalist Max Bennett Thrasher, who wrote *Tuskegee: Its Story and Its Work* in 1900 and was employed regularly as Washington's ghostwriter until his death in 1904 (Norrell 2009: 273). If *Working with the Hands* was ghostwritten, this would only make it typical of Washington's literary output (two ghostwriters helped with *Up from Slavery*).[2] Published in 1904, the lengthy subtitle of *Working with the Hands* is *Being a Sequel to "Up from Slavery" Covering the Author's Experiences in Industrial Training at Tuskegee*. Expanding on *Up from Slavery*, this autobiography acts as a sort of testimony to the success of the Tuskegee Institute and the value of educating a black citizenry in the trades.

Working with the Hands is an assemblage of shorter pieces intended for more transient consumption and arguably less aesthetically enduring than the painstaking art that Du Bois put into *The Souls of Black Folk*. Unlike *Up from Slavery*, which chronicles Washington's ascension from slavery to principal of Alabama's largest black college, *Working with the Hands* is nonlinear and focuses more on Tuskegee the school than Washington the man. The chapter titles reflect a preoccupation with skilled trades, domestic work, and agriculture: "Welding Theory and Practice," "Lessons in Home-Making," "Outdoor Work for Women," and "The Tillers of the Ground." Interspersed with these are more philosophical chapters: "Building up a System," "Head and Hands Together," and "The Value of Small Things." The book ends with a defense of Tuskegee against vocal detractors such as novelist and white supremacist Thomas Dixon, author of *The Leopard's Spots* (1902) and *The Clansman* (1905).

Recognizing some kind of doublespeak in Washington's political rhetoric has become customary for civil rights advocates, historians, and literary critics. In *Modernism and the Harlem Renaissance*, Houston A. Baker Jr. celebrates the chiastic coding of Washington's "mastery of form" and "deformation of mastery" in *Up from Slavery* (1987: 15). In that book, Baker argues, Washington dons the minstrel mask and masters its form in order to dupe a white audience into lending him financial and political support for his Tuskegee project. For example, in the opening passages of *Up from Slavery*, Washington casts his mother as a "chicken-stealing darky"—a "formidably familiar image of 'Negro behavior,'" Baker says, that would have been "soothing and reassuring" to white readers (1987: 27). Minstrel jokes such as these canvas the text, in effect encoding it for white and black readers: whites will see Washington's deferential mask, while black readers will be in on the game. For Baker, Washington's appropriation of the minstrel mask and use of it to bamboozle donations transforms him into a Promethean figure, a thief of finance capital who offers *Up from Slavery*. Pull away this minstrel mask of political compromise and behind it lurks a long-term agenda to lift the black masses and the South as a whole out of poverty.[3] Deception lies at the heart of the Washingtonian program, which is why it is so hard to pin down his authentic views on racial politics.

Ascribing intentions to Washington's writings, therefore, is a uniquely fallacious enterprise. Two more examples should suffice to highlight this gap between intention and equivocation, author and text, conscious and unconscious meanings. First, *Up from Slavery* was based on a previous pseudo-autobiography, *The Story of My Life and Work* (1900), ghostwritten by the black journalist Edgar Webber; however, that work proved so inadequate that Washington hired lawyer Max Thrasher to revise and republish it in 1901 (Norrell 2009: 216). The resulting *Up from Slavery* became a revised version of Thrasher's revision of Webber's narrative (Norrell 2009: 217). Second, Washington's books were shrewd persuasive acts. Tuskegee rode a capitalist wave of philanthropy with thousands donated by Andrew Carnegie, J. D. Rockefeller, George Eastman, and Julius Rosenwald (Harlan 1983: 130). Carnegie saw in Washington's program and writings a version of his own "Gospel of Wealth," commenting in his autobiography that "[n]o truer, more self-sacrificing hero ever lived: a man compounded of all the virtues" (1920: 266).

Decades of criticism has been leveled at Washington's racial uplift strategy, but Du Bois's critique in *The Souls of Black Folk* is still the most popular and enduring. In the early chapter "Of Mr. Booker T. Washington and Others," Du Bois attacks Washington's tacit support of African-Americans' status as a political and civil underclass. He first concedes that the Tuskegee Institute has achieved the impossible and its principal's "very singleness of vision and thorough oneness with his age is a mark of the successful man" (1903: 36). Tuskegee thrived in the heart of Alabama's racially hostile, lynch-crazed Black Belt, which impressed Du Bois enough for him to teach there in 1903. What Du Bois really opposes is Washington's de facto position as national race leader—a position that came on the heels of what Du Bois pejoratively dubs the "Atlanta Compromise," a speech Washington delivered to a southern white audience at the Atlanta Cotton States and International Exposition in 1895. For Du Bois, the speech inaugurates the elevation of the limited Tuskegee worldview to a universal prescription for the Negro problem. He condemns the speech's central metaphor for its preemptive support for the 1896 *Plessy v. Ferguson* "separate but equal" Supreme Court ruling: "[i]n all things that are purely social we can be as separate as the fingers, yet one as the hand in all things essential to mutual progress" (Washington 1901: 134). Du Bois argues that by stressing economic gain over such issues as voting rights, desegregation, and anti-lynching laws, Washington's Gilded Age "gospel of Work and Money" comes to "almost completely overshadow the higher aims of life" ([1903] 2003: 41). Ultimately, Du Bois sees more of a reduction to mere labor than an exaltation of black citizenship in Washington's ideas.[4]

Ecocritics such as Carolyn Finney, Scott Hicks, Evora Jones, and Anne Raine have recognized the prominence of ecological themes in the work of Washington and Du Bois.[5] Hicks makes a case for the value of rereading Washington ecocritically, though mainly in terms of what such a rereading contributes to the field of ecocriticism. Such an undertaking begins to construct a twentieth-century genealogy of what Hicks calls an "ecocriticism of color"—a type of ecocriticism that redefines what counts as nature writing (Hicks 2006: 202). Hicks's interpretation reproduces the reductive binary of Du Bois the radical and Washington the conservative: "[w]hereas Washington posits the land of the South as a space that predates historical inscription, repudiates racial categorization, and offers nothing but infinite potential, Du Bois denaturalizes and defamiliarizes such assumptions by seeking to speak for the mute subject" (2006: 209). Hicks infers this conclusion from a few passages from the Atlanta address and *Up from Slavery*, and fails to take a broader, more contextualized look at Washington's literary output. However valuable such a reading may be for ecocritics, if it reproduces conventional wisdom, then it contributes little to racial uplift debates and to African-American literary history in general. My reading of Washington is more symptomatic and focused on the texts rather than the views of the author himself. Hicks ends his article with a call for the examination of "the scientific history of farming in the postbellum South as a means to concretize further Du Bois's and Washington's ecocritical praxis" (2006: 218). A more historical look at Washington's writings and the Tuskegee Institute actually unmasks an added complex awareness and engagement with nature, southern environmental history, and the long shadow of slavery.

The Plantation Zone and Ecological Agencies

Working with the Hands and its underlying politics of ecological agencies repeats with a difference the practices of colonial-era and antebellum maroon settlements, although marronage is more a specter that haunts Tuskegee than something embodied in Tuskegee itself. The South emerges in Washington's prose as a gothic space haunted by the past and other places. In a humorous anecdote about a Georgia funeral, Washington points to the ironic inefficiencies of commodity production and long-distance trade. A man's grave, he recalls, was "dug in the midst of a pine forest, but the pine coffin that held the body was brought from Cincinnati" (1904: 21). The coffin was transported on a wagon made in South Bend, Indiana; the wagon's mule was from Missouri; and the shovels used to dig the grave were imported from Pittsburgh (1904: 21). In a rare display of gallows humor, Washington concludes that the "only things supplied by the county, with its wealth of natural resources, was the corpse and the hole in the ground" (1904: 21). In capitalism's version of a Frankenstein monster assembled from parts drawn from all over the country, the text critiques the unnaturalness of such geographical displacement. The choice of using a funeral as an example also evokes the destructive tendencies of this economic system on black labor and the environment.

The past that haunts Tuskegee originates in the colonial era. The English explorer Thomas Harriot's *A Briefe and True Report of the New Found Land of Virginia* (1590) exemplifies settler anxiety about native knowledge of local ecologies that could threaten European conquest. In his description of native fishing practices, Harriot marvels: "[t]her was never seene amonge us soe cunninge a way to take fish withal" ([1590] 1972: 56). He is puzzled by their motivations, which appear "free from all care of heaping opp Riches for their posteritie, content with their state" (Harriot [1590] 1972: 56). The accompanying illustration shows the natives' various methods of catching fish in a river: setting traps, using canoes, and spearing fish ([1590] 1972: 57). The river is full of species: catfish, eel, turtles, crabs, rays, and other assorted water-dwellers. The illustration echoes Harriot's earlier taxonomy of the commodities the new colony could yield: silk worm, hemp, turpentine, wine, cedar, furs, copper, iron, and dyes, to name a few ([1590] 1972: 7–11). While to the European gaze this river landscape showcases the abundance of wildlife in the new colony, it also conflates the natives with local ecology and places them on an ontological continuum with animals and plants. The illustration threatens such a disassembly by suggesting an alliance between natives and nature against the white colonial gaze.

In her analysis of William Bartram's *Travels* (1791), Allewaert argues that the English explorer's account of the southeast US region betrays a white colonial subject's fear—both real and imagined—of a type of human agency and resistance that she defines as ecological. A historical narrative of these "agents who gained power by combining with ecological forces" challenges the "assumption that colonial and later national ventures were largely uncontested and hegemonic" (2013: 30). Such forms of African and Native American resistance emerged as the dialectical negation of colonialism and the Atlantic Slave Trade, leading to what the ruling classes imagined, in Peter Linebaugh's and Marcus Rediker's terms, as a "many-headed hydra" that threatened their power (2000). Named after the monster from Greek mythology, this metaphorical hydra often found its material base on maroon settlements in the uncharted wilderness, existing off the grid of the plantation zone and outside white spheres of power. Bartram's *Travels* reveals that African maroons and natives used their environments to gain a degree of agency that negated the dominant, metropolitan print culture within which the Englishman writes. Bartram's travel account attempts to sell the Virginia region as a settler-friendly temperate zone. He carefully catalogues each plant or animal species he encounters, fitting them into taxonomies of nature. Yet, Allewaert argues, the "tropical, the useless, and the cataclysmic continually set [Bartram] off course" (2013: 31). The chaotic elements of the local ecology rendered the master–slave distinction ambiguous. Swamps, in particular, "sheltered diasporic Africans who, in refusing slave status, repudiated the prevailing organization of Virginia's plantation economy" (2013: 33). Slaves had the opportunity to settle these "Africanized spaces" that rivaled the carceral space of the plantation zone (2013: 33).

The power of these spaces stems partly from the intimacy with local ecologies that slaves gained from exploring and laboring the land. In one illustrative moment from *Travels*, Bartram is riding his horse on the outskirts of a South Carolina plantation when he encounters a group of slaves. He fears them, realizing that he is "unarmed" while the laborers carry their farm tools, which double as potential weapons in his imagination: "I mounted and rode briskly up; and though armed with clubs, axes and hoes, they opened to right and left and let me pass peaceably" (Bartram [1791] 1928: 379). He keeps a "sharp eye," however, as he anticipates a sneak attack might "their intentions [be] to ambuscade and surround me" (Bartram [1791] 1928: 379). As Allewaert observes, Bartram is not sure whether to identify the Africans as slaves or maroons, for he "expects that both slaves and Maroons have a particularly proximate relation to tropical terrains, and he also expects that this proximity has military significance" (2013: 38). This ambiguity of slave–maroon identity would later play out in the doubling and equivocations in Washington's own writing. *Working with the Hands* would also go on to reinscribe the ecological forms of this resistance from within the plantation zone itself.

Allewaert's analysis can be tied to ecological agency in the larger history of marronage across the North America and the Caribbean. In *Black Marxism*, Robinson uncovers a relation between the twentieth-century black radical tradition and the history of marronage. Though he does not articulate it in ecological terms, his account obliquely alludes to the type of ecological practices identified by Allewaert. From the beginning of the Atlantic slave trade, slaves found ways to defy the plantation zone: "resistance among the enslaved Africans took the form of flight to native or 'Indian' settlements" (Robinson [1983] 2000: 130). Maroon settlements sprung up in colonies such as Jamaica, Colombia, Venezuela, Guiana, and Suriname, to name a few (1983: 135–9). While Marx calls slavery a form of primitive accumulation wherein resources are forcibly extracted from humans and the earth, maroons negated this violent expropriation by retaining their own African ways of life and trying to reestablish them in new, non-plantation settlements (1983: 121). According to Robinson, the "transport of African labor to the mines and plantations of the Caribbean" also meant the "transfer of African ontological and cosmological systems" (1983: 122). This cultural transport provided a deep well of values for establishing and organizing maroon communities. Some maroon communities even achieved official recognition such as the San Lorenzo de los Negros in Mexico (1983: 132). One Virginia planter compared maroons plotting in the Dismal Swamp with Romulus and Remus, the founders of Rome (1983: 14). The specter of these communities haunted white colonizers.

In another account of this alternative history, C. L. R. James chronicles the Haitian Revolution. In *The Black Jacobins*, in which maroons and ecological agencies played a key role. James gives an account of the 1791 San Domingo uprisings that launched the revolution. The highly organized Dutty Boukman, a Voodoo priest, led this initial assault on white dominance of the plantation zone ([1938] 1963: 87). The circumstances of the revolt could have flowered from Bartram's fearful imagination:

> On the night of the 22nd a tropical storm raged, with lightning and gusts of wind and heavy showers of rain. Carrying torches to light their way, the leaders of the revolt met in an open space in the thick forests of the Morne Rouge, a mountain overlooking Le Cap. There Boukman gave the last instructions and, after Voodoo incantations and the sucking of the blood of a stuck pig, he stimulated his followers by a prayer spoken in creole, which, like so much spoken on such occasions, has remained. "The god who created the sun which gives us light, who rouses the waves and rules the storm, though hidden in the clouds, he watches us." ([1938] 1963: 87)

In James's account, the leaders use the cover of nature—the tropical storm and the thick forests—to coordinate the mass uprising, impressive in its scale. From the mountain, they perform a Voodoo ritual that mixes Catholicism with elements of earthly paganism. As the Creole prayer emphasizes, their deity governs nature and passes a damning judgment on the whites—a judgment carried out by the revolutionaries themselves. Soon afterward, the slaves across the plantations of San Domingo would revolt and burn down the plantations, with the goal of exterminating the whites ([1938] 1963: 88). Similar to the Haitian Revolution, maroon settlements and flights into wilderness provided the staging ground for acts of rebellion across North and South America, as in the cases of Gabriel Prosser and Denmark Vesey in the colonies (Robinson [1983] 2000: 149).[6]

While maroons developed autonomous social formations outside the plantation system through ecological agencies, *Working with the Hands* reflects ecological agencies working from inside the plantation system. Washington necessarily engages the public sphere, but in a masquerade that entails a close relationship between text and environmental action. Insofar as Washington's writings are like extended fundraising letters with the purpose of securing funds for the campus's construction from wealthy white donors, his writings are as much action as they are literary. In Laura R. Fisher's words, they bear an "instrumental relation to literary practice" that she calls "vocational realism" (2015: 711). New materialists such as Stacy Alaimo (2010) and Jane Bennett (2010) go further in their views on the interflow of bodies, environments and texts; they argue for an ontology that is a "complex intersection of bodies, natures, and political discourses—a being-in-the-world where embodiment and discursivity are co-extensive and mutually permeable" (Iovino 2012: 135).[7] Read through the lenses of new materialism and the eco-unconscious, the environment affects Washington's writings and those writings in turn have real material effects: the environment mediates the text just as the text mediates our perception of the environment. The Tuskegee Institute is an exemplary case of the reciprocal impact of representation and reality, of writing on the page and "writing" the environment by working with the hands. Framed in this *longue durée* of environmental history and black forms of ecological resistance to the plantation form in the United States and the Caribbean, Washington's *Working with the Hands* can be read as the haunted reflection of these colonial pasts.

Experimental Farming as Ecological Agency

In *Working with the Hands*, the chapter "On the Experimental Farm" represents ecological agencies that challenge centuries of environmental practices by attempting to replenish southern soils and recognizing restorative "natural agencies" (1904: 165). Rhetorically, the soil plays a central role in the book's vision of racial uplift; in fact, Tuskegee's history curriculum shows the "student how the American people, as is true of all great nations, began as cultivators of the soil" ([1904] 1969: 89). In *Up from Slavery*, Washington proclaims that the soil is the "solid and never deceptive foundation of Mother Nature where all nations and races that have ever succeeded have gotten their start" (54). He ends one of his most famous lectures, "Industrial Education for the Negro," with an ecstatic image of ascension that gains its initial foothold in the soil: "[o]ur pathway must be up through the soil, up through swamps, up through forests, up through the streams, the rocks, up through commerce, education and religion!" (1903: 360). Yet this rhetoric also has a materialist, scientific orientation in *Working with the Hands* that springs from the text's eco-unconscious engagement with southern environmental history.[8]

In the decades preceding the 1880s, the plantation economic form domi-nated and exploited the South's already poor-quality soil. In *This Land, This South: An Environmental History*, Albert E. Cowdrey discusses the precolo-nial and colonial-era southern environmental history that gave rise to the plantation form. For Cowdrey, the strangest and most significant charac-teristic of southern soils is how "old" they are (1996: 2). Unlike soils north of the Ohio River, the South was not covered by glaciers during the last Ice Age (c. 20000–10000 BCE), consequently they lack the mineral-rich layer of topsoil that the North has. Tuskegee sits at the end of what geographers call the Atlantic Piedmont, which spans from mid-Virginia to eastern Alabama (Cowdrey 1996: 76). This sloping stretch of land is prone to erosion during periods of heavy precipitation—a regional peculiarity that turned into a major concern for later agrarian reformists such as Washington. For Cowdrey, human activity and environmental history cannot be separated: "[i]ntriguing is the extent to which the natural environment of the South, including much that is usually termed primeval, is an artifact of sorts, shaped if not invented during the millennia of human occupation" (1996: 5). Early colonial farming of tobacco began to exacerbate the exhaustion of the southern soil (1996: 31). With continuing market demand for only a few cash crops, farmers cleared large areas of forest and confined their work to growing as much of one crop as possible. This system of monocultures and the resulting reduction in bio-diversity contributed to the erosion and depletion of nutrients from the soil. Even as early as the 1700s, there were calls for agricultural reform, soil conser-vation, and crop diversification. Thomas Jefferson, for example, experimented with crop rotations and plowing, but these reform efforts did not catch on broadly (Cowdrey 1996: 58).

After the early colonial period, the plantation economic form took hold and fostered large commercial farms of three hundred acres or more (Aiken 1998: 5–6). Emerging simultaneously with this form was the rapid expansion of slavery in the 1700s. For over two centuries, slavery and the plantation system became a "human factor of incalculable importance to the southern environment" (Cowdrey 1996: 36). Ecofeminist Carolyn Merchant argues that "[s]lavery and soil degradation are interlinked systems of exploitation, and deep-seated connections exist between the enslavement of human bodies and the enslavement of the land" ("Shades" 2003: 380). The demand for slave labor increased when cotton boomed on the world market as a cash crop. Because slavery deprived the region of a local consumer base and therefore of a local food market, agriculture was wholly geared toward profits and commercial exports (Cowdrey 1996: 78). The lack of markets for diverse crop commodities, in turn, stifled the incentive to grow non-cotton and non-tobacco plants, leading to the further destruction of biodiversity (Hurt 2003: 222). With the invention of the cotton gin in 1793, the so-called Cotton Kingdom—which Cowdrey dubs the "row-crop empire" to emphasize the erosive, canal-like watercourses that formed when it rained—saw rapid growth between 1790 and 1837, thus amplifying the human impact on the southern environment (1996: 71). The production of cotton bales rose from 3,135 in 1790 to 208,986 in 1815, and cotton became the country's leading export (Cowdrey 1996: 72). As a result, these cotton monocultures tended to spawn soil toxins and parasites, such as the boll weevil in the 1910s—one of the "push" factors that set the Great Migration in motion (Cowdrey 1996: 79–80).

Washington saw the correlation between slavery and the environment geographically inscribed in the "Black Belt," a strip of fertile soil stretching from Georgia westward to Mississippi. The Black Belt, Washington says, was "the part of the South where slaves were most profitable, and consequently they were taken there in the largest numbers" ([1904] 1969: 65). In essence, slavery was a form of mechanized labor that degraded the worker and the land, much like northern factory work: the "whole machinery of slavery was not apt to beget the spirit of love of labor" ([1904] 1969: 17). Here, *Working with the Hands* echoes *The Souls of Black Folk*, in which Du Bois also establishes

a direct causal connection between slave labor and agricultural degradation: "[t]he harder the slaves were driven the more careless and fatal was their
farming" (1903: 91). Thus, one can find a "geographical color-line" across
the South, a physical connection between race and environment (Du Bois
1903: 119).

When Washington first arrived at the school grounds in 1881, the Tuskegee
property reflected this environmental legacy of slavery. Landscape architect
historian Kenrick Ian Grandison points out that the school's land "bore the
scars of war and abandonment after years of abusive cotton cultivation"
(1996: 344). It consisted of a mere three buildings (a stable, a chicken coop,
and a kitchen) and one-hundred acres of eroded soil (Grandison 1996: 345–6).
It was, in short, one of the "waste places" (1901: 133) Washington spoke about
in his Atlanta address—a waste place that Alabama funded at only $2,000 per
year to get the school going (Harlan 1983: 128). Most of the school's budget
went to acquiring land and expanding the agricultural program. By 1895,
a large portion of the school's 1,810 acres had been set aside for crop cultivation. When NAACP activist Kelly Miller visited the campus in 1903, he
recorded the spectacle of students struggling with the depleted soil:

> The soil is generally thin and well exhausted. It almost makes the heart
> bleed to see those hard-working, honest, ignorant men wearing out soul
> and body upon a barren hill-side, which yielded up its virgin strength a half
> century ago, and whose top soil has been washed away, and can be restored
> only by another geologic epoch. A careful and dispassionate analysis of all
> the facts and factors leads plainly to two conclusions, (1) the Tuskegee idea
> alone cannot solve the race problem, and (2) the race problem cannot be
> solved without the Tuskegee idea. (1903: 3–4)

To Miller, the students were fighting with superhuman patience and persistence against centuries of entropy: the slow violence of antebellum agricultural practices and the ecosystem's slow healing processes. Tuskegee's
agricultural policy was in a way necessarily geared toward subsistence and
replenishing the soil rather than cash crops.

Working with the Hands, however, announces ambitions in "On the
Experimental Farm" that far exceed necessity. The chapter "On the
Experimental Farm" contains a staged photograph of Tuskegee student

workers cultivating a patch of cassava (a food staple grown in tropical areas) on the school's agricultural experiment plot. This photograph counters the image of the vagrant farm hand or slave laborer drudging away in the cotton field. Eight young black men are busy hoeing the plot, all with heads down intensely focused on work. These workers appear dapper in vests and dress pants; they look like a black bourgeoisie engaged in respectable, profitable, and intellectualized labor. The caption indicates that these men work on an "experiment plot," intellectualizing their labor by suggesting that it is a form of scientific inquiry tied to black masculinity. The page adjacent from the photograph proudly announces that "present experiments are in progress with ten varieties of corn, with vetch, clovers, cassava, sugar beet, Cuban sugar cane, eight kinds of millet, the Persian and Arabian beans, and many other food and forage plants" ([1904] 1969: 164). The landscape behind them is bordered by a fence and displays the property's managed environment. More importantly, the background landscape shows that this patch of land is a small plot, not an extensive and ecologically destructive cotton or tobacco monoculture. The multiple workers also indicate that this experimental plot requires coordinated group effort, a microcosm of racial solidarity and group economic action.

In addition to the photograph, key to this chapter's narrative of scientific labor and environmental practice is the innovative botanist and director of Tuskegee's Agricultural Experiment Station farms, George Washington Carver. Kimberly K. Smith observes that Washington became an "important voice for scientific agriculture in the South," as he "supported the work of black scientists such as George Washington Carver, held agriculture conferences for local farmers, and employed extension agents to travel to black farmers demonstrating new tools and techniques" (2007: 76). If *Working with the Hands* has a protagonist, a heroic figure other than Washington himself, then it is Carver. Carver's scientific innovations, Washington says, culminate a progressive narrative of science that originates in ancient Egypt. The Egyptian farmer "knew that if he let his land lie idle—'rested,' as he termed it—he was able to produce a much better crop" (1904: 165). Carver's own letters and scientific writings reveal a quasi-mystical attitude toward nature that contrasts with Washington's pragmatism. Carver's scientific mysticism shows a preference for an intuitive approach to ecological investigation that is similar to Allewaert's claims about black maroons' knowledge of local ecologies. Though Carver was a professed Christian, many of his beliefs amount to a form of nature-worship where nature as Gaia seems interchangeable with the Holy Spirit. In one letter to a friend, Carver professes that the "greatest of all teachers" is "Mother Nature," for "nature in its varied forms are the little windows through which God permits me to commune with Him, and to see much of His glory, majesty, and power by simply lifting the curtain and looking in" ([1930] 1987: 143). Many mainstream white scientists attempted to discredit Carver's studies because of this mysticism, to which he responded with a defense of intuitive scientific methods: the "master analyst needs no book; he is at liberty to take apart and put together substances, compatible or non-compatible to suit his own particular taste or fancy" ([1924] 1987: 130).

In his letters from this early period in Tuskegee's history, the mystical Carver seems to subscribe to the *longue durée* view of history's geological time. He claims to find God through geological inquiry into a mineral specimen: "I have dissolved it, purified it, made conditions favorable for the formation of crystals" ([1927] 1987: 135). The resulting crystal formation reminds him of God's "omnipotence, majesty and power" for the immense stretch of time embodied in the crystal ([1927] 1987: 135). He teaches the *Genesis* creation story to his students "in the light of natural and revealed religion and geological truths" ([1907] 1987: 134). Carver, the text summarizes, understands the "value of scientific cultivation," and finds ways to improve soil beyond merely resting it ([1904] 1969: 165). Beginning in 1898, Washington held Carver in such high regard that he publicized his methods and distributed his agricultural pamphlets across the South (Norrell 2009: 199). These pamphlets disseminated the school's scientific knowledge about crop rotation, fertilizers, replenishing the soil, and growing vegetable gardens (Norrell 2009: 199).

As evidence for the value of experimental farming, Washington cites Carver's development of new methods for growing that can increase the quantity and quality of the crop. On average, cotton-growing in the South only produces 190 pounds per acre, an "astonishingly low figure, and, except when high prices rule, below the paying point" ([1904] 1969: 164). On the experimental station, Carver has figured out a way to yield "nearly 500 pounds of cotton on one acre of poor Alabama land" (1904: 165). Moreover, Carver has produced varieties of "hybrid cotton" that are "vastly superior" in quality to the cotton typically grown in Alabama. The ability of crop rotation to restore nutrients to depleted soil is Tuskegee's "special study" (1904: 166). Rotation potentially solves problems such as how to "build up the poor upland soils of Alabama," to mitigate erosion, to reduce the need for costly fertilizers, to determine how many years it would take to reverse the soil-depleting effects of monocultures, and to discover the "smallest amount of such [purchasable] land the farmer should buy expecting to make a living off it" (1904: 166–7). An analysis of the existing soil reveals that it is "seriously deficient" of nitrogen, phosphoric acid (a mineral nutrient), and potash (a salt form of potassium) (1904: 168).

While these passages in "On the Experimental Farm" embody vocational realism with their detail and precision, they also show how experimental farming can undermine the human and ecological damage done by cotton monocultures. First, Carver, Washington, and the students worked to improve the physical condition of the soil by "deep plowing, rebuilding terraces and filling in washes" (1904: 168). The text breaks down the crop rotation plan for a farm of forty acres, as developed by Carver:

> First year, sixteen acres of cowpease [a legume], eight acres of cotton, two acres of riboon cane [a form of sugarcane], three acres of corn, one acre of sorghum [a cereal grain], one acre of peanuts, three acres of sweet potatoes, one acre of teosinte (a green fodder plant), one acre of pumpkins, cushaws [a kind of squash], squash, etc.... The second year it will be observed that the pease change places with the cotton, corn, ribbon cane, sorghum, teosinte, pumpkins and sweet potatoes ... With few exceptions mentioned, the third year is identical with the first. (1904: 168–9)

Washington uses technical, soil chemistry terms to emphasize farming as an intellectual enterprise. In 1897, they planted cowpease, using kainite and acid phosphate as fertilizer, and sold the crop for a profit of $2.40. In 1898, they planted sweet potatoes on the same acre as the cowpease, again using kainite and acid phosphate, and sold the crop for an increased profit of $22. In 1899, they rotated the cowpease back in, using the same methods as in 1897, for a substantial profit increase of $19.25, nearly ten times the profit in 1897. In 1900, they planted sorghum cane with kainite and acid phosphate, naturally fertilized with "swamp muck" and "decayed forest leaves," yielding a profit of $22 (1904: 170). In 1901, cowpease were planted again for another profit gain of $28.75. The next year they planted a "garden truck" of cabbage, onions, beets, squash, tomatoes, melons, beans, turnips, mustard, and more, yielding a $39 profit. In 1903, they planted the cowpease again for a profit of $43.85 (1904: 171). For Washington, this drastic increase in profit shows that even a small two-acre farm can help black farmers (1904: 172). Within seven years, this crop rotation plan turned a profit of $96.22 per acre on land that had previously lost $2.40 per acre (1904: 170). Though framed in terms of the profit motive, this carefully planned system of crop rotation restores the metabolic cycle of the soil.

Working with the Hands discusses the consumption as well as the production side of agriculture. Early on, it criticizes the southern black masses' consumption of imported food, seeing the lack of a local food market as an obstacle to crop diversification and black self-reliance. Seeing them as role models for the masses (and since they are the principal profession of Tuskegee graduates), the text targets teachers in particular: "school teachers were eating salt pork from Chicago and canned chicken and tomatoes sent from Omaha. While the countryside abounded in all manner of beautiful shrubbery and fragrant flowers, few of these ever found their way into the houses or upon the dinner tables" (1904: 14). Washington advocates subsistence gardening over cash crops, reflecting on how "[o]ne feels, when eating his own fresh vegetables, that he is getting near to the heart of nature; not a second-hand stale imitation, but the genuine thing" (1904: 156–7). The South is a veritable Eden of abundant food, if it would only be recognized and cultivated as such.

If conservation focuses on long-term profit over short-term gain, then *Working with the Hands* is a work of conservation as well as racial uplift. Tuskegee's aim, under the direction of Carver, is to invent "right methods" for teaching black farmers of Alabama how to make their land "yield unfailing profit" and "win in the fight against the deadly mortgage system" (1904: 163). Here and throughout, *Working with the Hands* expresses concern that the southern system of sharecropping and tenant farming stifles the development of new methods; this stifling helps to continue slavery by other means and thus has negative environmental consequences similar to those of slavery itself. For instance, the "wrong," unscientific method can be embodied in the "farm hand" type. In the chapter "Making Education Pay Its Way," Washington advocates the use of improved farming technologies and discusses how white planters "refused to encourage the use of much agricultural machinery" for fear that it would "spoil the Negro 'farm hands'" (1904: 46). Farm hands form a sort of rural southern peasantry who do not own land and are "ignorant and unskilled, with little conscience" (1904: 47). This destitute laborer, utterly lacking in ecological agency, cares nothing for knowledge, for learning how to use "labor-saving machinery," and for the wider community of "progressive agriculture" (1904: 47). Appealing to his white audience, Washington veils his criticism of white property owners with the farm-hand type. In reality, the farm hand shows how racism blocks advances in soil conservation. Scientific innovations, along with property acquisition, are the two key components to reconstructing the plantation environment. Though explicitly couched in the capitalist language of the profit motive, such innovations implicitly contribute to sustainable farming practices. The short-term view of capitalism prioritizes profit over a twenty- to thirty-year span, whereas the vision in *Working with the Hands* of ecological agencies and economic advancement dovetail in scientific practices of soil conservation. If this conservationist approach had worked in its idealized form portrayed in *Working with the Hands*, black-owned farms would become more profitable than white-owned farms. Soil conservation, then, is a form of ecological agency that dismantles the legacy of the white master's environmental practices.

The Tuskegee Georgic and the Mastery of Nature

In *Working with the Hands*, Washington so intertwines "nature" and "work" that they become central to the Tuskegee project and his engagement with African-American autobiography, particularly slave narratives, and his vision of southern history. For Washington the philosophical materialist, nature is foremost an object to be worked on, the material substratum that enables "working with the hands" and offers the "bedrock" foundation for a politics of racial uplift. It is this working on nature and especially the emphasis on agricultural labor that puts Washington in the georgic tradition of other African-American writers such as Paul Laurence Dunbar and Sterling Brown. The georgic mode differs from the pastoral in its emphasis on laboring the land, whether that labor is given a pessimistic or redemptive framing. According to Timothy Sweet, this difference goes back to Virgil: "in the *Eclogues* Virgil understands the natural world primarily as a site of leisure, [but] in the *Georgics* he understands it primarily as a site of labor" (2). The georgic mode is also agrarian and tends to be didactic, using representations of agricultural labor to philosophize about larger questions of citizenship and government.

The Tuskegee variation on the georgic mode emphasizes the productive power of labor both as an end in itself and as a pathway to citizenship.[9] As Janet Fiskio claims, "[c]ultivation of a sense of place through long-term inhabitation and labor is central to the American georgic and to its embrace by the field of American ecocriticism" (2012: 301). But labor as pathway to citizenship is first of all a pathway to personhood and agency. As explained earlier, manual labor has intellectual as well as practical dimensions. With this valorization of self-directed black labor, a form of colonial-era ecological agency meets the Tuskegee georgic and its environmental reconstruction of the plantation zone.

For Washington, his pragmatic and georgic approach to reconstructing the plantation also leads to a philosophy that promotes the hard-won mastery of nature—a philosophy that makes him vulnerable to criticism from ecocritics and environmental historians. For instance, in *Up from Slavery*, Washington plans to show Tuskegee students "how to make the forces of nature—air, water, steam, electricity, horse-power—assist them in their labor" (1901: 89). Following a line of thought similar to the Frankfurt School, Kimberly K. Smith has criticized Washington's views on nature. Smith concludes that Washington's "chief means of achieving individual autonomy is to impose one's will on the natural world, and most of the benefits of manual labor derive from the experience of successfully mastering nature" (96).[10] One can read Washington's Atlanta address for its promotion of an anthropocentricism that elevates human interests above environmental stewardship:

> Cast down your bucket among these people who have, without strikes and labour wars, tilled your fields, cleared your forests, built your railroads and cities, and brought forth treasures from the bowels of the earth, and helped make possible this magnificent representation of the progress of the South. Casting down your bucket among my people, helping and encouraging them as you are doing on these grounds, and to education of head,

hand, and heart, you will find that they will buy your surplus land, make blossom the waste places in your fields, and run your factories. (1901: 133)

Cultivating "waste places" may be construed as a pro-environmentalist statement, insofar as it shows a form of reparative engagement with nutrient-depleted soil. Yet it also seems clear that Washington is strategically adopting the capitalist rhetoric of the Gilded Age in order to turn black labor into a marketable commodity.

Given the context of Reconstruction and the larger environmental history of the South, Washington had his reasons for promoting this mastery of nature—reasons that bear an unconscious relation to ecological agencies and the history of resistance to colonialism and slavery. In perhaps his second-most popular lecture, "Industrial Education for the Negro" (1903), he repeats his views of nature and labor from *Up from Slavery*: training "consists in teaching [the Negro] how not to work, but how to make the forces of nature—air, steam, water, horse-power and electricity—work for him" (359). Under slavery, Washington asserts, "the Negro was worked; as a freeman he must learn to work. There is a vast difference between working and being worked" (1904: 16). The slave is a victim of system rather than creator and applier of it. That work be voluntary and that the worker owns the final product are essential for deriving benefits from it; to be free is to own land. Washington reasons that because "the man who tilled the land did not own it, his main object was to get all he could out of the property and return to it as little as possible" (1904: 34). As long as the farmer does not own his land, he will exploit it without concern for the long-term impact on the soil's health. Under this sharecropping system, the "land, of course, was more impoverished each year" (1904: 35). As suggested earlier, the then-current system establishes a causal connection between slavery (and sharecropping) and ecological degradation. Only free, property-owning laborers can break this cycle. Black farmers, Washington asserted, needed to diversify their cultivation and to escape the socially and ecologically destructive cash crop system. This policy translates practically into subsistence farming and livestock raising, while also reducing cash crop cultivation (1904: 33). Otherwise, black farmers would have to pay inflated rates for their food, thus cementing their entrapment in the tenant farming system (1904: 34).

The Tuskegee project, geared toward cultivating free labor, was pushing back against decades of the plantation system and redesigning the Black Belt environment through cultivation of ecological agencies. In the chapter "Building up a System," Washington describes how he expanded this pragmatism to the Tuskegee Institute's campus construction and environment. Student labor built most of the campus, doubling the value of all student labor projects: students learned their trades by doing, while also making real, material contributions to the campus (1904: 56). At the time of the book's writing, seventy-two buildings had been erected by students attending the school on Tuskegee's work-study plan (1904: 58). This method saves money and teaches construction skills, while also providing a "more natural process of development" than hiring contractors (1904: 90). In this narrative, the students' educational development and the development of the Tuskegee environment are harmonious. A system of black labor brought into sync with natural forces and the post-plantation environment, then, replaces a previous system of exploitation that pitted black labor against the land. In this instance, *Working with the Hands* shows an acute awareness of Tuskegee as a former plantation, as a historical–environmental space layered with decades and even centuries of ad hoc practices and economies.

Working with the Hands contains a number of photographs of the Tuskegee campus that provide visual evidence for the Tuskegee georgic mode. Michael Bieze points out that the book's visual appeal made it more marketable to northern whites used to "highly romantic artistic representations of black life" (2008: 98). Most of these photographs show the campus at various stages of construction with students performing and learning "handwork," contributing to the work's georgic celebration of labor and the land. They consistently portray abundance, action, and efficiency: students grinding sugarcane, repairing furniture, building roads, woodworking, dressmaking, typesetting, and cultivating crops, to name a few examples. Intended for a predominantly white audience, *Working with the Hands* offers an idealized portrait of Tuskegee's everyday operations.

While white readers might read an innocuous narrative of an expanding college campus and free black labor force, the Tuskegee campus also became a militarized, black reconstruction of the plantation zone. Landscape architecture historian Kendrick Grandison argues that the Institute's campus environment developed dialectically with the rise of Jim Crow and southern white hostility. A bizarre incident illustrates the severity of the potential threat, as well as Washington's diplomatic skill at negotiating it. One night, a local black man fleeing a lynch mob sought refuge at Washington's home, the Oaks, across the street from the campus. Though Washington publicly stated he turned the fleeing man away (and was ridiculed as a coward by other black leaders), in reality Washington found the fleeing man a doctor and helped him secure refuge elsewhere. Washington feared that if he openly sheltered the man, he would incur the wrath of the white mob on his entire campus.

This incident and the campus layout show the presence of very real dangers—dangers that Washington always downplayed in his writings for fear of antagonizing the white enemy. The existence and proximity of a school focused on "the education of laboring masses," Grandison claims, was a "threat to the viability of the Southern plantation economy" (1996: 336). Located one mile from the town of Tuskegee, physical distance and natural barriers offered the institute greater autonomy and protection from a potential Ku Klux Klan attack (350–1). The school was built like a fortress, with "imposing classical architecture" facing inward and modest brownstone backs facing outward (365), limited entry points for vehicles (359), and the men's dormitories positioned strategically at entrances to the campus while women's were built in the interior (360). The men's dorms lined Montgomery Road, the main access road to the campus, and "could potentially serve as a first line of defense in case of hostile intrusion" (362). The campus entrance was gated and guarded by uniformed Tuskegee students working as a security force.

Working with the Hands equates "mastery" not with the exploitation of nature but with reconstructing the plantation zone and turning slave labor into a form of ecological agency and long-term sustainability. Labor itself becomes a form of aesthetic experience. The text's georgic vision requires the pragmatism of an experience-based study of nature; it demands a methodical approach to the worker's interaction with nature. Given the *longue durée* context of environmental history, the eco-unconscious of *Working with the Hands* reveals this web of landscape architecture and sustainability—that is, environmental reconstruction—as a form of ecological agency and thus a covert form of black resistance.

Conclusion

In the "Getting Down to Mother Earth" address, with which I started this chapter, Washington charges future Tuskegee graduates with a task: "[o]ne of the highest ambitions of every man leaving Tuskegee Institute should be to help the people of his race find bottom—find bed-rock and then help them to stand upon that foundation" ([1902] 2008: 342). Invoking a focus on economic nationalism and capital accumulation, this address does not—as Washington's contemporaries Roosevelt or Sierra Club founder John Muir might—urge his graduates to escape the trappings of modernity and venture into the wilderness to find themselves. What he sees, instead, are the possibilities contained within the toolbox of nature to bring a generation reared by former slaves to economic prosperity. From an ecological perspective, this metaphor also evokes an ontology of nature as a race-less substratum of being that recognizes the quantity of sweat instead of the quality of skin.

In *Working with the Hands*, Tuskegee emerges not as a machine but as a local instance of a black southern nation-to-come grounded in overcoming the historical sediment of the plantation zone through soil conservation, scientific farming, and a georgic vision of redemptive labor. In his final autobiography, *My Larger Education* (1912), Washington continues to hold on to georgic portraits of agricultural labor. Black farmers, in particular, appear as intuitive poets of the practical: "the Negro farmer has a rare gift of getting at the sense of things and of stating in picturesque language what he has learned" (155). They are naturalists, experts at learning by experience, studying the "soil, the development of plants and animals, the streams, the birds, and the changes of the seasons" (155). For Washington, Tuskegee's construction and continued growth aimed at a southern environmental reconstruction of the plantation zone antithetical to the tenant and sharecropping systems. As the Washingtonian program attempts to alter, resist, and reconstruct the order of the plantation zone, it repeats with a difference, a hidden African-American history of resistance. Placed in a historical and environmental context, Washington's version of "mastery" becomes not an exploitive dominance of nature, but rather black labor and land redefined as powerful forms of ecological agency.

While this chapter has undertaken an against-the-grain reading of Washington's work, revealing the textual eco-unconscious by reading it in the context of environmental history, this politics of ecological agencies remains unconscious and historically displaced. Even though it is unconscious, it is still materialist in its concern with ecological agencies and the environmental reconstruction of the plantation. By the time of Du Bois's *The Souls of Black Folk* and *Darkwater*, we move to a more conscious, if less material, engagement with the conservation movement and its politics. For Du Bois, especially in *Darkwater*, conservation becomes the occasion for an aesthetic project of conscious figurations, metaphors, and objective correlatives put into the service of a critique of segregation and an affirmation of integration and democratic pluralism.

W. E. B. Du Bois at the Grand Canyon: Nature, History, and Race in *Darkwater*

Introduction

While Booker T. Washington's autobiographies promote a racial uplift agenda through ecological agencies, W. E. B. Du Bois's *Darkwater: Voices from within the Veil* (1920) cultivates an aesthetic project in his quest for integration. Du Bois's essay "Of Beauty and Death" appears as a culminating experimental effort near the end of *Darkwater*, his modernist text par excellence: a semiautobiographical callaloo of poems, essays, and short stories. "Of Beauty and Death" contains much of the biting social critique one would expect from the then-editor of the NAACP's *The Crisis*: depictions of black life behind the Veil, studies of whiteness, and applications of his theory of double consciousness. What come as a surprise, however, are its Thoreauvian thick descriptions of the Grand Canyon, the Rocky Mountains, and Maine's Acadia National Park. Romantic and social realist modes occupy the same page: lyrical accounts revering the "glory of physical nature" and "all the colors of the sea" are interspersed with anecdotes about his journey to the national parks in a train's Jim Crow car (1920: 174–5). Despite these themes, Kimberly K. Smith observes that "we don't read this essay as an expression of progressive environmentalism at all; we read it as a discourse on social justice" (2007: 2). Why, then, does Du Bois mix environmental, racial, and existential themes in this often overlooked essay? How is it that natural beauty gives rise to this combination of strident antiracist protest and an imported German romanticism?

Even more eclectic than its predecessor *The Souls of Black Folk*, *Darkwater* assembles poems, essays, and short stories into a fragmented work.[1] Du Bois's method throughout is juxtaposition: he pushes the reader to make thematic and historical connections among the book's varied genres. Scholarly insights and emotional lyric exist side by side in *Darkwater*. For example, the essay "The Souls of White Folk" dissects the "discovery of personal whiteness among the world's peoples" as a "very modern thing" (1920: 21); it is then followed by the poem "The Riddle of the Sphinx," which seethes disgust at the "white world's vermin and filth" (1920: 39). Along with this formal experimentation, Du Bois brings to the parks the experience of double consciousness, or the "sense of always looking at one's self through the eyes of others, of measuring one's soul by the tape of a world that looks on in amused contempt and pity" (1903: 9). In *The Souls of Black Folk*, he claims that this cognitive and affective doubling of the black self means that African-Americans are "gifted with second-sight in this American world," a way of seeing themselves and the country differently (1903: 9). Later, in his 1940 autobiography *Dusk of Dawn*, he speaks of a "double environment," a concept that merges double consciousness with "environment":

> Not only do white men but also colored men forget the facts of the Negro's double environment. The Negro American has not only the white surrounding world, but usually, and touching him much more nearly and compellingly, is the environment furnished by his own colored group. (1940: 173)

African-Americans experience their own immediate environment as it is moated by the larger white environment. They experience environments doubly, as both white and black enfolded in one another. The concept of double consciousness can be augmented to include the psychic internalization of double environments.

Du Bois maps the disjunctive spaces of modernity and the double environments of the color line by engaging with the discourses of emergent environmentalist movements—a loose, mostly conservationist coalition that Roderick Frazier Nash dubs the "wilderness cult"—at the turn of the twentieth century (1967: 141). Writers, naturalists, and politicians such as Muir, Gifford Pinchot, and Roosevelt saw the federal government as protector of the nation's resources from unchecked profiteering and they campaigned for and secured the first national parks. Works such as Roosevelt's *The Wilderness*

Hunter (1893), Muir's *Our National Parks* (1901), and Pinchot's *The Fight for Conservation* (1910) came to embody an increasingly mainstream, white-dominated, and nationalistic environmentalist discourse. At the same time, many of these early environmentalists, particularly Roosevelt, deployed "nature" as an ideology meant to justify white supremacy, social Darwinism, and a cult of masculinity. While the mode of nature writing characteristic of Sierra Club founder John Muir contains exhaustive phenomenological detail, Du Bois's writing employs formal experimentation that gestures at a fragmented grasp of totality. For Du Bois, the sublimity of the Grand Canyon becomes an analog for the inaccessibility of the social totality.

Darkwater is significant for the literature of the civil rights and environmental movements because it bridges disparate histories and aesthetic modes. It developed out of two events that seem to belong separately to environmental history and African-American history: the passage of the 1916 National Parks Act and the Red Summer of 1919. The 1916 Act created the National Park Service and maneuvered into place the state apparatus needed to administer the nation's designated wilderness spaces, including the Grand Canyon (Merchant 2007: 151). The 1916 Act seemed to have caught the eye of the increasingly socialist Du Bois, for the power to administer the parks involved the massive and unprecedented expropriation of land away from private (and, perhaps unknown to Du Bois at the time, Native American) hands and into public control. Fueled by urban segregation, the bloody riots of the Red Summer ravaged the country's cities from May to September of 1919. For Du Bois, the riots were stoked in part by the unjust treatment of black soldiers during the First World War—a subject he analyzes and condemns throughout *Darkwater*. But the riots were also triggered by a drowning "accident" on a segregated Lake Michigan beach. Environmental historian Colin Fisher argues that the Chicago race riot reflected a longer struggle in the black community for access to public parks and other urban natural spaces (Fisher 2006: 63–76). In responding to these events, Du Bois racializes romantic modes of nature writing through the lens of double consciousness, double environments, and modernist aesthetics.

This chapter first explores the concept of wilderness in *The Souls of Black Folk* and Du Bois's 1904 "Credo," a short prayer-like piece he later reprinted as the opening of *Darkwater*. I then contextualize my reading of *Darkwater* by examining the wilderness discourse of Muir, Roosevelt, and Pinchot, whose works came to dominate the conservationist movement that had arisen between Du Bois's writing of *The Souls of Black Folk* and *Darkwater*. In the next section, I show how Du Bois's explorations of the double environments of Jim Crow and national parks in *Darkwater* foreground practices of segregation across both natural and urban spaces. Such practices involve managing and controlling space in order to include or exclude racial groups—to enforce a color line of physical space and aesthetic experience. At the same time that he racializes the nature discourses of the conservationist movement, Du Bois also revises their tropes in his own *Crisis*-style critique of these segregating practices. Du Bois uses Colonel Charles Young as a figure who unites the spaces and histories of Jim Crow and conservation. Du Bois's patchwork of nature writing ends with portraits of urban nature—portraits that anticipate the Harlem Renaissance project of reimagining an American cultural nationalism. Du Bois rearranges the opposition between natural and urban spaces, substituting a more differentiated, heterogeneous sense of modern space.

Wilderness in *The Souls of Black Folk* and the 1904 "Credo"

The environmental themes in *Darkwater* appear less anomalous when placed in the context of Du Bois's literary and sociological work at the dawn of his scholarly career in the late-nineteenth century. Much of his late-nineteenth-century work analyzed the economic plight of southern black folk, most notably his 1893 University of Berlin doctoral thesis, "The Large and Small-Scale System of Agriculture in the Southern U.S., 1840–1890" (Lewis 1993: 143). Du Bois brings a scholar's eye to the same region Washington wrote about. While this early work shows a primary concern with race and economics, the material relations within and across environments—whether they be rural or urban, swamps or plantations, national or global—increasingly come to the fore.

The Souls of Black Folk combines historical, sociological, and economic insight with what Leo Marx would describe as a "complex pastoral" mode of representation.[2] In contrast to sentimental depictions of an unspoiled nature, the complex pastoral imagines a landscape inscribed with the traces of modernization and, in Du Bois's case, the histories of slavery and Jim Crow (L. Marx 1964: 14–15). In the chapter "Of the Meaning of Progress," for example, Du Bois recounts his two summers spent teaching in rural Tennessee, where he often "lingered to look at the blue and yellow mountains stretching toward the Carolinas" (1903: 49). This reverie is framed within a racial and social context: Du Bois was at the time a student at the all-black Fisk University and received his summer school training at a segregated teachers' institute. He characterizes his journey to dine with the white school commissioner's family as idyllic: the "sun laughed and the water jingled" as he walked through the woods. The idyll suddenly takes a wrong turn when he arrives and sits down to eat with the family: "even then fell the awful shadow of the Veil, for they ate first, then I—alone" (1903: 50). This complex-pastoral mode is mixed with the experience of double consciousness and double environment.

My foremost concern here is to sketch Du Bois's early, complex-pastoral figuration specifically of wilderness rather than a generalized environment in *The Souls of Black Folk*. This early figuration of wilderness previews the even more complex representation of race and nature in *Darkwater*. To understand wilderness in *The Souls of Black Folk*, it is important to contextualize it with other romantic discourses circulating about wilderness at the time. Du Bois's contemporary Roosevelt romanticized and politicized wilderness in his frontier memoir *The Wilderness Hunter*, published ten years before *The Souls of Black Folk* in 1893. Roosevelt is exemplary here because of his key role in the conservationist movement. Among his many accomplishments, he successfully lobbied for the Forest Reserve Act of 1891 and served as president of the Boone and Crockett Club, an influential conservation lobbying group, for six years (Cutright 1985: 182). As US president, he worked closely with Pinchot to establish the national parks and federal bureaus that managed forests and game. His many writings about his frontier sojourns helped him fashion a self- and public-image as an amateur naturalist and "wilderness warrior," in Douglas Brinkley's words, which in turn motivated his conservationist policies. *The Wilderness Hunter* offers an account of the future president's hunting and ranching experiences in the Dakota Badlands—a "devil's wilderness"—during the last days of the Western frontier (Roosevelt 1893: 71). Environmental justice critic Mei Mei Evans contends that there is a close relation between wilderness and American cultural identity in popular narratives like Roosevelt's: the "conception of wilderness or Nature in U. S. American popular culture is the site *par excellence* for (re)invention of the self" (2002: 182). Roosevelt's memoir, then, is an act of political self-invention, as he "finds" the essence of that political identity in the Dakotas, far removed from his comfortable New York lifestyle.

In *The Wilderness Hunter* Preface, Roosevelt begins by remarking that he spent much of his life "either in the wilderness or on the borders of the settled country" (1893: xxi). He goes on to paint his romanticized view of wilderness, linking it to nationalism, democracy, and masculinity:

> In hunting, the finding and killing of the game is after all but a part of the whole. The free, self-reliant, adventurous life, with its rugged and stalwart democracy; the wild surroundings, the grand beauty of the scenery, the chance to study the ways and habits of the woodland creatures—all these unite to give to the career of the wilderness hunter its peculiar charm. The chase is among the best of all national pastimes; it cultivates that vigorous manliness for the lack of which in a nation, as in an individual, the possession of no other qualities can possibly atone. (1893: xxi)

For Roosevelt, wilderness is both "inside" and "outside" of civilization. On the one hand, removal from civilization forces him to cultivate the manly virtues of self-reliance and rugged individualism. On the other hand, this very removal "civilizes" or anthropomorphizes the wilderness as an ideal training ground for the hard-hitting political life that someone born into the comfortable and well-connected life of New York City's elite would need.

The rest of Roosevelt's memoir seldom refers back to civilized life, creating the effect of the solitary frontiersman in the Dakota territories and reflecting the disjunctive space of modern capitalism. Typifying the nature writing genre, he provides exhaustive phenomenological detail of the various species he encounters and hunts: blacktail and whitetail deer, prong-horn antelope, mountain sheep, white goat, caribou, round-horned elk, and moose. Interspersed with thrills of the chase are contemplative, pastoral moments, as when Roosevelt stops to listen to a mockingbird sing: "theme followed theme, a torrent of music, a swelling tide of harmony, in which scarcely any two bars were alike" (1893: 47). Moments of rapture like this one reveal a romantic sensibility at work or, in Leo Marx's lexicon, sentimental pastoralism. However, political life creeps back into the text through analogy. For example, Roosevelt likens the teamwork required of ranchers in order to round up cattle to a "real and healthy democracy" (1893: 69).

The memoir concludes with a form of politicized wilderness hero-worship akin to the romanticism of Thomas Carlyle. Life in the wild is a "rugged and stalwart democracy; there every man stands for what he actually is" (1893: 161). He then lists a number of exemplary great men, American leaders who "sought strength and pleasure in the chase" and in the process discovered their essence: George Washington, Abraham Lincoln, Andrew Jackson, Daniel Webster, Henry Clay, and Henry Cabot Lodge (164–7). For the romantic Roosevelt, wilderness discloses the essence of great men; it helps realize a masculinized democracy and American nationalism, and lies at the core of American identity.

Du Boisian and Rooseveltian conceptions of wilderness cannot be reduced to opposing viewpoints, especially given *The Souls of Black Folk*'s ready use of a German romantic aesthetic and Herderian philosophy of the *Volk* in order to promote a black nationalism. Just as white America's strength is drawn from nature in *The Wilderness Hunter*, so too is an emergent black nationalism drawn from the black folk's connection to the southern soil in *The Souls of Black Folk*. To do this, Du Bois draws on the eighteenth-century *Sturm und Drang* rhetoric of early German romanticism, with a focus on the landscape as an objective correlative for the "storm and stress of human souls" (1903: 129). Similarly, Roosevelt valorizes frontier travel and hunting as correlatives of the human spirit, in which rugged conditions dish out chicken soup for the sportsman's soul: "[n]o man who, for his good fortune, has at times in his life endured trial and hardship, ever fails to appreciate the strong elemental pleasures of rest after labor, food after hunger, warmth and shelter after bitter cold" (1893: 57). Placed in its context, Roosevelt here plays the role of the white, European frontiersman "going native."

However, despite their shared romanticism, Du Bois and Roosevelt also work within divergent traditions of American and African-American wilderness thinking and imagery. Where Roosevelt sees the wilderness as a proving ground for a future great leader, Du Bois works within an African-American tradition that sees wilderness more ambivalently as both a refuge and a difficult spiritual trial for downtrodden black masses. In his study of metaphorical geography and identity, Melvin K. Dixon argues that spatial metaphors of mountaintops, wilderness, and the underground, structure a figural as well as often literal topography of an African-American quest for selfhood. Such metaphors create "alternative landscapes where black culture can flourish apart from any marginal, prescribed 'place'" (1987: 2). During slavery, wilderness takes on special symbolic status as a pathway to freedom and a space of flight from the plantation zone, as dramatized in the slave narratives of Frederick Douglass and Henry Bibb (1987: 26).

The slave song "Go in de Wilderness," published in an 1867 collection, combines many of the themes seen in the various "Sorrow Songs" Du Bois analyzes toward the end of *The Souls of Black Folk*:

> I found free grace in de wilderness,
> in de wilderness, in de wilderness,
> I found free grace in de wilderness
> For I'm a-going home. (qtd. in Dixon 1987: 18)

The wilderness offers a spiritual and physical alternative to the plantation, an oppressive pastoralized space cultivated and "conquered" by slave labor. Du Bois generalizes that in slave songs the "'Wilderness' was the home of God" (1903: 82). The wilderness here, as in the trials of biblical figures, is also a space that both tests the individual and, through this test, offers the possibility of salvation and refuge.

For Du Bois, laboring and pastoralizing the American wilderness is one of the "gifts" of black folk to the country's early formation. In the context of arguing for the integration of a black nation into the nation as a whole, Du Bois observes that slaves have, in an "ill-harmonized and unmelodious land," given their "sweat and brawn to beat back the wilderness, conquer the soil, and lay the foundations of this vast economic empire" (1903: 187). In *The Gift of Black Folk*, he would later reiterate the role of black labor in taming the American wilderness and modernizing the "new world": the "black man was the pioneer in the hard physical work which began the reduction of the American wilderness" (1924: 13). For Du Bois, conquering the wilderness becomes the occasion for locating a black nationalism at the forefront of an American nationalism and expansionism. Much like it did for Washington, this black environmental reconstruction turns the alienated labor of slavery into a case for the kinship between African-Americans and nature, and thus to the kind of American national identity advocated by Roosevelt.

While the "Forethought" of *The Souls of Black Folk* draws the bulk of critical attention for famously announcing the problem of the twentieth century as the "problem of the color-line" and for introducing the concept-metaphor of "the Veil," the single-paragraph "Afterthought" employs a new concept-metaphor: the "world-wilderness" (1903: 189). This metaphor becomes important from an ecological perspective and for understanding some of *Darkwater*'s environmental themes. Additionally, Du Bois thought the concept-metaphor significant enough to decide to conclude the book with it. The concept also helps to frame the color and ecological lines as more than a national problem, as well as to preview the transnational turn of *Darkwater*. "World-wilderness" appears in the context of an apostrophe to the reader and a prayer to "God the Reader." The whole "Afterthought" also employs an extended nature metaphor that invokes a menacing atmosphere indicative of a complex-pastoral aesthetic mode:

> *Hear my cry, O God the Reader; vouchsafe that this my book fall not still-born into the world-wilderness. Let there spring, Gentle One, from out its leaves vigor of thought and thoughtful deed to reap the harvest wonderful. (Let the ears of a guilty people tingle with truth, and seventy millions sigh for the righteousness which exalteth nations, in this drear day when human brotherhood is mockery and a snare.) Thus in Thy good time may infinite reason turn the tangle straight, and these crooked marks on a fragile leaf be not indeed.* (1903: 189)

In the context of the extended metaphor, "world-wilderness" refers to the world of print culture and an international readership. These "crooked marks" (writing) on a "fragile leaf" (the book's pages) pun on the materiality of the book—it is as though the book starts to spring to life in the reader's hands in an instance of the trope of the talking book. But the metaphor "leaf" suggests the material origin of books in wood pulp, in trees, and thus in nature and out of the soil. The wilderness here pointedly suggests hostility, for the book is like the infant Oedipus abandoned to the wild. But it also suggests the world-wilderness as a space of trial for the souls of black folk.

The year after publishing *The Souls of Black Folk*, Du Bois's "Credo," a short prayer-like work he would later choose and leave mostly unchanged for the opening of *Darkwater*, appeared on a single page in an October 1904 issue of the *Independent*. Though it does not mention "wilderness," it includes pastoral and racial themes that help to bridge *The Souls of Black Folk* to *Darkwater*. The "Credo" professes a series of beliefs: in God, in the "Negro Race," in "humble, reverent service," in the "Prince of Peace," and in the "Training of Children" (1904: 787). Like so much of the work produced by African-American writers at the time, "Credo" appears doubly coded for white and black: white audiences would read expressions of Christian piety, whereas black audiences would read a profession of racial pride and spiritual uplift. "Credo" enjoyed immense popularity, suggesting that its racial, religious, and pastoral themes must have touched the pulse of the country's black masses. It was reprinted throughout the black press, and a member of Du Bois's short-lived but significant Niagara Movement read it aloud at the group's second meeting (Lewis 1993: 12; 328–9). When it was published again in *Darkwater*, which sold well to the working class and Talented Tenth African-Americans alike, families across the nation hung it on their walls (Lewis 1993: 312–13).

"Credo" strategically muddles black nationalism with a mainstream American nationalism. Echoing the religious and egalitarian sentiments expressed in the Preamble to the US Constitution as well as the Catholic "Apostles' Creed," Du Bois begins: "I believe in God, who made of one blood all races that on earth do dwell" (1904: 787). He changes "races" to "nations" in the *Darkwater* version, reflecting again the book's globalist turn. About halfway through the Credo, Du Bois condemns the "scramble for Africa": "I believe that the wicked conquest of weaker and darker nations by nations whiter and stronger but foreshadows the death of that strength" (1904: 787). Careful to distinguish his more German-romantic religious vision from Washington's pragmatism, Du Bois exhorts the races / nations to strive for the "possibility of infinite development" (1904: 787). Listing "black and brown and white" races, he singles out the exceptional potential of the "Negro Race": he believes in the "beauty of its genius, the sweetness of its soul, and its strength in that meekness which shall yet inherit this turbulent earth"

(1904: 787). In a preview of Du Bois's later, more explicit brand of socialism, labor serves as the great equalizer and builder of interracial solidarity, for there is "no distinction between the black, sweating cotton hands of Georgia and the first families of Virginia" (1904: 787).

Along with black nationalism and an expressed belief in a possibly Christian deity, free movement within national space is a central motif of the "Credo." Du Bois believes that everyone should have the "space to stretch their arms and their souls; the right to breathe and the right to vote" and to "enjoy the sunshine and ride on the railroads"—freedoms that can only be fully realized through desegregation. Under the category of "Training of Children" in the Credo's penultimate paragraph, Du Bois champions a pastoral pedagogy, advocating that "little souls" be led out into the "green pastures and beside the still waters, not for pelf or peace, but for life lit by some large vision of beauty and goodness and truth" (1904: 787). The distinction between venturing out into the wilderness not for "pelf or peace" but for "life lit" by the good, the true, and the beautiful challenges the popular, contemporaneous view of nature as a relaxing retreat for nerve-wracked, white bourgeois urbanites. This pastoral scene appears to reconcile racial conflict, as black and white children enjoy an idyll in the country. It also echoes the idea of nature as training ground in Washington's *Working with the Hands* and Roosevelt's *The Wilderness Hunter*. Nature for Du Bois is not an upper-class white playground but a space where sublime and existential truths are revealed. In Du Bois's early work, he sets up a discourse of nature and wilderness that parallels those of other writers such as Roosevelt. For Roosevelt in *The Wilderness Hunter*, the wilderness is a proving ground where he shapes his political identity. For Du Bois in *The Souls of Black Folk*, wilderness is filtered through both his Germanromantic sensibility and his invocation of wilderness tropes in Negro spirituals, or "Sorrow Songs." His writing is a version of complex pastoral: he frames nature and wilderness tropes within a larger social critique of racism and the experience of double environments. "Credo" extends this complex pastoral, linking travel and free movement to the experience of the overall national space. In this way, he sets up an African-American counter-discourse about wilderness that becomes more evident and fully developed in *Darkwater*.

National Parks and Race: John Muir, Gifford Pinchot, and the Grand Canyon

By the time Du Bois wrote *Darkwater*, the wilderness preservationists had been fighting for the establishment of national parks for decades. The recognition of the Grand Canyon as a national park in 1919 marks a symbolic culmination of this history of the struggle to preserve supposedly pristine natural spaces. In the dominant reading of this history, preservationists such as Sierra Club founder John Muir saw this push as a noble resistance to the expansion of eastern capital set on consuming the nation's natural resources. Against this reading of the history of the parks, Richard Grusin, borrowing a notion from nineteenth-century landscape architect Frederick Law Olmstead, argues that the formation of the parks functioned as part of a national project of "postbellum reunification"—an attempt to unify the country geographically and culturally after the North/South division of the Civil War (2004: 23). The way people experienced wilderness and the national parks at the time depended largely on the discursive frames of writers such as Roosevelt, Muir, and Pinchot. Works such as Muir's *Our National Parks* and Pinchot's *The Fight for Conservation* helped shape the parks as aesthetic, political, and cultural constructions—constructions that Du Bois challenges with his own reconstruction. As the myth of the frontier ebbed, their rhetoric sought what Terry Gifford calls a "rediscovery" of the western frontier as an "essentially inner experience," though access to this "inner experience" would for a while only be available to wealthy white tourists (2006: 19). These works also codify and popularize the dominant environmentalist discourse that Du Bois critiques and reframes in *Darkwater*.

Conservationists such as Pinchot advocated the "wise use" of natural resources, while preservationists such as Muir were more romantic in outlook, calling for large wilderness areas to be set aside, unused, and uninhabited (Nash 1967: 129). Beginning in the 1870s, Muir began publicizing the beauty of places such as Yosemite Valley in magazines such as *Century Magazine* and *Harper's* and in a number of bestselling books (Gifford 2006: 29; 39). His *Our National Parks* celebrates and commodifies various national parks, emphasizing their aesthetic attraction to wealthy easterners and centering on

Yosemite, Yellowstone, Sequoia, and General Grant National Parks. Muir's passages celebrating the Grand Canyon (not yet a national park) helped sell the idea of the park to the federal government and to tourists: "so incomparably lovely and grand and supreme is it above all other cañons in our fire-moulded, earthquake-shaken, rain-washed, wave-washed, river and glacier sculptured world" (1901: 35–6). He repeatedly stresses the canyon's transcendence and otherworldliness: "as unearthly in the color and grandeur and quantity of its architecture, as if you had found it after death, on some other star" (1901: 35). With the "you" directed at the tourist-reader, Muir functions as a sort of guide who will lead the visitor to the romantic sublime. *Our National Parks* is full of descriptions like these, framing these wilderness spaces as singular, sublime, sacred, and almost entirely devoid of any sign of civilization.

Though he does champion the public good over private profit, Muir's writing also participates in a discourse of enclosure that assumes a division between culture and nature—a division that Du Bois implicitly challenges as racially codified. Outka chronicles Muir's latent racism, arguing that his account of the western frontier "traces the process of forgetting the explicitly racialized geography of the east and south" (2008: 156). Muir's project continues the postbellum reunification that, Outka argues, sought to repress the national trauma of slavery and the Civil War. Despite such repression and even as they espouse the interconnectedness of all things, Muir's writings reflect a Jim Crow mentality of segregation. Though not explicitly stated, Muir's target audience is clearly white, city-dwelling bourgeois eastern-ers: "[a]wakening from the stupefying effects of the vice of over-industry and the deadly apathy of luxury, they as do best they can to mix and enrich their own little ongoings with those of Nature, and to get rid of rust and disease" (1901: 1). This appeal is a strategic attempt to translate Muir's own values into the utilitarianism of the urban-dweller and to advertise the parks to potential tourists. This passage also reflects white male fears of, as Nash puts it, "over-civilization" that could lead to a national crisis of masculinity and the degeneration of the white race (1967: 152). Roosevelt and George Bird Grinnell, the editor of *Forest and Stream*, would say in a coauthored 1893 publication laying out the principles of the Boone and Crocket Club that without the manly virtues cultivated in the wilderness "no race can do its life work well" (qtd. in

Nash 1967: 152–3). The solution to the feminizing force of modernity would be a return to a primitive condition, in which the cure is, as Muir famously said, to "go home" to nature: "going to the mountains is going home."

Muir more directly manifests his racism in his attitude toward Native Americans. In *Our National Parks*, a racially charged moment occurs when he describes his visit to Alaska. While studying the various Alaskan plant and animal species, he encounters a group of Inuit and proceeds to compare them with animals: "men, women, and children, loose and hairy like wild animals" (1901: 9). He objectifies them and places them in a picturesque landscape: a "lively picture they made, and a pleasant one" (1901: 10). Elsewhere, he describes Yosemite's Native Americans as "lazy" and reassures those white tourists who might fear that the park harbors hostility: "As to Indians, most of them are dead or civilized into useless innocence" (1901: 193; 28). Merchant also charts examples of Muir's racism toward Native Americans, citing numerous cases where Muir characterizes Indians as "dark and dirty" contaminants in his vision of a human-free wilderness (Merchant 2003: 382). These are not "gotcha" racist moments incidental to Muir's nature writing, but rather evidence of his participation in a discourse of enclosure and segregation between culture and nature that had larger material and historical effects.

This conservationist discourse of enclosure helped create the cultural environment that would validate the removal of Native Americans from these wilderness areas. In the case of the Grand Canyon, there was a decades-long struggle between the Havasupai tribe and the federal government over control of the land and resources. According to historian Karl Jacoby, Native American experiences from Wisconsin and Michigan to Minnesota and Colorado reveal that "Indian peoples offered a powerful collective dissent from the official mores of conservation" (2001: 150–51). For the Havasupai, conservation merely continued a history of conquest over their land and resources. In 1893, President Benjamin Harrison issued an executive order to create the Grand Canyon Forest Reserve, federalizing tribal hunting land and turning the Havasupai into a "solitary island in a sea of conservation land" (Jacoby 2001: 165). The final designation of the Grand Canyon as a national park led to the construction of ranger stations, warehouses, mess halls, administration buildings, roads, and trails along the canyon's rim. Ironically, many of the Havasupai were employed as wage laborers for these various construction projects (Jacoby 2001: 187–8). The Havasupai experienced the park's establishment as a "narrative of loss" rather than national gain (Jacoby 2001: 149).

While Native Americans make occasional appearances across Muir's oeuvre, African- Americans appear mainly in the posthumously published *A Thousand-Mile Walk to the Gulf*.[3] As "natural" objects Muir encounters on his wilderness journeys, African-Americans are sentimentalized from within an equally sentimental view of nature as a passive landscape painting put there for the white gaze to behold. Like the naïve and cheery Captain Delano of Herman Melville's *Benito Cereno*, Muir cannot imagine black agency or culture. Stumbling across some playful black children in Florida, Muir concludes that they do not live "in harmony with Nature," for "[b]irds make nests and nearly all beasts make some kind of bed for their young; but these negroes allow their younglings to lie nestless and naked in the dirt" (1916: 107). Paradoxically, African-Americans are both discordant with nature and "beasts" segregated into it—they are *in* nature but not *of* it. "Harmony" with nature, it seems, is best achieved by a well-traveled, white naturalist like Muir himself. This culture–nature opposition clears the ground for a pernicious white supremacy that sees African-Americans as less than animals, for at least birds know how to make shelter.

Muir's much-maligned contemporary Gifford Pinchot held more controversial views about the relation between the social and natural worlds. His views build a sort of bridge between Muir and Du Bois. Much of Pinchot's negative reputation originates in the Hetch Hetchy Valley Dam controversy, when he approved the construction of a dam in the Yosemite National Park (1967: 161). But Pinchot combined his national park and wise-use advocacy with a strong, progressive stance on issues of social and economic justice—issues that merge in his nationalist rhetoric of domestication. His conservation manifesto *The Fight for Conservation* is strewn with metaphors of domesticating wilderness for the nation: the "nation that will lead the world will be a Nation of Homes. The object of the great Conservation movement is just this, to make our country a permanent and prosperous home for ourselves and for our children" (1910: 23). Functioning both as an agent of westward expansion and an idea to rally against, Pinchot argues that the profit-motive was also at work in this westward expansion and enclosure. He saw an opposition between narrowly defined profit and the public good, seeing conservation as a way of protecting people (and nature) from the powerful interests of the captains of industry and their "great concentrations of capital" (Pinchot 1910: 26). Rather than repudiate the profit-motive altogether, he sought to redefine it in democratic and quasi-socialist terms: "natural resources must be developed and preserved for the benefit of the many, and not merely for the profit of a few" (1910: 46–50). Pinchot's redefined notion of profit and attempt to synthesize conservation with cultural and economic demands offers a philosophical bridge between conservation and Du Bois.

Du Bois at the Grand Cañon: "Of Beauty and Death" and the Sublime

The Grand Canyon passage in "Of Beauty and Death" paints the park as sublime, while at the same time drawing on the racialized, complex pastoralism and double environments found in *The Souls of Black Folk* and other parts of *Darkwater*. That Du Bois (or any black writer for that matter) writes about the parks at all is significant in 1920, given the perceived lack of African-American interest in wilderness spaces. This passage also challenges Outka's white sublime / black trauma opposition, revealing a tradition of African-American writing on the natural sublime that will be further explored in later chapters. By representing the Grand Canyon or "Grand Cañon" (Du Bois uses the Spanish name), Du Bois engages in the American cultural nationalism of representing the parks, but he rejects Olmsted's project of postbellum reunification. Rather than conceal the trauma of civil war, Du Bois seeks to denaturalize segregation and naturalize integration in defiance of Jim Crow and early environmentalist discourse.

The Grand Cañon passage gains much of its implied meaning through the essay's overall context. The essay's experimental form redefines and widens the scope of conventional nature writing with a modernist aesthetic of juxtaposition. In the essay, Du Bois actually visits both the Grand Canyon National Park and Maine's Acadia National Park, where he marvels at the "glory of physical nature," though he describes the cañon in greater detail (1920: 174). Beginning early on with the essay's fourth fragment, the Acadia section previews what is to come and establishes the centrality of the national parks to the essay's themes. With careful attention to place names, Du Bois describes Bar Harbor, Mount Desert, and Frenchman's Bay off the coast of Maine, where he admires the variety of intermingling colors: "white, gray, and inken" clouds, a "shadowy velvet" that "veiled the mountain," the sea's "gray and yellowing greens and doubtful blues, blacks not quite black, tinted silvers and golds and dreaming whites" (1920: 174–5). This motif of integrated colors in nature will become even more evident in the later Grand Canyon section. Evoking a key concept-metaphor from *The Souls of Black Folk*, Du Bois repeatedly puns on "veil," for nature is continually veiling and unveiling itself: "[b]efore the unveiled face of nature as it lies naked on the Maine coast, rises a certain human awe" (1920: 175). This unveiled space offers Du Bois a respite from the social world, someplace where he can rejuvenate and where, echoing Muir, "in the tired days of life men should come and worship here and renew their spirit" (1920: 175).

The Grand Canyon section is sandwiched between a tale of segregation in the military during the Great War and a number of fragments critiquing Jim Crow. Earlier in the essay, Du Bois explicitly characterizes his overall method as "juxtaposition" in order to "compare the least of the world's beauty with the least of its ugliness—not murder, starvation, and rapine, with love and friendship and creation—but the glory of sea and sky and city, with the little hatefulnesses and thoughtlessnesses of race prejudice" (1920: 174). Juxtaposition shows that the "truth" of the ugliness of Jim Crow and the beauty of the national parks (or natural beauty in general) exist in the same world: "[t]here is not in the world a more disgraceful denial of human brotherhood than the 'Jim-Crow' car of the southern United States; but, too, just as true, there is nothing more beautiful in the universe than sunset and moonlight on Montego Bay in far Jamaica" (1920: 177). Further juxtapositions of about twenty separate fragments make "Of Beauty and Death" into a sort of montage capable of producing unexpected connections and third meanings similar to the later dialectical montage of 1920s Soviet cinematic style of Sergei Eisenstein. It can produce meanings and associations that would usually escape the intentional control of the author, allowing a textual unconscious to run wild. Rather than writing a philosophical tract, Du Bois hopes that "out of such juxtaposition we may, perhaps, deduce some rule of beauty and life—or death?" (1920: 174). The logic of juxtaposition defies the Aristotelian syllogism, for it seeks to deduce underlying truths about the social totality by means of aesthetic accident instead of philosophical deliberation.[4]

The Grand Canyon passage must be placed in the context of the passage immediately preceding it, where Du Bois describes a conversation with a multiracial group of friends. He draws an analogy to colors mingling in nature: "[a]round me sat color in human flesh—brown that crimsoned readily; dim soft-yellow that escaped description; cream-like duskiness that shadowed to rich tints of autumn leaves" (1920: 176). A white companion suggests that the group travel for recreation, but the "thought of a journey seemed to depress" the others at the table (1920: 176). An unnamed black friend (who could be Du Bois himself) then gives an account of the arduous process of traveling by train. Petty Jim Crow "thoughtlessnesses" harass the black passenger before she has even boarded the train: "to buy a ticket is torture; you stand and stand and wait and wait until every white person at the 'other window' is waited on" (1920: 176). After dealing with the agent's racially motivated contempt, the black passenger must then ride in the segregated Jim Crow car:

> Usually there is no step to help you climb on and often the car is a smoker cut in two and you must pass through the white smokers or else they pass through your part, with swagger and noise and stares. Your compartment is a half or a quarter or an eighth of the oldest car in service on the road ... The white train crew from the baggage car uses the "Jim-Crow" to lounge in and perform their toilet. The conductor appropriates two seats for himself and his papers and yells gruffly for your tickets before the train has scarcely started ... As for toilet rooms,—don't! (1920: 176–7)

National park enthusiasts extolled the virtues of visits to wilderness spaces as a rejuvenating escape from the claustrophobia of the cities, yet the punishing ride in a Jim Crow car undermines this particular value of the parks—or specifically the journey to the parks—for African- Americans. Du Bois exposes park tourism as not just bourgeois escape, but also an activity of white privilege. Railroad companies themselves possessed a huge economic stake in establishing the parks for tourism, prospecting for new vistas as one would for gold. Railroad companies such as Northern Pacific, for example, lobbied for the establishment of Yellowstone National Park in 1872. They and others in the tourism industry sought to make the national parks, in Grusin's words, an "idealized commodity" for tourists as well as armchair tourists eager to consume verbal and visual representations such as those of Muir and land-scape painter Thomas Moran (2004: 12). In helping to commodify and pro-mote the parks, the railroad companies also succeeded in expanding their Jim Crow policies westward. To be sure, the reasons Du Bois gives for visiting the parks are similar to Muir's: bourgeois exhaustion with urban life and war. He affirms, too, that actually being in the national parks can offer African-Americans temporary respite from racism. But Du Bois asks a question about the infrequency of visitors to these places, which leads him directly to issues of race: "[w]hy do not those who are scarred in the world's battle and hurt by its hardness travel to these places of beauty and drown themselves in the utter joy of life?" (1920: 176). Whatever their value as escape for Du Bois, getting to the parks requires disposable incomes and navigation of the Jim Crow gauntlet—petty, everyday intrusions when set next to the grandeur of the Grand Canyon.

The travel passage that follows this description of a Jim Crow car offers an unusual moment in Du Bois's prolific corpus. It begins by charting Du Bois's "great journey" that spans "over seven thousand mighty miles" across the United States (1920: 182).[5] He begins with the fairy-tale opening "Once upon a time," which suggests this journey is somewhat imaginary—a fan-tasy confabulated to illustrate his form of social protest (1920: 182). Traveling through deserts, mountains, and cities, he visits, among other places, the Rocky Mountains, "the empire of Texas," and finally the Grand Canyon (1920: 182). He also intersperses visits to cities on this trip: Seattle, Kansas City, Chicago, Los Angeles, and Manhattan. The journey, then, is diverse and sweeping both in its geographical and environmental range, for Du Bois moves from the most natural spaces to the most built and human-centered environments. In its inventorial geography marked by the essay's fragmen-tary, elliptical prose, the journey also invokes the close relation between natu-ral resources and nationalism in conservationist discourse. In *The Wilderness Hunter*, for example, Roosevelt performs a similar inventory of the country's earthly gifts, naming places, regions, and animal species: the Atlantic Coast, the Mississippi Valley, "magnificent hardwood forest[s]," "fertile prairies," "tepid swamps" that "teem with reptile life," Texas, the Rocky Mountains, the "strangely shaped and colored Bad Lands" (1893: 1–11). Contrary to Du Bois, Roosevelt does not list any cities, showing the latter's sense of a distinct separation between natural and built environments. By intertwining such seemingly disparate and opposed spaces, Du Bois forces us to compare them according to the logic of double consciousness and double environments.

In contrast to the more static natural beauty of Acadia, Du Bois represents the Grand Canyon as a sublime landscape that is dynamic and even somewhat menacing. This representation of the canyon as sublime follows in a long tradition of nature writing about the southwestern desert region. Grusin observes that from its initial exploration in 1869 to 1919, the Grand Canyon has been troped as "cognitively inaccessible" and the "preservation of this inaccessibility is critical to the establishment and continued attraction" of the park (2004: 103). Here, Du Bois's writing typifies both representations of the canyon and the ambivalence toward wilderness found in African-American slave narratives and sorrow songs. The tradition of black wilderness ambivalence that emerged in *The Souls of Black Folk* reaches its apotheosis in *Darkwater*. The Grand Canyon, then, is the perfect landscape for a meeting between African-American ambivalence and sublime representations of nature.

Such ambivalence toward the canyon follows the same structural logic between the human observer and nature found in Kant's theory of the sublime. According to the *Critique of Judgment*, the sense of the sublime differs from beauty: the "beautiful in nature relates to the form of the object, and this consists in limitation, whereas the sublime is to be found in an object even devoid of form" (1793: 306). For Kant, natural beauty "conveys a finality in its form" and suggests a systematic ordering even if the whole cannot be comprehended by the observer (1793: 307–8). Du Bois's visit to Acadia exemplifies the beauty both in Kant's sense and in the title "Of Beauty and Death." Du Bois claims, following Kant, that beauty has a certain completeness to it: "for beauty by its very being and definition has in each definition its ends and limits" (1920: 190). In contrast to beauty, the sublime provokes an "image of *limitlessness*, yet with a super-added thought of its totality" (Kant 1793: 306). The sublime is nature as excess, as a break from form and systematic ordering that produces a "negative pleasure" in the subject, who is, ambivalently, "alternately repelled" and attracted to the sublime object (Kant 1793: 307).

The ambivalence built into the experience of the sublime suggests that it has more to do with culture than with nature, with subjective feeling than the perceived thing-in-itself. In Spivak's reading of the Kantian sublime, the subject's "feeling for nature" operates according to a metalepsis, a substitution of effect for cause (in this case, of nature for culture) (1793: 11). For Kant, sublime feeling is the result of receptivity to aesthetic experience that must be cultivated, for it is the "attitude of mind that introduces sublimity into the image of nature" (Kant 1793: 308). Spivak argues that because the sublime depends on the subject's cultivated sensibility, it is a cultural aptitude belonging, by way of implication, to the enlightened, European subject. This aesthetic capacity is important in the Kantian philosophical system because, in addition, it reveals the capacity for freedom, which for Kant is also the capacity to make ethical choices and to be fully human. Opposed to the cultured European, Spivak argues, is the "man in raw," who corresponds to the "savage," or, adjusted for the context of the Jim Crow era, African- Americans. Pseudo-scientific studies such as Charles Carroll's *The Mystery Solved: The Negro a Beast* (1900), novels such as Thomas Dixon's *The Leopard's Spots* (1908), and D. W. Griffith's film *The Birth of a Nation* (1915) consistently portray African-Americans as animalistic, uncultured raw men (1993: 276). As shown earlier, Muir portrays the black children in Florida as incapable of aesthetically (and spiritually) experiencing the nature around them. For Kant, Spivak goes on, the raw man experiences the sublime as "*Abgrund*-affect," as terror before an abyss (1999: 26).

Pushing back against these popular portrayals, Du Bois offers a decidedly "cultured" experience of the canyon. He begins his sublime portrait with a Miltonic trope of the wounded, feminized earth: "[i]t is a sudden void in the bosom of earth, down to its entrails—a wound where the dull titanic knife has turned and twisted in the hole" (1920: 182-3). The "sudden" appearance of the "void" mimics or attempts to recover the affective response of the first discoverers of the Canyon. The sublime, expressed as an act of phallic violence inflicted on the earth, functions as a strategy to recuperate and represent an authentic encounter with nature. Given its context in the essay, the image also suggests the trauma of racial violence. Du Bois then moves on to describe the colors of the Canyon—a tactic he uses throughout the essay to contrast the fluid mingling of colors in nature with the social rigidity of the color-line problem. The Grand Canyon "hole" leftover from the knife leaves the anthropomorphized canyon's "edges livid, scarred, jagged, and pulsing over the white, and red, and purple of its mighty flesh" (1920: 183). The land-scape of the canyon is like an inverted mountain, drawing its sublime power from the radical uniqueness—the seeming unnaturalness of the canyon itself. "It is awful," writes Du Bois, and because it appears as nature violently attacking herself (in reality, the "slow violence" of the Colorado River), "[t]here can be nothing like it. It is the earth and sky gone stark and raving mad. The mountains up-twirled, disbodied and inverted, stand on their peaks and throw their bowels to the sky. Their earth is air; their ether blood-red rock engreened. You stand upon their roots and fall into their pinnacles, a mighty mile" (1920: 183). Here, Du Bois gives us a black experience of the sublime.

Du Bois goes on in a mode of fervent questioning and Old Testament bom-bast, adopting rhetoric similar that of Muir's almost twenty years before:

> Behold this mauve and purple mocking of time and space! See yonder peak! No human foot has trod it. Into that blue shadow only the eye of God has looked. Listen to the accents of that gorge which mutters: "Before Abraham was, I am." Is yonder wall a hedge of black or is it the rampart between heaven and hell? I see greens,—is it moss or giant pines? I see specks that may be boulders. Ever the winds sigh and drop into those sun-swept silences. Ever the gorge lies motionless, unmoved, until I fear. It is a grim thing, unholy, terrible! It is human—some mighty drama unseen, unheard, is playing there its tragedies or mocking comedy, and the laugh of endless years is shrieking onward from peak to peak, unheard, unechoed, and unknown. (1920: 183)

The repetition of "ever" and "mocking of time and space" suggests the can-yon's seeming eternity, created long before humans—before Abraham—ever existed. The sublime comes close to what Kant calls the "horrible," an ambig-uous variant on the sublime that closely resembles his youthful definition of the "dynamic sublime" or "terrifying sublime" in *Observations on the Feeling of the Beautiful and Sublime* (1764). Because, for example, a storm-wracked sea can present imminent danger to the viewer, it is "horrible," unless one has cultivated the subjective feelings capable of receiving it (Kant 1793: 308). The landscape gains some of its horror through the simultaneous absence of human presence—"No human foot has trod it"—and the canyon's uncanny anthropomorphism. This simultaneity makes the canyon a human-like alien, capable of the same or even greater acts of violence similar to those perpetrated by humans overseas in war-torn Europe or the 1919 race riots. By the measure of typical ecocritical litmus tests, such blatant anthropomorphism may undermine the possibility of a more ecocentric perspective in Du Bois's work. In this case, however, anthropomorphism functions more as rhetorical strategy than evidence of insensitivity to the landscape's alterity. Personifying the canyon as a "mighty drama" brings it closer to the social world, just as the natural colors—"mauve," "purple," "blue shadow," "greens"—evoke the problem of the color line. The gorge thus becomes a symbol of racial integration.

A series of short meditations on the African-American experience in Europe during the Great War immediately follows the Grand Canyon passage. Du Bois begins with an idyllic description of everyday race relations in Paris. Enjoying an evening out among "civilized folk," Du Bois feels thankful for the absence of the "hateful, murderous, dirty Thing which in American we call 'Nigger-hatred'" in the evening's "community of kindred souls" (1920: 184). The black intellectual's cultivated sensitivity to the natural sublime—expressed in the Grand Canyon reverie—manifests itself in a European social context as a "reverence for the Thought" that transcends the "commonplaces" of race (1920: 184). Through juxtaposition, Du Bois implies that the only escape from white America's racism is either into the bourgeois playground of the national parks or Europe. Set against the spirit of Roosevelt's nationalist "democracy" of American wilderness is Du Bois's exhortation to African-Americans: "[f]ellow blacks, we must join the democracy of Europe" (1920: 165).

Parisian intellectual life, however, is no paradise: the cityscape bears the traces of the war, itself a product of European colonialism turned against itself, as Du Bois argues in "The Souls of White Folk." The next fragment describes a haunting image of invasion: "[t]hrough [Paris's] streets—its narrow, winding streets, old and low and dark, carven and quaint,–poured thousands upon thousands of strange feet of khaki-clad foreigners" (1920: 185). The sublime feelings induced by the Grand Canyon transform into the terror of the cityscape. The streets are "feverish, crowded, nervous, hurried; full of uniforms and mourning bands, with cafes closed at 9:30" (1920: 186). In Du Bois's view, France is saved by black American soldiers drawn from every part of the United States. Ironically for Du Bois, the war affords African-Americans the opportunity to travel to Europe and witness its democracy. If Paris and the Grand Canyon can be seen as urban and natural democracies of color, then they are hard fought and hard won, for both mix "beauty and death." By juxtaposing this social expression of racial community in Paris with nature's mixing of colors at the Grand Canyon, Du Bois continues to naturalize desegregation and transnationalize a vision of democracy across the color line.

Actually being in the national parks can only offer African-Americans a temporary respite from racism. The reasons Du Bois gives for visiting the parks are similar to Muir's: bourgeois exhaustion with urban life and war. But he asks a question about the infrequency of visitors to these places, which leads him directly to issues of race: "[w]hy do not those who are scarred in the world's battle and hurt by its hardness travel to these places of beauty and drown themselves in the utter joy of life?" (1920: 176). Whatever their value as escape for Du Bois, getting to the parks requires the navigation of many obstacles set by Jim Crow—petty, everyday intrusions when set next to the grandeur of the Great War and black soldiers sacrificing their lives for France.

By intertwining the Grand Canyon with Jim Crow in these fragments, Du Bois strategically subverts the racialism of Kantian and conservationist discourses. He demonstrates not only an African-American aptitude for the aesthetic experience of nature, but also its superiority to a form of nature writing that erases signs of the social world. That Du Bois, or any African-American, proves capable of writing about nature so eloquently makes his nature writing an act of social protest. Unexpectedly, it is the experience of racism, which would seem to (and indeed threaten to) foreclose this aptitude in the first place that bestows the advantage of second-sight and a challenge to discourses of segregation. The black subject's second-sight saves her from the white bourgeois tourist's commodified experience of nature.

A few years later, in his Harlem Renaissance manifesto "Criteria of Negro Art" (1926), Du Bois shows his contempt for white American "excursionists," who interrupt his pastoral reverie at the Scottish lake of Sir Walter Scott's poem "Lady of the Lake" (1810). He sets the idyllic scene: "[i]t was quiet. You could glimpse the deer wandering in unbroken forests; you could hear the soft ripple of romance on the waters. Around me fell the cadence of that poetry of my youth. I fell asleep full of the enchantment of the Scottish border" (1926: 778). Into this scene, much like Leo Marx's machine in the garden, intrude the vulgar Americans:

> They were mostly Americans and they were loud and strident ... They all tried to get everywhere first. They pushed other people out of the way. They made all sorts of incoherent noises and gestures ... They carried, perhaps, a sense of strength and accomplishment, but their hearts had no conception of the beauty which pervaded this holy place. (1926: 778)

Here, it is the white American tourists who are the "men in the raw"; they are philistines without the capacity for aesthetic experience and they profane the "holy place." Worse yet, they drag along the noisy, frenzied rush of the city into the pastoral idyll, turning it into another urban space. Furthermore, Du Bois inverts white supremacy and reduces them to creatures incapable of speech or the ability to communicate at all.

Precisely because of their marginalization from this vulgar version of white American culture, African-Americans have an escape hatch out of philistinism. Du Bois states: "pushed aside as we have been in America, there has come to us not only a certain distaste for the tawdry and flamboyant but a vision of what the world could be if it were really a beautiful world" (1926: 778–9). Through this reversal of cultural taste, Du Bois transforms a perceived weakness into strength: African-Americans become "co-worker[s] in the kingdom of culture" (1903: 9). The ironic gift of second-sight becomes another Kantian faculty, a unique capacity for experiencing natural beauty that not only grants African-Americans access to the cultural–nationalist project of the national parks, but also reconfigures the opposition between culture and nature. Showing the influence of his study abroad in Germany, Du Bois even gives this African-American exceptionalism a flavor of German romanticism, seemingly to respond to Poundian exhortations to "make it new" with a "gift" of black folks' "new appreciation of joy, of a new desire to create, of a new will to be" (1926: 779). Continuing in this vein, he claims that the "bounden duty of black America" is to step forward as "custodian" of the beautiful, "to begin this great work of the creation of Beauty, of the preservation of Beauty, of the realization of Beauty" (1926: 782). Through participation in the cultural project of representing the sublimity of the cañon, Du

Bois invokes an African-American exceptionalism that previews the Harlem Renaissance. For Du Bois, Colonel Charles Young embodies this exceptionalism and plays a crucial role in connecting the essay's themes of segregation, national parks, and the war.

Charles Young at Sequoia National Park

Appearing immediately before the Grand Cañon passage, the longest section of "Of Beauty and Death" narrates the segregation of black soldiers during the First World War. Du Bois argues that this ultimate outrage (depriving black soldiers of their rights even as they died for their country) set in motion the "extraordinary series of events" that pushed black anger to a "fever heat" and culminated with the 1919 race riots (1920: 179). The historical and thematic links between this passage and the Grand Canyon seem unclear at first: what does anger about segregated soldiers have to do with national parks? Following the essay's method of juxtaposition, segregation and the national parks converge in the figure of Charles Young. A paragon of the Talented Tenth, Young was the third African-American to graduate from West Point Academy and the highest-ranking black officer in the US Army at the time. Promoted to colonel by the time he died in 1923, Young served in the military for twenty-eight years, commanding the all-black Twenty-fifth US Infantry and the Ninth US Calvary. Du Bois celebrates his friend's military accomplishments: "[i]n Haiti, in Liberia, in western camps, in the Sequoia Forests of California, and finally with Pershing in Mexico—in every case he triumphed" (1920: 181). Though Du Bois gives a brief account of Young's work at Sequoia, that account becomes significant to the essay because of its context among passages on Acadia and the Grand Canyon national parks.

Prior to the creation of the National Park Service, the caretaking duties fell to the US Army. In summer 1903, while serving as captain of the Ninth Calvary, Young was appointed to supervise the Sequoia and General Grant National Parks in the Sierra Nevada (Kilroy 2003: 60). Young himself helped literally and discursively to build the national parks as part of a larger project of American cultural nationalism, as well as perform his summer job as "custodian of the beautiful" (Du Bois 1926: 782). By focusing on the circumstances surrounding Young's discharge from the Army, Du Bois further connects segregation and the First World War to the cultural project of the national parks.

During the war, when many black leaders thought Young would have been promoted to general if he were white, he was unexpectedly forced to retire on the dubious grounds of high blood pressure (1920: 181). Du Bois fought hard on Young's behalf during this time—a fight that, according to David Levering Lewis, scarred Du Bois emotionally. Young's and Du Bois's friendship went back to their days teaching at Wilberforce College in Ohio from 1894 to 1896, where Du Bois taught classics and Young taught military science (Lewis 1993: 176; Kilroy 2003: 47). They would spend many evenings playing music together, occasionally accompanied by the poet Paul Laurence Dunbar (Kilroy 2003: 33). In public speeches, Young, though he admired and emulated the militaristic discipline at the heart of Washington's philosophy, would advocate Du Bois's Talented Tenth theory of an educated black leadership as the best path to full black citizenship (Kilroy 2003: 64). He campaigned on behalf of civil rights, contributing to and raising money for the NAACP's anti-lynching fund (Kilroy 2003: 110). Soon upon (what would prove to be) his temporary retirement, Young accepted a position on the NAACP board and toured the country speaking on behalf of civil rights (Kilroy 2003: 139). He even joked that he "fathered" *Darkwater*, because he saw so many of his conversations with Du Bois reiterated in that book. It is possible that one of those conversations revolved around Sequoia National Park, for which Young frequently waxed nostalgic later in life (O'Connell 2003). Du Bois responded by sending Young an autographed copy of *Darkwater* when it was published (Kilroy 2003: 150).

When the Great War came, however, Du Bois's friendship and loyalty to Young embroiled him in political debates with other civil rights leaders. Risking charges of nationalistic chauvinism from his Talented Tenth cohort, Du Bois supported the war in Europe. He reasoned that the sacrifice of African-American soldiers on European battlefields might, for all its necessary evil, pave the road to integration and full citizenship (Lewis 1993: 530). He thought (wrongly) that the gravitas of such large-scale war would squash the triviality of racism: "[w]hat were petty slights, silly insults, paltry problems, beside this call to do and dare and die?" (1920: 178). To Du Bois's chagrin, however, the war calcified the color line in the military. First, the US Army refused black volunteers, and then when a draft was implemented, black soldiers were segregated into separate regiments and used for labor purposes—a fate that befell 89 percent of black soldiers (1920: 179; Kilroy 2003: 119). Moreover, the black officers leading these soldiers would have to be trained at the segregated Camp Des Moines (Lewis 1993: 530). This caused Du Bois to proclaim that possibly "never before in the history of the United States has a portion of the citizens been so openly and crassly discriminated against by action of the general government" (1920: 179). Deciding that African-Americans had opportunistically to "take advantage of the disadvantage," he reasoned that the officer training camp set up at Des Moines was better than nothing, and rallied wavering civil rights leaders to support it. Du Bois, working in an uncharacteristically pragmatic mode and conciliatory mood, successfully advocated that black officers lead black soldiers (1920: 180). His support of the war and the camp stirred controversy among some of his closest allies, including Archibald Grimké of the Niagara Movement, *The Messenger* editors Asa Randolph and Chandler Owen, and William Monroe Trotter (Lewis 1993: 531).

In the midst of this less-than-ideal compromise, the dismissal of Young in the summer of 1917 (the first year the US entered the war) struck a significant blow to Du Bois's morale and that of black masses in general (Kilroy 2003: 120). To Du Bois, it was a major personal and political affront. Perhaps he speaks especially of his own feelings about the bad news when he writes: "[t]o say that Negroes of the United States were disheartened at the retirement of Colonel Young is to put it mildly" (1920: 181). There seemed to be no doubt surrounding Young's fitness: in protest against his racist superiors, the colonel even rode five hundred miles on horseback from his home in Ohio to Washington DC (Kilroy 2003: 120). Du Bois mobilized all the resources of the NAACP and *The Crisis* to lobby for the colonel's reinstatement, but to no avail (Kilroy 2003: 130). Young even had the backing of former president Roosevelt, who fantasized about Young leading a black version of Roosevelt's Spanish-American War era "Rough Riders" into European battlefields (Kilroy 2003: 124–5).

Young's forced retirement was emblematic of what was happening within the military across the United States. Everywhere, Du Bois protests, a black soldier would be "separated like a pest" from his regiment (1920: 181). He laments that "one poor fellow in Ohio solved the problem by cutting his throat" (1920: 181). White paranoia conjured the specter of "German plots" seeded among a disgruntled black populace, making "Negroes too dangerous an element to trust with guns" (1920: 179). *The Crisis* further testified to the poor treatment of black soldiers: the magazine reported on harassment of black soldiers by military police; the constant barrage of racial epithets from white soldiers and officers; the lack of USO facilities for black soldiers; and denials of recreational activities such as going to the movies (Lewis 1993: 135–6). A young George Schuyler, a sergeant, reported that black officers-in-training at Camp Des Moines received none of the study courses available to white officers (Lewis 1993: 542). In a foreshadowing of the 1919 riots, in 1917 a resentful black regiment attacked a police station and shot sixteen whites in Houston (Lewis 1993: 541). Du Bois compares the incongruous justice served against the perpetrators in Houston to those in the 1917 East St. Louis riots: "[a]t East St. Louis white strikers on war work killed and mobbed Negro working-men, and as a result 19 colored soldiers were hanged and 51 imprisoned for life for killing 17 whites at Houston, while for killing 125 Negroes in East St. Louis, 20 white men were imprisoned, none for more than 15 years, and 10 colored men with them" (1920: 182). Still embittered about all these events years later, Du Bois gave a eulogy in 1923 at Young's memorial service, taking advantage of the occasion to protest racism in the military and to pin the responsibility for Young's early death to the despair brought on by his forced retirement (Kilroy 2003: 157).

Du Bois's visit to the Grand Canyon recalls the moment fourteen years before the calamitous events just recounted when captain Young served as acting superintendent for a summer in Sequoia National Park. Sequoia was the second national park designated by the federal government in 1890 in order to protect the heavily forested area from the lumber industry (Kilroy 2003: 60–61). The park is so named after the Sequoias or giant redwood trees, often referred to simply as the "Big Trees." Muir writes about them in *Our National Parks*, stressing their enormous size and old age, calling them "Nature's forest masterpiece" (1901: 268). Measuring approximately three hundred feet high and thirty feet in diameter (269), the trees are so big, Muir notes, that one could hollow them out and live in them—as some people actually did (1901: 306). He writes of the destructive threat of the lumber industry to the forest, noting the necessity for their supervision at the hands of the US Army, though he does not mention much about the soldiers or Young's role (1901: 328).

Though the park was thirteen years old when Young arrived on the scene, its infrastructure remained rudimentary. A workaholic like his hero Booker T. Washington, Young was one of the most industrious park supervisors up until that time. Historian David P. Kilroy summarizes the young officer's industrious approach: "[w]here previous acting superintendents perhaps saw this assignment as a temporary summer sojourn, Charles Young committed himself body and soul to the parks" (2003: 61). In addition to having his troops clear and improve park trails, Young constructed more miles of road in one summer than previous supervisors did in three. He completed a wagon road that gave tourists access to the Giant Forest and Moro Rock, the park's main attractions. They also built a road connecting the General Grant National Forest to the nearby town of Visalia. Young's exemplary custodianship earned him unprecedented respect for an African-American in the local community. Leaders of the local town of Visalia publicly thanked him for his work as the town stood to benefit greatly from increased tourism to the parks (Kilroy 2003: 61–2). The park's next superintendent lauded the improvement to the park's roads and trails, which he ascribed to the "strict personal supervision of the work given by Captain Young" (Young 1903: 3).

While Young's experiences in the park were not devoid of racial tensions, he did often succeed in smoothing over race relations that were also strained by the complicating factor of locals resenting any form of federal government intrusion, let alone an all-black cavalry. Generally, however, the California was friendlier than the Jim Crow South. Upon Young's arrival, the local newspaper, *The Tulare County Times*, printed a sympathetic press release. It reported that Young is a "man of brilliant parts. His career has been one of hard struggle against the prejudice of race. He has, however, risen above all these difficulties by force of character and inherent ability" (O'Connell 2003). When Young completed the roads, he gave what the local newspaper called a "great feast" to a "hundred or so" of all those involved in the work and the elites of the area. The paper concludes that "Those from this city who sat about the festal board speak in glowing terms of the hospitality of Captain

Young and his ability to entertain" (O'Connell 2003). Anecdotal evidence reveals that there were some moments of racial tension: at least one Visilia restaurant owner refused to serve Young (Kilroy 2003: 62). In another incident, two white lieutenants once passed the African-American captain without saluting. This act of disrespect prompted Young to remove his uniform and hang it on a fence, proclaiming to the offenders that they did not have to salute him, but they did have to salute the uniform (O'Connell 2003).

Young's final report to the Department of the Interior (DOI) reads as though it spilled from the pen of John Muir. In words echoing the opening passages of *Our National Parks*, which Young may have read, he dreams of a future where "overworked and weary" Americans can escape the frenzy of urban life during the summers:

> The trees of the park consist of pines and cedars and firs in general and of the giant redwoods, or sequoias, in particular, all of which are well worth protecting. It has been previously remarked that the Sequoia National Park is the Giant Forest, but it is believed by many that even without the grandeur of the Giant Forest, which is matchless anywhere else in the world, there are enough beautiful mountain views, delightful camping sites, and water courses stocked with fish to constitute a national park where the overworked and weary citizens of the country can find rest, coolness, and quiet for a few weeks during the hot summer months, and where both large and small game can have a refuge and be allowed to increase. (1903: 6–7)

He goes on in this nature writing mode to celebrate Sequoia and General Grant parks for their beauty and sublimity.

While Young waxes poetic about the forests, he also warns the US Interior Secretary about the destruction of the Sequoia trees and the parks; he urges the federal government to take more drastic steps to protect the forests against the exploitation of local interests and to promote their preservation. Thinking pragmatically and willing to lay the groundwork necessary to facilitate his preservationist vision, Young prodded the DOI to purchase 3,877 acres (O'Connell 2003) of private property in the park at nineteen dollars an acre per request of the owners (Kilroy 2003: 62). Muir likewise advocated the purchase two years earlier: "[p]rivate claims cut and blotch" the park, "every one of which the government should gradually extinguish by purchase"

(1901: 329). The DOI delayed this acquisition for about fifteen years, and in the end the federal government payed inflated prices for the land (Kilroy 2003: 62).

Evoking the conservationist and nationalistic spirit of Roosevelt's presidency, Young recommended to the DOI that the government adopt a tradition of christening the giant redwoods with names "acceptable to the entire nation" (1903: 10). In an attempt to memorialize the Civil War in the West, Young named a tree for the Grand Army of the Republic, a Union army veterans' organization (Young 1903: 10). To help preserve the memory of African-American labor in the parks, he named another tree after the "great and good American, Booker T. Washington" (Young 1903: 10).[6] Though locals insisted that the tree be named after Young himself, he stuck to the Washington name, perhaps realizing that his soldiers had performed the sort of physical laboring of the environment preached by Washington. In this politics of tree naming, the size of the Sequoia would symbolize the stature of the man to hikers passing by, for Washington was at his peak of power and fame in 1903.

Du Bois works within the tradition of this African-American discursive construction of the parks that emerged with Young in order to create a counter-narrative. Though Du Bois focuses on the First World War, Young's biography also clears space for inclusion in an American cultural nationalism through an early contribution to the national parks. As a figure, he helps Du Bois facilitate an integrationist vision of the parks as a cultural space that simultaneously transcends race and bears the marks of an ideology of segregation.

Urban Nature: Toward the Harlem Renaissance

Du Bois argues that stories such as Young's and other acts of discrimination against black soldiers during the war contributed to the 1919 race riots. But other factors were involved too. Because of the dense cityscape and influx of African-Americans to the city in the Great Migration, opportunities for outdoor recreation in urban spaces became increasingly vital by 1919. African-Americans' limited access to officially or de facto segregated parks, beaches, and other spaces of urban nature became a growing source of racial tension and violence. As noted in the introduction to this chapter, Fisher has argued that segregated parks and beaches played a determining factor in the Chicago riots. Prior to this tragic event, urban nature spaces such as Washington Park or Cook County Forest Preserves in Chicago were valued by African-Americans as an escape from the claustrophobic South Side. In defiance of "forced exclusion from parks, playgrounds, and beaches, blacks struggled for access to open space" (Fisher 2006: 64). Many black children were left to play in marginal spaces of urban nature: open dumps, vacant lots, and roughshod playgrounds. Culminating a series of smaller skirmishes of racial violence, the riots started in July 1919 on the segregated beaches of Lake Michigan. The "black beach" was nicknamed "Hot and Cold" because it was near the industrial area of the shore (Fisher 2006: 64). When fifteen-year-old South Side working-class resident Eugene Williams drifted into the "white" section of Lake Michigan beach, angry whites perceived this breach as "polluting" their water. They began throwing rocks at Williams and the boy drowned. The resulting outrage from both black and white Chicagoans made for the worst rioting in the city's history, lasting four days and leaving thirty-eight dead, 537 injured, and about one thousand homeless (Fisher 2006: 64–75).

Though the end of "Of Beauty and Death" does not represent race riots directly, it does draw attention to spaces of urban nature that set the pre-conditions for the riots. By referring to the East St. Louis riots in the frag-ment just prior to the travel account of the Grand Canyon, Du Bois makes a direct link with the sociological study "Of Work and Wealth" in *Darkwater*. In that essay, Du Bois writes extensively about the 1917 East St. Louis riots. He frames the study as a lesson in sociology, taking the 1917 riots as a case study in urban race relations and interspersing it with the language of what ecocritic Lawrence Buell calls a "toxic discourse" (2001: 30). According to Buell, toxic discourse draws on the trope of "Gothicized environmental squa-lor" that dates back to early industrialization (2001: 43). Toxic discourse also previews the environmental justice movement of the 1980s. Using similar Gothicized rhetoric, Du Bois describes St. Louis as a place where "mighty riv-ers meet" (1920: 64), but this convergence results in the opposite of a pastoral scene, for these "rivers are dirty with sweat and toil" (1920: 69) and the "city overflows into the valleys of Illinois and lies there, writhing under its grimy cloud" (1920: 64). He casts St. Louis proper as a "feverish Pittsburg [sic] in the Mississippi Valley" (1920: 64) full of "Nature-defying cranes" (1920: 70). If St. Louis is an industrial landscape comparable to Pittsburgh, then East St. Louis, across the river in Illinois, is a toxic one. It has "no restful green" and smells of "ill-tamed sewerage." The cityscape also shows the lingering "ruins" of the 1917 race riots (1920: 65).

The final fragments of "Of Beauty and Death" continue the urban nature thread begun in "Of Work and Wealth," as Du Bois turns his eye toward the Manhattan cityscape. These fragments paint the frenetic energy of city life through images of urban nature, eventually returning to the philosophical themes of beauty, death, ugliness, and their relation to the Veil. Formally, the fragments become increasingly shorter and disconnected. This movement from the national parks of the west to the more urban east suggests a frontier reversal, an importation of wilderness into urban space. After describing the broken Paris of the First World War, Du Bois sketches New York in language that echoes his portrait of the Grand Cañon: "white cliffs of Manhattan, tier on tier, with a curving pinnacle, towers square and trim, a giant inkwell daintily stoppered, an ancient pyramid enthroned" (1920: 187). By characterizing the cityscape in such terms, Du Bois makes it a kind of second (mediated) nature in an example of urban nature writing.[7] Du Bois also invokes the seasonal cycles: "[w]e would see spring, summer, and the red riot of autumn, and then in winter, beneath the soft white snow, sleep and dream of dreams" (1920: 190). The "red riot" conflates two events, one social and the other natural: the Red Summer, which actually continued into late September, and the changing colors of leaves in the autumn.

At the same time that it represents urban nature, the end of "Of Beauty and Death" and *Darkwater* also reflect the 1919 race riots. After the riots, Lewis says that Du Bois's mood "verged on apocalyptic bitterness"—a mood clearly reflected in the sardonic humor of the apocalyptic short story "The Comet," which follows "Of Beauty and Death" (2000: 13). Finalized for an early 1920 publication in the midst of the riots and at the close of the First World War, *Darkwater* is usually read within the context of these violent episodes in the long history of the United States and global race relations. Though Du Bois claimed to have finished the manuscript in February 1918, he continued revising it until September 1919—before reverberations of the riots across the county had died down (Lewis 2000: 11). Oswald-Garrison

Villard's review of the book for *The Nation* frames it in terms of the race riots, praising the artistry of "A Litany at Atlanta," a poem about the Atlanta race riots (1920: 726). But such proximity to the violent events, Villard continues, produces excessive affect, for the book "carries with it a note of bitterness, tinctured with hate, and the teaching of violence which often defeats his own purpose" (1920: 727). Some whites but mostly black residents were killed during the rioting. These riots were for Du Bois, in a sense, the First World War brought home from Europe.

These last fragments of the essay, then, are permeated with the tense urban atmosphere that sparked the riots. Punning on "riot," Du Bois describes the Harlem streets as a dense space, a double environment segregated from the "white world" and full of "black eyes, black and brown, and frizzled hair curled and sleek, and skins that riot with luscious color and deep, burning blood" (1920: 188). He invokes claustrophobic living conditions: "[h]umanity is packed dense in high piles of close-knit homes that lie in layers above gray shops of food and clothes and drink" (1920: 188). Du Bois's and writers such as McKay's pastoralization of urban nature would later permeate much of the work of the Harlem Renaissance.

By making nature part of the color-line problem, Du Bois maps double environments and disjunctive social and natural spaces. In his second-sight, the wilderness becomes simultaneously an ideal "integrationist" space of intermingling natural colors—an objective correlative for a desegregated society—and a compromised, fraught space mediated by the problems of the color line and modernity. This counter-narrative challenges the dominance of white supremacy and social Darwinism as well as an emergent environmentalism. Ultimately, for Du Bois there is no "nature" without the baggage of the color line, no Grand Cañon without Jim Crow, and no wide-open landscapes without claustrophobic cityscapes. These concerns carried over to Du Bois's editorship.

The Crisis, the Politics of Nature, and the Harlem Renaissance

Effie Lee Newsome's Eco-poetics

Introduction

The cover of the February 1915 issue of *The Crisis*, the NAACP monthly edited by Du Bois, displays a Henry David Thoreau quote framed with prominent borders and flanked by sketches of factories with large smokestacks. The smoke, which rises to twice the size of the buildings themselves, wends its way up the sides of the page, tangling into the magazine's large-font title at the top. This image of a northern industrial landscape draws a line between Great Migration narrative tropes and Thoreau's critique of industrialization in *Walden* (1854). The quote itself, however, comes from Thoreau the abolitionist rather than Thoreau the naturalist: "Do you call this the land of the free? What is it to be free from King George and continue the slaves of King Prejudice? What is it to be born free and not to live free?"[1] This cover creates a number of unusual associative links: the natural rights doctrine of the US Constitution, abolitionism, industrial capitalism and urbanization, the NAACP's civil rights crusade, and New England Transcendentalism.

The Crisis Thoreau cover reveals a great deal about the political agenda and strategy of Du Bois and editorship of the NAACP magazine. While Washington's *Working with the Hands* advanced an economic strategy of racial uplift via ecological agencies, Du Bois politicized representations of nature by extending double consciousness to his portrayal of natural environments in *The Souls of Black Folk*, *The Quest of the Silver Fleece*, and *Darkwater*. These thematic concerns with race and darknature continued in his role as founder and editor of the NAACP's *The Crisis*—which reached peak circulation in the early 1920s—from 1910 to 1935. A perusal of issues from this period reveals the magazine's ongoing engagement with conservation, natural history, natural sciences (e.g., biology), pastoralism, and primitivism. In order to trace these themes in *The Crisis* during the 1910s and 1920s, this chapter focuses on the prolific writings of the now mostly forgotten poet, essayist, and amateur naturalist Effie Lee Newsome.

Verbal and visual representations of nature in *The Crisis* expand Du Bois's vision of "Liberty for all men" and the "Training of Children, black even as white" espoused in his 1904 "Credo." For Du Bois, "liberty" means access to open spaces and physical mobility; voting rights and interracial friendship; and desegregated railroad cars and "sunshine" (1920: 2). "Training" requires that children venture out to natural spaces, to "green pastures" and "life lit by some large vision of beauty and goodness and truth" (1920: 2). As editor, Du Bois fosters these varied connections among integration, mobility, pedagogy, and nature, and gives them further expression in a number of essays, fiction, poems, and short histories published in *The Crisis* throughout the 1910s and 1920s. This body of environmental writing by African-American (and sometimes white) authors includes published excerpts from Jean Toomer's regionalist masterpiece *Cane* (1923); the urban–pastoralist poetry of Arna Bontemps, Langston Hughes, and Claude McKay; John Matheus's short stories such as "Fog" and "Swamp"; Yolande Du Bois's[2] nature meditations; prose sketches of black recreational spaces such as segregated beaches and city parks; and critical histories of natural disasters such as the 1927 Mississippi flood.

These trends found exemplary expression in Newsome's writings, many of which appeared in *The Crisis* between 1915 and the early 1930s as frequently as those of Harlem Renaissance luminaries such as Hughes, McKay, and Countee Cullen. Scholars know Newsome more for her work as an early writer of African-American children's literature than for her role in the Harlem Renaissance and as *Crisis* contributor. Not yet compelling to scholars of the literary Left, Newsome's musings on nature and relatively conservative religious views seem to have more affinities with Washington than such radicals as Du Bois and McKay. But her writings are still political, even if they usually do not fit into the recognizable categories of black nationalism or the literary Left. In the pages of *The Crisis*, Newsome wrote on topics and themes unusual—even radical—for African-Americans at the time: birdwatching, entomology, ethology (animal psychology), and other forms of amateur nature study. Placed in their context in *The Crisis*, Newsome's writings perform a sort of double movement; they work at the levels of text and context, of verbal icon and print culture. At one level, Newsome's writings attempt to substitute the observational study of natural history and conservationist politics for the omnipresent burdens of the color-line problem seen on every page of *The Crisis*; they are, in short, a form of productive escapism. On one side, natural history and conservation become more overtly racialized and politicized when they resonate in the pages of *The Crisis*; on the obverse, this encourages racial readings of otherwise white-dominated scientific fields and political movements.

First, Newsome champions conservationist policies, which gained major traction in the Progressive Era with the presidency of Roosevelt and the nationwide effort to establish national parks, forest reserves, game preserves, and policies to regulate and manage the country's natural resources. Her concern with birds also typifies white middle-class women's conservationist values and pedagogical aims—a concern that offers, especially for black children, a political alternative to and respite from the ubiquitous problem of the color line. But according to Spencer Schaffner, "popular and familiar forms of anthropomorphism, sentimentalism, taxonomic discourse, nationalism, racism, and taste were all mobilized" in the field guide genre, making it inherently political (2011:17). Second, Newsome's writings also use nature to enact a subtle racial critique that the publishing context of *The Crisis* further amplifies. A nature poem about a bluebird, for example, might follow articles on the "lynching industry" or studies of black women factory workers. This proximity to articles about Jim Crow and black workers demands a racial reading of Newsome's poems. Rather than verbal icons isolated on the page, Newsome's writings form composites with other, more race-centric texts that thread through *The Crisis*.

This chapter first considers the Harlem Renaissance concern with pedagogy, children, the role of black women, and the use of nature imagery and metaphors to advance a strategic black nationalism. It then examines the politics of the most predominant concern of Newsome's prose and poetry: birds. Through tropes of integrated nature, taxonomy, and disembodied voice,

Newsome's work critically signifies on discourses of bird conservation institutionalized and professionalized through such organizations as the Audubon societies in the late 1800s. The multi-generic forms of knowledge she produces—short essays, children's poems, her *Crisis* columns, and drawings—intervene in both the conservationist and the civil rights discourses by promoting the pedagogical and affective benefits of birding and nature study in general. The final section of this chapter focuses on Newsome's more political poems and prose, which often target both child and adult audiences with their focus on futurity. These writings conjure tropes that have as much to do with conservation as they do with strategies of racial advancement through cultural achievement.

Newsome, New Negro Poetics, and the Organic Trope

Born into Philadelphia's Talented Tenth in 1885, Newsome was heavily influenced by her father, who served as an African Methodist Episcopal (AME) bishop and president of the country's first all-black college—Wilberforce University in Ohio—from 1873 to 1881. For its day, the AME Church had a radical orientation, founded in 1787 through an act of social protest against the mainstream, white Methodist church. In her *Crisis* eulogy to her father, Newsome compares Bishop Lee's love for home and nature with the nineteenth-century nature writer John Burroughs (1926: 69).[3] Newsome recalls his fondness for exploring "cranberry bogs" and listening to the "kill-dees" at his childhood home in New Jersey. She portrays him as an amateur naturalist who treated home as a veritable botanical garden: "[h]e studied the trees and knew them. The grand elms and oaks, the gracious beech trees—but he loved them *all*" (1926: 70). Between 1901 and 1914, Newsome studied art at a number of colleges, including Wilberforce University. Though she lived much of her life in Wilberforce, where she enjoyed the rustic setting that allowed her to gain an immense knowledge of nature, Newsome spent most of the 1920s in Birmingham, where her husband served as pastor of an AME church (K. C. Smith 2004: 46-7).[4] The bulk of Newsome's poetry appeared between 1915 and 1940 in *The Crisis*, occasionally in the National Urban League's *Opportunity*, and, later, in Atlanta University's *Phylon* (founded and edited by Du Bois). Her work also appeared in the short-lived, Du Bois and Fauset–edited children's periodical, *The Brownies' Book* (1920–22). Though her output was prolific, her only full-length poetry book, *Gladiola Garden*, appeared in 1940, collecting many poems written during the 1920s and 1930s. Most of these poems fall into two kinds of nature poetry: pastoral and more scientifically oriented poems about birds, insects, and other animals.

Newsome's work functions within the larger cultural field of the Harlem Renaissance, known more for its urbanism than its concern with nature.[5] New Negro arbiter of literary taste, William Stanley Braithwaite, summarized the movement's cultural nationalism with gendered terms in "Some Contemporary Poets of the Negro Race": the "present revival of poetry in America could scarcely advance without carrying in its wake the impulse and practice of a poetic consciousness in the Negro race" (1919: 275). This poetic consciousness, though in its nascent stage, contains "intense emotionalism," "folk-qualities," and "primal virtues" springing from spirituals and other folk-vernacular forms such as the blues and ragtime. A concomitant Apollonian "grounding in the technical elements of the science of versification" balances out these Dionysian elements (1919: 277). When characterizing black women poets such as Georgia Douglas Johnson, Braithwaite invokes Victorian assumptions about women's hyper-affective, sentimental, and "subjective lyric emotion": "[w]hether in religion or love, or in the descriptive rendering of nature, they always extracted the substance to which clung the mist of tears" (1919: 279). Johnson, as well as Newsome, Anne Spencer, and Angelina Grimké, to name a few, all performed such descriptive renderings of nature. That women would be expected—and often did fulfill this expectation—to write about nature repeats the centuries-long association of the feminine with the organic.[6] Readers', editors', and publishers' expectations about black women's writing at the time would also tend to mitigate against militant forms of racial protest, such as those found in Du Bois's *Darkwater* or McKay's "If We Must Die."

For Barbara Foley, Leftists and New Negro writers and artists turned the dominant racist ideology on its head by linking Harlem and the southern black folk to an emerging black nationalism (2003). While Foley claims that this "welding of place to race" functions as the "distinctive contribution" of the movement, it also, ironically, succeeded in reaffirming racial essentialism (2003: 6–7). For example, Alain Locke drew on organic tropes to theorize the movement as distinctly cultural in his introduction to *The New Negro* anthology (1925). There, Locke brought together the Herderian keywords of nationalism: folk-spirit, self-determination, and group expression. This nationalism followed a cultural and spiritual, rather than economic, impulse. One of the extended metaphors of Locke's introduction is the impending "flood" of black mass migration and cultural production. The "tide" of the Great Migration is not, Locke argues, a haphazard "blind flood" breached by external forces (the Great War, the boll weevil, etc.), but rather "successive wave[s]" of a black folk-spirit propelling itself onto the "beach line" of northern cities (Locke 1925: 6). This ocean metaphor suggests a flowing unity between the rural South and the Harlem ghetto.

For Foley, the organic trope appears most pointedly in the poetry of the period. Langston Hughes's "Earth Song," which appeared in *The New Negro* (1925), typifies this poetic–political strategy:

> It's an earth song—
> And I've been waiting long
> For an earth song.
> It's a spring song!
> I've been waiting long   5
> For a spring song:
>   Strong as the bursting of young buds,
>   Strong as the shoots of a new plant,
>   Strong as the coming of the first child
>   From its mother's womb—   10
> An earth song!
> A body song!
> A spring song!
> And I've been waiting long
> For an earth song.   15

The seasonal motif, quasi-Gaia hypothesis, and image-constellation—earth, spring, plants, childbirth, and body—act to make this poem an exemplar of the organic trope. Foley argues that the "hyper-materiality of the organic trope functions metonymically to naturalize identity as a function of place, thereby largely occluding both historical and structural understandings of the 'roots' of racism" (2003: 237). But Foley's Marxian narrative of the New Negro organic trope overlooks certain material and discursive contexts of the complex and contradictory politics of the Progressive Era. What she sees as the organic trope's ideological betrayal of the "good" nationalism espoused by the New Negro and black-belt-thesis Communists, I see as more an encroachment of early-twentieth-century conservation and environmentalism into black politics.

Harlem Renaissance concerns with organic tropes, a cultural black nationalism, and a black women's aesthetic dovetail with what Katherine Capshaw Smith characterizes as a deep investment in "building a black national identity through literary constructions of childhood" (2004: xiii). Examined in Chapter 2, Du Bois's "Criteria of Negro Art" (1926), for example, appears in *The Crisis*'s annual "Children's Number" alongside dozens of photographs of African-American infants submitted by readers. Extending statements made in the "Credo," Du Bois's *Darkwater* essay "The Immortal Child" makes the case for the central role black children play in future racial and democratic progress. In typical Du Boisian hyperbole, he starts the essay with the pronouncement: "our children's children live forever and grow and develop towards perfection as they are trained. All human problems, then, center in the Immortal Child and his education is the problem of problems" (1920: 151). In broad, vitalist strokes, Du Bois charges black parents—and, by implication, the Talented Tenth—with the duty "to accomplish the immortality of black blood, in order that the day may come in this dark world when poverty shall be abolished, privilege be based on individual desert, and the color of a man's skin be no bar to the outlook of his soul" (1920: 158). He admits the difficulty of such a grandiose task: on the one hand, parents can shield their children from racism as much as possible, but this strategy makes the child vulnerable to the possibly avoidable traumatic coming to awareness of racism and double consciousness. On the other hand, parents can throw their children into the "sea of race prejudice," but such an approach, while beneficial to some stronger types, would be "brutal" to the majority of black children. Instead, Du Bois preaches moderation and care: with "every step of dawning intelligence, explanation—frank, free, guiding explanation—must come" (1920: 159). A progressive education rooted in Platonic (and, later, pragmatist) values of the true, the good, and the beautiful is the Du Boisian ideal. Du Bois also criticizes industrial capitalism and the reduction of public education to training workers in improving the "land's industrial efficiency" (1920: 162).

Education fell mainly to African-American women in their roles not just as mothers, but also a prominent position in such feminized professions as teaching. Elise Johnson McDougald's typology of black women in *The New Negro* describes two categories that would apply to Newsome: the bourgeois woman of leisure and the teacher. Teachers, McDougald explains, who bring to the classroom "sympathy and judgment" form a "mighty force" in the struggle to uplift black youth (1925: 376). Newsome periodically worked as a librarian. Women of leisure constitute a "very small" group of wives married to professional men, like Newsome's husband, who can support them. Ultimately, literary constructions of black childhood found their vehicle in the more feminized publications of the Harlem Renaissance: *The Crisis*'s annual Children's Number, the mostly Fauset-edited *The Brownies' Book* (1920–21), Newsome's "Little Page" column (appearing in *The Crisis* from 1925 to 1929), and the plethora of children's poetry, prose, and visual art published in various African-American periodicals.

Newsome often employs what children's literature scholars call "cross writing," a technique that double-voices a text for both child and adult audiences. The practice of cross-writing possesses elements of reformist education and even indoctrination in it: "the cross writing employed by southern reform movements uses children's texts to instruct an adult reader, who is imagined as culturally and intellectually regressive, about health and labor modernizations; the child becomes primarily a conduit to reach the adult" (K. C. Smith 2004: xix). In the case of African-American readers in the 1920s and 1930s, the wildly disparate levels of literacy (often split along generational lines) meant that many children found *The Crisis* more accessible than their less educated elders. As Smith puts it, children's literature "became the means to breach the divide between the progressive black child and unschooled adults, offering interesting inversions and subversions of power and authority" (2004: 274). Examples of such children's writing include Newsome's whimsical "March Hare" (1925), which uses simple rhymes and adopts the perspective of a rabbit in order to appeal to children:

> It makes me feel so sad
> When people call me "mad,"
> Nor can I find out why,

For I am very shy.
I'd rather far take flight   5
Than ever just make fight.
But only let me run,
And folks will yell in fun,
"Why, there goes old March Hare,
He's mad yet, I declare!"   10

The March Hare is marginalized as "mad" for fulfilling his nature to run, offering the reader a modest form of subversive identification. Similarly, the speaker of "Mariposita" (1926c) is a butterfly—"Born in Old Mexico"— who tells its story in rhyme (l. 2). Children's literature also has an element of indoctrination to it, particularly work that instills younger readers with conservationist values or that portrays white children as superior to black children.

For Du Bois and *The Crisis*, the entire "future of the race" is at stake in black children's literature because of its ideological effects on children. Always haunting Newsome's work and any work written for black children is the potential regression into abolition- and Reconstruction-era, Uncle Tom caricatures and depoliticized, sentimentalized racial stereotypes of what Braithwaite calls the "happy, care-free, humorous Negro" (1925: 31). She avoids this problem by writing more about nature than humans and she does not condescend to her child (or adult) audience but rather seeks to prime their curiosity in nature, particularly birds. It is as though the future of the race were intertwined with nature itself and African-American attitudes toward nature. As the next section demonstrates, Newsome's poetry supplements organic tropes with species-specific, scientific "studies" and a pedagogical approach that goes beyond black nationalism and shows the pluralist politics of the Harlem Renaissance.

Birds, Pedagogy, and *The Crisis*

Newsome's prose and poems on birds engage the discourse of white, middle-class women's natural history writing on birds as well as bird conservation. Newsome's short photo essay, "Birds and Manuscripts," appeared in the June 1915 issue of *The Crisis* after articles and editorials on the release of

The Birth of a Nation, lynching, segregation, and the Great War. Appearing immediately before Newsome's essay, "Fighting Race Calumny," an article condemning D. W. Griffith's pro-KKK film as libel and recounting nation-wide protests against the film's screening, jarringly contrasts with Newsome's essay. Reading as though it could have appeared in *Bird-Lore*—the leading ornithology magazine at the time—"Birds and Manuscripts" speaks to the political context of the early-twentieth-century "plume wars."

In the late 1800s, the feather trade exploded when bird-hats became fashionable among urban, bourgeois women. Species such as humming-birds, sparrows, owls, egrets, warblers, and many others could be spotted on women's heads as they walked down the street (Price 1999: 58–9). Historian Jennifer Price explains the obsession with women's hats at the time:

> [F]ew topics evoked the nether definitions of womanhood more effectively than hats: spring, summer, fall and winter hats, and morning, afternoon and evening hats. Walking and traveling hats. Church, garden, mourning, golf and carriage hats. Women's elite fashions—which achieved such byz-antine dimensions in the late nineteenth century, when they became the stuff of Edith Wharton novels—mandated a devotion to hats that can now seem wondrous in a more hat-free age. (1999: 75)

Partly motivated by late-Victorian ideals casting women in the role of society's moral legislators, state Audubon societies protested this fashion in the 1890s. Unlike the male-dominated campaign for national parks championed by Muir and Roosevelt (as well as the Du Boisian twist on this campaign, as shown in Chapter 2), women played a larger role in bird conservation due to the help of the "women's club" movement of the Progressive Era (Price 1999: 63). Price argues that this "bird-hat campaign marks an even earlier, essential shift into new ways of thinking about nature" (1999: 61). Audubon activists won a vic-tory with the passage of the federal Lacey Act in 1900, which banned the inter-state and international millinery trade (Merchant 2007: 277). Later, in 1918, the federal government passed the Migratory Bird Treaty Act, thus protect-ing birds from profit-hungry traders by banning the selling and shipping of migratory birds between the United States, Canada, and Mexico (Merchant 2007: 279). By the time Newsome began writing, the need for bird protection and sanctuaries still existed, however, and new laws needed enforcement.

Newsome's "Birds and Manuscripts" (1915) speaks to the politics of the plume wars. It begins not with birds but a demonstration of contrasting pedagogical methods, that is, the "manuscripts" part of the title. Set in a classroom, Newsome's composition instructor—metonymically identified as a "blue pencil"—criticizes her writing's disorganization and flowery stylistic flourishes. In a commanding Strunk-and-White tone, the instructor stresses the "orderly and responsible" business of formal writing. Like a burgeoning nature writer on the verge of an epiphany, Newsome sighs at the constricting classroom atmosphere, with its indoor claustrophobia enhanced by the relentless criticism of the blue pencil: "[s]o, tireless devotion to composition for composition's own dear sake had brought me to this, a realization that I was creator of pen chameleons, narrow, wriggling color studies that spent their time shifting shades. I felt wounded" (1915: 89). Newsome emphasizes the materiality of the manuscript as it seems to come alive, to become animated with the instructor's marks on the page in an echo of the trope of the talking book (Gates 1988: 127). These authoritarian "color studies" will contrast with the more affirmative color studies of birds that Newsome will soon undertake. She asks the instructor if she can write on her own chosen theme, making her even more of a "peculiarity" in the class in the essay's only explicit reference to race: the "fact that the one colored member of the class might hereby be further establishing herself as a peculiarity troubled me little then" (1915: 89). As she steps outside, she pauses to watch sparrows, for which she "even felt grateful" (1915: 89). The "even" probably refers to how sparrows were widely regarded at the time as pests.

The essay then proceeds in a vein of nature writing about birds that seems modeled after John Burroughs's *Wake-Robin* (1871) and, later, the more scientific writing of white women such as Mabel Osgood Wright. Newsome's essay includes photographs of robins building nests, a birdhouse of a bluebird, and orioles perched in a tree. She decides to write about a "mocking bird in honeysuckles" and the once-stodgy instructor immediately praises her work, for it has the "naiveté of a folk-tale" (1915: 90). Basking in this approval, Newsome realizes that her "best of friends were likely to prove nature and her birds" (1915: 90). As she would later perform in her poetry, Newsome begins cataloguing bird families, placing them in the "scene" of their habitats and geographical locations: "[f]rom the mocking birds in reeds by Florida lagoons; white herons on white oyster bars; cardinals swinging amidst scarlet cassesnas" (1915: 90). She continues to identify families throughout the rest of the essay: chickadee, titmouse, oriole, chewink, bluebirds, cow bird, catbird, and dove. The birds are mixed with scenes of seasonal change and motherhood: it is spring and there is a "wealth of bird-land incident," especially birds laying eggs.

Newsome's trope of taxonomy in "Birds and Manuscripts" borrows from the numerous field guides and manuals filling bookshelves at the turn of the century. Published in 1897, Wright coauthored with Elliot Coues the novelized field guide *Citizen Bird: Scenes from Bird-Life*, which, like Newsome's work, targets mostly a child audience. Written in a narrative form, it follows Dr. Roy Hunter as he instructs four children (his daughter, nephew, niece, and Rap, a "country boy") on how to study and identify various bird species around their orchard farm, including the kingfisher—one of the species most prevalent in Newsome's work. As the title suggests, Wright grants citizenship to birds and uses strategies of anthropomorphism to build the children's identification with the birds. Dr. Hunter's goal, he states, is to teach that "every bird you can find is such a citizen of this country" and to "show you why we should protect him" (1897: 52).[7] The children, Dr. Hunter argues, belong to a world of urban "House People" who "grow selfish and cruel" unless they "visit the homes of the Beast and Bird Brotherhood, and see that these can also love and suffer and work like themselves" (1897: 12). Learning about nature also improves the humanity of the children. Dr. Hunter draws various analogies between birds and humans: nests are like homes where parent-birds take care of hatchlings, feathers are like clothes, and the like. The book's conservation politics, then, are clear: education of future generations in nature appreciation will lead to the expansion and institutionalization of bird protection.

Wright's book, however, targets white children, and like much of the children's literature at the time, it offers only racial stereotypes to black children. In *Citizen Bird*, Mammy Bun, an "old colored nurse," appears as a background figure used to punctuate various scenes. For example, after discussing their plans for the day's bird excursions, Mammy Bun appears with a "plate of steaming hot flannel cakes" at the end of one chapter, to which the Doctor proclaims "[n]ow let us eat to the health of Birdland and a happy season at Orchard Farm!" (1897: 86). The Mammy character is not invited to learn and explore, nor does she show an interest except for one scene where she describes the behavior of mockingbirds—long associated with African-Americans, perhaps most notably in the characterization of all-black poetry from Phyllis Wheatley to Dunbar as the "mockingbird school"—to the children (Gates 1988: 113). She speaks in the dialect style of Joel Chandler Harris's Uncle Remus plantation tales or Jim in Mark Twain's *The Adventures of Huckleberry Finn* (1885). As the doctor's niece says, Mammy has a "sort of language all her own" (1897: 132). In describing the mockingbird's mimetic qualities, Mammy uses the minstrel stereotype of the "stealing darky" (a stereotype Washington also put to use in *Up from Slavery*): "[n]ow lots o' coon darkies dey uster steal de youn' Mockers jes' afore dey lef' de nest and sell 'em to white trash dat ud tote 'em down the ribber an' sell 'em agin in N'Orleans, to be fotched off in ships" (1901: 134). This anecdote refers to the feather trade, in which birds were hunted for bird-hats and entrapped as caged animals. As Jennifer Price has observed, it also points to the classism of the Audubon movement, which pitted bourgeois women against poor whites and people of color (1999: 97). Still, the use of dialect here draws on a white supremacist tradition of Jim Crow-era literature that Dunbar and other black authors tried, with controversial success, to appropriate in their own dialect fiction and poetry.

Writing against Wright's use of racial stereotypes, Newsome inflects her taxonomy with subtle racial critique, thereby "Signifyin(g)" on—in Gates's sense of "repetition with a signal difference"—texts of white women bird-watchers (1988: xxiv). Scenes of domesticity and motherhood in "Birds and Manuscripts" are not, as one might expect, marked by sentimental conventions, but rather a tragic revision of domestic tropes in nature writing: the "mourning dove's" home is a "pitiful nest of weeds" where she lays "colorless eggs" accompanied by her "plaint, 'Here's another new-u-u-found woe-o-o'" (1915: 90). This image displaces onto birds a trope found in the African-American literary tradition that associates childbirth with tragedy and despair because of the likelihood of a bleak future for the newborn, as in Georgia Douglass Johnson's "Motherhood," or later, much of Gwendolyn Brooks's poetry.

When Newsome speaks about enjoying the sparrow, she offers a positive valuation of a bird highly racialized at the time, for it was associated with "dirty" immigrants—a foreign nuisance according to nativist and segregationist discourses. During the late-nineteenth-century Great English Sparrow War, which tried to eradicate the bird-pest, Elliott Coues performs what Fine and Christoforides call "metaphorical linkage," joining sparrows with urban black residents: "Washington harbors and encourages a select assortment of noise-nuisances—the black newspaper imps who screech every one deaf on Sunday morning; the fresh-fish fiends, the berry brutes ... but all these have their exits as well as their entrances; the Sparrows alone are tireless, ubiquitous, sempi-ternal" (1991: 382). In *Citizen Bird*, Wright and Coues deem English sparrows "detestable" (1897: 181), a "very bad" citizen who "ought to suffer the extreme penalty of the law" (182), "criminals" who are "condemned by everyone" (204), and a "disreputable tramp" (204).[8] This rhetoric that denies citizenship to certain species follows an exclusionary logic of segregation that the civil rights movement sought to counter with a politics of inclusion.

In "Birds and Manuscripts," Newsome also engages in a class critique of pastoral design involving access to "picturesque places" that "seemed only for the rich" (1915: 90). She sees "small sweet Sonora doves flitting from the Phoenix rich man's olive groves to the pepper trees of my humble stopping-place" (1915: 90). A bird she pursues and observes on the wealthy property, however, is a class-blind "impartial friend" who "flutters reassurance" from "among the live-oak, maple or cotton-wood boughs" (1915: 90). She also refers, unexpectedly, to Native Americans—Apache and Hopi—as belonging to the spaces where sparrows and killdeer fly. Following on her own racial "peculiarity" in the classroom, as well as the class critique of the well-managed, pastoral estate, birdwatching becomes the occasion for solidarity among people of color, African and Native American: the impartial "birds befriend us all" (1915: 90). As Norwood argues, many writings by African-American and Native American women reflect a "shared tradition of organicism" and sense of solidarity cathected around nature (1993: 192). Eventually, for their "courage and care," these birds play the role of teachers as well as friends: "I would have for teachers the robin and the oriole, symbols, respectively, of hardihood and subtility [subtlety]" (Newsome 1915: 90).[9] In this instance, Newsome portrays an inclusive community, where citizenship extends to all species, including sparrows.

Newsome persisted in writing light verse about birds, usually aimed at children, in *The Crisis* throughout the 1920s. While her black nationalist poems such as "The Bronze Legacy" often use organic tropes, these poems simply describe the appearance and behavior of various bird species. "Pigeons," "Chickadee," "The Blue Jay," "The Peacock Feather," "Capriccio," and "Bluebird" all center on taxonomy; their brevity is reminiscent of Imagism. Other bird poems include "Young Birds' Mouths," "Pigeons and People," "Birds at My Door," "The Peacock Feather," and "The Wet Pigeon." Appearing in April 1927, "Bluebird" stresses sound over sense, and is simple in its short length, use of alliteration, and the *a a b c c b* end-rhyme scheme:

> I just heard your soft smothered voice today!
> I'm sure you'll flit on in your light-winged way,
> Unmindful, undreaming of me,
> Who have not yet seen you in blue and brown,
> But just heard your lush notes drip down, drip down
> As showers from the black ash tree. (ll. 1–6)

The poem's mode of address suggests a double movement: on the one hand, the speaker anthropomorphizes the bird by speaking directly to it, as though it could understand and respond to her; on the other, the bird's musical presence and physical absence asserts, simultaneously, its relation—its "soft smothered voice"—to the speaker and its alterity in its disembodied voice, "Unmindful, undreaming" of her (l. 3). Perhaps more perceptible to contemporaneous black readers than white, the "blue" of the bluebird creates an associative link to race. In his poem "Mulatto" (1927), Hughes refers to the blue-bruised black body. Popularized by Louis Armstrong, Andy Razaf's song "What Did I Do (To Be So Black and Blue)?" was a jazz-blues staple with lyrics that pun on "blue" to connote both physical and emotional bruising (having "the blues"). Given this association, the bluebird's music is described in words that could apply to a country blues singer: "your lush notes drip down, drip down" (l. 5).

The subtle racial associations internal to the poem become overdetermined by its context, not just as a poem printed in *The Crisis,* but also with its arrangement on the page. Under the heading "Poetry and Painting" and a photo portrait of Arna Bontemps (often considered the "father" of African-American children's literature) followed by a biographical blurb, "Bluebird" is surrounded by other race-themed poems that employ organic tropes: John Strong's "The True American," Edward Silvera's "Color," Bontemps's "Tree,"

Frank Marshall Davis's "Portrait of an Old Woman," and Sterling Brown's "After the Storm." These poems, especially "Tree" and "After the Storm," similarly adopt a pastoral mode, but their allegorical and political meaning is more explicit. "Tree" describes a nondescript tree that grows near the "river of life" and functions as "an healing / To the nations" (Bontemps 1927: 48). By the end of the poem the tree is revealed as a symbol of "Love," figuring nature as a site of fantasy for resolving social rifts rather than using nature to buttress racist discourse.

Newsome's "The Bluebirds Are Coming" (1927d) provides another example of how the publishing context of *The Crisis* advances a racial reading of a seemingly simple poem about a bird and seasonal change. It adopts a blues-style form of repetition:

> The snow's on the bird house,
> On gable and eaves,
> The snow's on the bird house
> On gable and eaves.
> But still I feel merry,   5
> For here's February,
> And bluebirds are coming,
> The whole world believes,
> Yes, bluebirds will be here,
> The whole world believes.   10

The first four lines follow a blues structure in their *a b a b* repetition, followed by lines that respond to the previous ones. The poem then ends with another blues verse that goes unresolved, suggesting an incomplete or open-ended future where the "bluebirds will be here" (l. 9).

The poem "The Satisfied Swifts" (April 1926d) goes into more descriptive detail of bird behavior, movement, and hunting than "Bluebird." Newsome renders field guide entries on the Chimney Swift, exemplified by Wright's *Birdcraft* (1897), into a poetic idiom:

> Some chimney Swifts swirled overhead
> One pleasant April day.
> Their actions plainly said,
> "We're here to build and stay.

"We cannot tramp like Redbreast there,   5
But, my! we're nimble in the air.
We don't dig food in Flicker style,
And yet we're feasting all the while. (ll. 1–8)

The first image of the swirling chimney swifts echoes Wright in *Birdcraft*: "[n]othing, however, is more picturesque than these Swifts as they circle above the wide stone chimney of some half-ruined house" (1897: 194). *Citizen Bird* repeats a similar image when describing the chimney swift: "blackish birds kept streaming from the top [of the chimney], circling high in the air and darting down again" (Wright and Coues 1897: 296). Ventriloquizing the swifts, the second stanza compares it with other bird species, so as to make them more distinguishable from each other. In *Birdcraft*, Wright emphasizes many of these same features: Swifts are "constantly on the wing, either darting through the air, dropping surely to its nest, or speeding from it like a rocket" (1897: 193). According to Wright and Coues in *Citizen Bird*, the swift's wings are "very strong, and almost as long as all the rest of his body" (1897: 297). The next stanzas of Newsome's "The Satisfied Swifts" continue with behavioral observations and comparisons to other bird species:

"Flying to catch the bugs that fly
And make our lunch here in the sky.   10
We don't sing like the birds in trees,
But we can whistle, we can wheeze.

"Poor Meadow Lark warbles and sings,
But, my! He's hardly any wings.
Though Thrasher's coat is brilliant bay,   15
We're glad to have our sooty gray." (ll. 9–16)

"Lunch" and "coat" suggest artifacts of human culture, anthropomorphizing the birds in a way that serves as a mnemonic device for children to understand their behavior and appearance. The swift's affirmation of its "sooty gray" color implicitly models race-pride for African-American readers. The poem's final stanza directly appeals to the reader's sense of nature appreciation:

"His yellow eyes look brass-like, cheap.
Our eyes are dark and rich and deep.

> Of all of Nature's kindly gifts,
> First thank her, please, for making Swifts!" (1926: ll. 17–20)

By appealing to the swifts' dark, rich, and deep eyes, which suggest the birds' subjectivity or interiority, Newsome urges an affective, empathetic identification with the swifts. In doing so, Newsome advances an appreciation for birds while at the same time suggesting that these concerns are intertwined with the racial politics of *The Crisis*.

Published in the February 1927 issue of *The Crisis*, Newsome's "At the Pool" combines a pastoral idyll with a naturalist's and entomologist's eye for cataloguing insects. Consistent with many of her other poems, Newsome's aims seem to be pedagogical: to teach nature appreciation from a poetic–scientific perspective. Her aims are also philosophical, for as Zeigler observes, "At the Pool" expresses the "world's contradictions as well as its wondrous glories" (1988: 128). The first stanza, written in a conversational, almost defiantly prosaic style with a simple rhyme scheme, sets the pastoral scene and invites the child reader into its romantic vitalism:

> I like to stand right still awhile
> Beside some forest pool.
> The reeds around it smell so fresh,
> The waters look so cool!
> Sometimes I just hop in and wade,   5
> And have a lot of fun,
> Playing with bugs that dart across
> The water in the sun. (ll. 1–8)

The speaker inserts herself into the landscape, modeling and encouraging interaction with the insects of the pool. In the second stanza, the pool becomes a veritable ecosystem (before A. G. Tansley elaborated the concept in 1935), a laboratory for studying aquatic insects interacting with their environment. Newsome emphasizes the species names to make them stand out and to emphasize their variation:

> They lodge here at this little pool—
> All sorts of bugs and things   10
> That hop about its shady banks,
> Or dart along with wings,

Or scamper on the water top,
As *water-striders* go,
Or strange *back-swimmers* upside down,   15
Using their legs to row,
Or the stiff, flashing *dragon flies*,
The gentle *damoiselle*,
The clumsy, sturdy *water-bugs,*
And *scorpions* as well,   20
That come on top to get fresh air
From homes beneath the pool,
Where *water-boatmen* have their nooks,
On pebbles, as a rule. (ll. 9–24)

The speaker seems wonderstruck particularly by the movement of these creatures, painting the vitalism of this small world with action verbs and adjec-
tives such as "hop," "scamper," "row," "strange," and "flashing." Interestingly,
all these insects—water-striders, back-swimmers, dragonflies, damoiselles,
water-bugs, scorpions, and water-boatmen—are predators.[10]

That the insects are predators becomes relevant in the third stanza, when
the predators are outdone by the kingfisher, a small bird (more precisely, a
group of related bird species) that dives for fish. In Zeigler's reading of this
poem, the kingfisher also brings "death" (1988: 129):

And then, behold! Kingfisher comes   25
That great big royal bird!
To him what is the *dragon fly*
That kept the pool life stirred?
Or *water-tigers* terrible
That murder bugs all day?   30
Kingfisher comes, and each of these
Would hide itself away! (ll. 25–32)

The diction—"terrible" water-tigers that "murder" their prey—suggests some
kind of social Darwinian justice to the natural order of the food chain. As
described in *Citizen Bird*, the kingfisher dives into the water to hunt fish and
its length is about thirteen inches, making the bird a giant when compared
with the insects described in "At the Pool" (1927a: 318–19). In *Birdcraft*, the
kingfisher is described with violent rhetoric as a hunter who "seizes his prey

by diving, and if it is small and pliable swallows it at once, but if it consists of the larger and more spinney fish they are beaten to pulp against a branch" (Wright 1897: 205). In *Birds through an Opera Glass*, Florence Merriam calls the species a fearless "woodsman" that will "teach you the secrets of the forest" (1889: 60). Celia Leighton Thaxter's poem "The Kingfisher" portrays the bird with similar admiration and romanticization, though the presence of the speaker agitates the bird: "[h]e perched on the rock above me, and kept up such a din, / And looked so fine with his collar snow-white beneath his chin, / And his cap of velvet, black bright, and his jacket of lovely blue" (Thaxter 1894: ll. 5–7). Newsome's scientific, rather than merely descriptive, rhetoric shows her sense of the child reader's maturity and level of education.

Newsome turns the kingfisher into a German-romantic heroic figure that hunts for insects and brings death. The masculinized kingfisher terrorizes the pond's inhabitants:

> He swoops and swallows what he will,
> A *stone-fly* or a *frog*.
> Wing'd things rush frightened through the air   35
> Others to hole and log.
> The little pool that held them all
> I watch grow very bare,
> But fisher knows his hide and seek—
> He'll find someone somewhere! (ll. 33–40)   40

While this poem seems to characterize a flight from history into nature, effectively ignoring race, the naming of species anchors it in the history of the entomological taxonomy of insects. The focus on the interaction of the species, showing deference to scientific accuracy, reflects the history of ecological science as well.

Because of their scientific specificity, Newsome's writings on birds and natural history are irreducible to the notion of an organic trope that reinforces a New Negro black nationalism. Rather, she speaks to political and scientific discourses about birding and conservation that at first glance seem far adrift from the concerns of *The Crisis*. Such writings as "Birds and Manuscripts," "The Satisfied Swifts," and "At the Pool" engage the bird conservation ethos of the plume wars. They also critically signify on field guides such as *Citizen Bird*, which contains racist stereotypes of African-Americans and participates in a discourse environmental management and species seg-regation. Taken as a whole, these writings reveal the pluralism of New Negro politics and *The Crisis*, affirming the freedom of African-American readers to be concerned with something other than the "Negro problem."

Conservation and Black Nationalism

Yet Newsome's writings in the 1920s continually bear out a tension between explicitly promoting conservation and employing organic tropes in the ser-vice of black nationalism. Newsome's June 1928 "Little Page" column, for example, draws on the machine-in-the-garden trope to condemn the pollu-tion of paper mills in unusually direct and polemical rhetoric. She establishes a pastoral idyll by describing a bridge that crosses a creek, in which the lei-surely stroller "look[s] out upon the silver and green waters" and "smell[s] the cool high waters in spring," while cardinals are "flitting about the banks and haughty kingfishers enjoying their minnows" (1928: 195). A paper mill—the machine in the garden—interrupts this idyll: "[f]ish would perish in the stream of chocolate brown water with the white froth stirring dully on top, and people could be heard exclaiming, 'That horrid paper mill!'" (1928: 195). The description suddenly turns to a toxic discourse of pollution and ecological violence. When spring flowers tried to "perfume" the landscape, the "stealthy sickening smell would rise from the creek" (1928: 195). As though realizing her tone grows too angry for a child audience, she downshifts the pathos and describes the paper mill as, nonetheless, a deceptively "picturesque sight" that "sat so casually upon the hillside with banks of trees that changed colors all year furnishing a rich background" (1928: 195).

Newsome's poem "The Bird in the Cage," which won honorable mention in *The Crisis* prize contest of 1926, returns to more recognizably Du Boisian political ground. This poem echoes themes in Dunbar's "Sympathy" (1899) and seems cross-written for child and adult audiences. Dunbar's famous poem begins:

> I know what the caged bird feels, alas!
>> When the sun is bright on the upland slopes;
> When the wind stirs soft through the springing grass,

And when the river flows like a stream of glass;
    When the first bird sings and the first bud opes,   5
And the faint perfume from its chalice steals—
I know what the caged bird feels! (ll. 1–7)

The poem ends with the famous line, "I know why the caged bird sings!" (l. 21). As in much of Newsome's poetry, Dunbar finds an objective correlative and allegorical figure for black suffering in the caged bird. The affect is, as the title declares, one of intense sympathy naturalized by the speaker's spontaneous identification with the caged bird, which could symbolize slavery, Jim Crow, and the general carceral society of the South.

Another poem authored by an African-American that uses the trope of the caged animal is Countee Cullen's prize-winning "Thoughts in a Zoo" (1926), which appeared in *The Crisis* two issues prior to "The Bird in the Cage."[11] Cullen's poem makes explicit the analogy between imprisoned zoo animals and metaphorical human imprisonment: "They in their cruel traps, and we in ours, / Survey each other's rage, and pass the hours / Commiserating each the other's woe" (ll. 1–3). Yet the identification occurs between animals and humans in general, rather than specific minority groups: "[t]hat lion with his lordly, untamed heart / Has in some man his human counterpart" (ll. 7–8). The poem concludes with the question: "Who is most wretched, these caged ones, or we / Caught in a vastness beyond our sight to see?" (ll. 17–18). This couplet evokes the vertigo experienced by southern black migrants upon their arrival in northern cities, like King Solomon Gillis, the dazed protagonist of Rudolph Fisher's "City of Refuge." The metaphorical imprisonment of African-Americans is ironic: people are swallowed up in incomprehensibly vast space in a sort of urban sublime.

Newsome revises this caged animal trope in Dunbar's and Cullen's poems by turning the structure of identification into a triangular relation and focusing on the violence of the bird beating against the bars of the cage:

I am not better than my brother over the way,
But he has a bird in the cage and I have not.
It beats its little fretted green wings
Against the wires of its prison all day long.
Backward and forward it leaps. (ll. 1–5)

Instead of simply identifying with the bird or condemning her fellow human, the speaker first identifies with her "brother"—which suggests an intimate, familial link—who occupies the same ethical playing field as the speaker: "I am not better." In this way, too, Newsome revises sentimental women's abolitionist literature, which tends to invoke a clear distinction between good and evil and apostrophizes against the evils of slavery. The "brother," it seems, can be good if he just sets the caged bird free. Verbs such as "beats" suggest not only the violence of captivity, but also the persistence of the bird's natural will to freedom. The next few lines of the poem paint in idealized, pastoral strokes the freedom for which the bird longs:

> While summer air is tender and the shadows of leaves
> Rock on the ground,
> And the earth is cool and heated in spots,
> And the air from rich herbage rises teeming,
> And gold of suns spills all around,   10
> And birds within the maples
> And birds upon the oaks fly and sing and flutter. (ll. 6–12)

The variations and contradictions of the outside world represent freedom as mobility: the cool and heated spots, the tender summer air and rock on the ground, the welcoming abundance of the "gold of suns." The free birds offer a joyous, affective counterpoint to the caged bird's struggle. The speaker then turns the focus back to the caged bird: "And there is that little green prisoner, / Tossing its body forward and up, / Backward and forth mechanically!" (ll. 13–15). The word "little" implies the prisoner's child-like vulnerability, while its behavior becomes increasingly denaturalized and mechanized. The limited, rigid movements—"forward and up" and "Backward and forth"—along with the word "mechanically," also evoke factory workers under the conditions of assembly-line production. The speaker then establishes her identification with and sympathy for the bird:

> I listen for its hungry little song,
> Which comes unsatisfying,
> Like drops of dew dispelled by drought.
> O, rose bud doomed to ripen in a bud vase!
> O, bird of song within that binding cage!   20

Nay, I am not better than my brother over the way,
Only he has a bird in a cage and I have not. (ll. 16–22)

Newsome returns to a sentimental mode with the apostrophes and exclama-
tions, yet the sentimental affect is nuanced by the repetition of the poem's
opening lines, which stress ethical identification—a recognition of the brother's flawed humanity—rather than opposition. The owner of the caged bird is
not "evil" but ignorant of what he is doing.

A few months before "The Bird in a Cage" appeared, Newsome subtitled
a column of the "Little Page" "Something about Birds," in which she focused
on the trope of the caged bird (1926b). Newsome reads Dunbar's "Sympathy"
literally instead of allegorically. Dunbar's poem demonstrates an empathetic
identification with animals: he "could imagine what must be the feeling of
the caged bird as he listens to the free birds singing about him, taunting
in their boundless liberty" (1926: 25). While this may be a purposive mis-
reading urging her child audience to look beyond the poem's political allegory, she gets more mileage out of the poem as both a call for racial uplift
and a conservationist statement. She then turns to Leonardo Da Vinci, who,
she recounts, "used to buy caged birds whenever he was able and set them
free, and watch them with great joy flying into the turquoise skies of Italy"
(1926: 25). She directly addresses the reader in rhyme, saying "you read of
his art," but should also "think of his *heart*" (1926: 25). Da Vinci becomes
a figure of compassion in Newsome's attempts to teach conservationist values to African-American children. She then goes on to discuss cardinals,
which were "once commonly sold in this country for cage birds." She urges
empathetic identification with the bird through the rhetorical strategy of
anthropomorphism: "imagine gay Sir Cardinal in his grenadier's hat as
a prisoner." In this light, a reading of "The Bird in the Cage" nuances the
political allegory by urging a more literal interpretation of the caged bird
trope. Its dovetailing of Progressive-era conservation politics with African-
American (and romantic) tropes suggest parallels between that movement
and abolition: one day the (presumably white) owner of the caged bird will
realize his wrongs and set the bird free.

Further developing conservationist themes, Newsome's poem "Mattinata"
(1927f) laments the lack of access city children have to the countryside,

employing images of wildlife absence that anticipate Rachel Carson's *Silent Spring* (1962). The poem's title is Italian for morning and it meditates on the dawn:

> When I think of the hosts of little ones
> Who wake to a birdless dawn,
> Who know of no meadow that waits for them,
> No pool with its dragon flies
> All bathed with the silver of morning light   5
> Like the lights that flash on the pool. (ll. 1–6)

For Newsome, to lose contact with a rural setting is to be deprived of something essential. It bespeaks a sense of absence and loss. The poem concludes:

> I fear that the dawn's too rich for my share.
> I fear I have robbed some child
> Of the fragrance of dew,   15
> Of the birds' first notes,
> Of the warm kind light from God—
> All sent in tints of nasturtium blooms—
> For the little red hearts of childhood. (ll. 13–19)

The speaker moves into an adult role, expressing culpability for the child's life—the next generation—experienced without nature. She seems to be lamenting her inability to represent nature's sights and sounds, to render into words the "too rich" dawn for the city-dwelling child (l. 13). Again, Newsome affirms the value of nature.

Newsome's explicitly race-themed poems are perhaps her most anthologized and critically examined ones. Published under the name Mary Effie Lee, "Morning Light (The Dew-drier)" first appeared in the November 1918 issue of *The Crisis* before it became anthologized in Countee Cullen's landmark 1927 collection of Harlem Renaissance-era poetry *Caroling Dusk* and later *The Poetry of the Negro, 1946–1949*, edited by Langston Hughes and Arna Bontemps (1949). As children's literature scholar Donnarae MacCann observes, this poem "makes reference to some of Newsome's strongest interests: childhood, natural history, Christianity, and her African heritage" (1988: 64). A highly alliterative free verse poem, "Morning Light" employs an extended metaphor that likens an African boy leading a European traveler through the wilderness to a future generation of African-American race leaders. Set in an African jungle, it fits well into the Pan-Africanist sensibilities of *The Crisis* and reflects the (unfulfilled) hope for civil rights advancement after the Great War. Newsome prefaces the poem with an explanation of its inspiration:

> It is a custom in some parts of Africa for travelers into the jungles to send before them in the early morning little African boys called "Dew-driers" to brush with their bodies the dew from the high grasses—and be, perchance, the first to meet the leopard's or hyena's challenge—and so open the road. "Human brooms," Dan Crawford calls them. (1918: 17)

Having set the scene, the first stanza describes the tropical African setting and the second stanza envisions the dew-drier black boy as a symbolic agent of racial uplift:

> Brother to the firefly—
> For as the firefly lights the night
> So lights he the morning—
> Bathed in the dank dews as he goes forth
> Through heavy menace and mystery   5
> Of half-waking tropic dawns,
> Behold a little black boy, a naked black boy,
> Sweeping aside with his slight frame
> Night's pregnant tears,
> And making a morning path to the light   10
> For the tropic traveler! (ll. 1–11)

Though set in Africa, the more inclusive and African diasporic designation "black boy" is used to name the dew-drier instead of "African." Just as the assonant long "o" of Hughes's "The Negro Speaks of Rivers" resonates throughout that poem, so too does the consonant "black boy" form a veritable echo chamber of "b"-sounds here: brother, bathed, behold, blood, battle, body, bared, and bear. In the first line, the child bears a familial relation to nature, specifically an insect—the "firefly" that performs an analogous task to the child clearing a path. Despite the familial link to the firefly, to nature, the jungle is described as hostile, a "heavy menace and mystery" that places the vulnerable "naked" and "slight" black boy in peril. This hostility only enhances the black boy's bravery.

The "dank dews" that "bathed" the black boy suggest a sort of ritual purification or trial, especially as these dews become "dews of blood" in the poem's final line. The peculiar personified night's "pregnant tears" evoke themes of black motherhood tinged with tragedy. These lines also play on "morning" as mourning—perhaps for the slave trade or the late-nineteenth-century scramble for Africa—through which the black boy makes a "morning path," finds a way past the mourning of black history and to a new dawn.

The second stanza shifts from this particular scene to broader claims about the black diaspora as a whole, envisioning the dew-drier as the leader who will lead his race to future uplift:

> Bathed in the blood of battle,
> Treading toward a new morning,
> May not his race—its body long bared to the world's disdain,
> It's schooled to smile for a light to come—   15
> May not his race, even as the dew-boy leads,
> Bear onward the world toward a new day-dawn
> When tolerance, forgiveness,
> Such as reigned in the heart of One
> Whose heart was gold,   20
> Shall shape the earth for that fresh dawning
> After the dews of blood? (ll. 12–22)

The thumping, alliterative first line—"Bathed in the blood of battle"—suggests both black Buffalo soldiers in the Great War and the metaphorical battle against Jim Crow. If black soldiers help secure democracy abroad, as the poem suggests and as race leaders like Du Bois hoped, then they would gain democracy at home. The "body" of the race, which has been "long bared to the world's disdain," bears the marks of a traumatic history. But the face—"schooled to smile for a light to come"—looks to the future with hope. That the smile is "schooled" suggests that Jim Crow can be unlearned through the pedagogical tasks taken on by Newsome and *The Crisis*. The "dew-boy leads" because the next generation of children are the future of the race, perhaps the first generation to reap the benefits of full rights as US citizens. The race as well as the whole world will be uplifted: "May not his race, even as the dew-boy leads, / Bear onward the world toward a new day-dawn" (ll. 16–17). By ending with a question, the poem's final lines suggest a hesitant hope.

This poem does provide an example of Foley's notion of the black nationalist organic trope. However, placed in the context of Newsome's oeuvre and *The Crisis*, it also fits into a pattern of nature appreciation, of developing positive valuations of blackness in association with nature and showing how the African-American future is intertwined with the natural environment.

Perhaps Newsome's most well-known poem, "The Bronze Legacy (To a Brown Boy)," first appeared alongside Georgia Douglass Johnson's "Motherhood" in the October 1922 issue of *The Crisis*. The poem appears in the annual "Children's Number," among pages full of pictures of African-American infants and toddlers sent in by readers; its interpellative subtitle—"to a brown boy"—announces its pedagogical aims. These special issues devoted to children combined writing for child as well as adult audiences, and "The Bronze Legacy" is an expression of race-pride typical of the 1920s and similar to Hughes's "Earth Song." The optimism of "The Bronze Legacy," however, is balanced out by its juxtaposition next to Johnson's ironically titled "Motherhood." As Katherine Capshaw Smith observes, "Newsome's upbeat voice occupies the same space as does Johnson's pessimistic argument, a linkage that reflects the period's competing ideas about black childhood" (2004: 23). In Johnson's poem, the mother-speaker addresses a child waiting to be born, warning that the "world is cruel, cruel, child, / I cannot let you through" (ll. 7–8). Newsome's poem is more optimistic:

> 'Tis a noble gift to be brown, all brown,
> Like the strongest things that make up this earth,
> Like the mountains grave and grand,
>   Even like the very land,
>   Even like the trunks of trees—   5
>   Even oaks, to be like these!
> God builds His strength in bronze.
>
> To be brown like thrush and lark!
>   Like the subtle wren so dark!
> Nay, the king of beasts wears brown;   10
>   Eagles are of this same hue.
> I thank God, then, I am brown.
>   Brown has mighty things to do.

The lyric naturalizes race in such a way that inverts white supremacist and social Darwinist ideologies by valorizing brownness over whiteness. To be "brown" is to be related to the material foundation of the earth—what Washington calls the "bed-rock bottom"—expressed affectively through a series of amplifying similes: mountains "grave and grand," tortured into existence over long centuries, and the "very land" on which the southern economy depends (ll. 3–4).

The first stanza's comparisons of the brown boy to "trunks of trees" and, more specifically "oaks," anticipates the tree imagery of Angelina Wald Grimké's "The Black Finger" (1923), another poem about race-pride:

> I have just seen a most beautiful thing:
> Slim and still,
> Against a gold, gold sky,
> A straight, black cypress
> Sensitive   5
> Exquisite
> A black finger
> Pointing upwards.
> Why, beautiful still finger, are you black?
> And why are you pointing upwards?   10

The species-specific "oaks" in Newsome's poem and "cypress" in Grimké's suggest ecological knowledge as well as symbolism. Oak wood is ideal for housing construction and is not coincidentally the name of Washington's home, the "Oaks," as well as Dunbar's "The Haunted Oak," in which a speaking oak tree bears witness to the traumas of lynching.

While the first stanza of "The Bronze Legacy" deploys images of immanence, the second stanza, with the exception of the lion, deploys images of transcendence that reflect the poet's interest in bird families: thrush, lark, wren, and eagle. The bird reference speaks back to Newsome's interest in birding and natural history. Though the references to "God" in lines seven and twelve may show the poet's Methodism, the religious outlook seems more akin to Emerson's *Nature* (1836) and quasi-pantheistic, nineteenth-century Transcendentalism, which locates transcendence in immanence. In Newsome's poem, God expresses himself through nature: "God builds His strength in bronze" (l. 7). The poem's final line, as in "Morning Light," points toward the future fulfillment of promise: "Brown has mighty things to do" (l. 14). This black nationalist charge to the race reflects Newsome's and *The Crisis*'s emphasis on educating children for the future of the race.

Conclusion

From her "Little Page" columns to "At the Pool," Newsome's multi-generic writings engaged political issues of the historical period that have not traditionally been accounted for by literary critics and historians of African-American literature: the plume wars, the Great English Sparrow War, bird conservation, and interlinks between natural history and race. At the same time, she (and Du Bois in his editorial role) puts these histories and discourses into the unlikely context of *The Crisis* and its civil rights agenda. Natural history and conservation, in this context, become linked to problems of segregation and the naturalizing of racial difference. Newsome's work challenges these problems with the pedagogical aims of her writings, her taxonomies of bird species, her tropes of integrated nature, and the black nationalism of "The Bronze Legacy (To a Brown Boy)" and "Morning Light (the Dew-drier)."

In the process, her writings, along with those of other *Crisis* contributors interested in environments, complicate the politics of *The Crisis* by expanding the range of its political concerns. While attacking Jim Crow and promoting a politics of inclusion, *The Crisis*, guided by its editor, sometimes offered a productive alternative to the color-line problem. Its politics aims to denaturalize racial difference, to challenge a discourse of enclosure and segregation, and engage natural history and conservation.

Sawmills and Swamps

Ecological Collectives in Zora Neale Hurston's Mules and Men *and* Their Eyes Were Watching God

Introduction

Jonah's Gourd Vine (1934), Hurston's first novel, opens with a vision of the swamp as a chronotope of the southern environment. John, a young black teenager, works at sharecropping in a town moated by a swamp and isolated from the outside world. Nature's intractability expresses itself through the soil—the "barren hard clay yard"—and the undeveloped, impassable danger of the swamp, of which John's mother warns him not to get "snake bit" (1934: 12). Slavery also haunts this "over-the-creek" place: in the exploitative system of sharecropping and more subtly in the psychology of white supremacy and subservience that makes Ned, John's stepfather, threaten to beat him for staring at the "white folks" walking by their home (1934: 2). In *Jonah's Gourd Vine*, the swamp is an ambivalent space, temporally stretched across human and environmental time.

From the mid-state Orlando region to the Everglades, almost all of Hurston's fiction and ethnographic stories take place in swampy south Florida. In this chapter, I focus on Hurston's ethnographic engagement with the southern environment—and particularly her representation of swamps—in the frame narrative of *Mules and Men* and in the final third of *Their Eyes Were Watching God*. Ecocritics, ecofeminists, and black feminist critics have foregrounded the importance of the southern environment in Hurston's writings. Hurston does more than reflect the swamp tropes that pervade twentieth-century southern and African-American literature. Her work shows how ecological collectives are formed out of the shared exploitation of human, animal, and natural resources. This understanding informs her critique of environmental inequities and her approach to imagining civil rights. For Hurston, the swamp provides a space for ecological agencies that differ from those found in Washington's *Working with the Hands*. Much like Washington's representation of the plantation zone, Hurston represents the swamp space as existing outside the official public domain dominated by white supremacy; however, she focuses almost entirely on community and egalitarian collectives that resist this white domination. While Washington attempted to develop a program of racial uplift through ecological agencies, Hurston imagines the swamp as a space for ecological community.

In order to provide a literary and environmental context for Hurston's work, I briefly examine several figurations of the swamp in early-twentieth-century African-American literature. Swamps are prominent in Du Bois's *The Souls of Black Folk* (1903) and *The Quest of the Silver Fleece* (1911); two short stories published in *The Crisis* during the Harlem Renaissance; Hurston's first novel, *Jonah's Gourd Vine* (1934); and Arna Bontomps's 1936 novel *Black Thunder*. These figurations show the swamp as a contradictory space of regulation and wilderness, of menace and utopia. Drawing on work in environmental history, I then approach the depiction of the southern environment in *Mules and Men* through its narrative framing device and the displacements and sublimations enacted in the folktales Hurston collects and recounts. The exploitive and utopian possibilities of the swamp come into focus in *Their Eyes Were Watching God*, when Janie and Tea Cake live "on de muck" or the Everglades (1937: 122). While the ontological gaps among species collapse in the swamp to form an ecological collective, racial segregation is quickly restored in the aftermath of a hurricane, showing the possibilities and limits of Hurston's vision of civil rights and environments.

Swamp Figurations: A Short Literary History

The swamp itself, while textually mediated, is also irreducible to the text, to figurations and tropes, for it contains real dangers of disease and violence, and the history of anonymous suffering under slavery and Jim Crow. Variously called bogs or marshes, swamps are officially known to ecologists as "wet-lands." The word "swamp" came into prominent use to describe the Americas, particularly the southern United States, during the colonial era. Swamps are numerous in the South; 50 percent of the states of Florida and Louisiana, for example, are wetlands (Wilson 2006: xiii). Abundant with cypress and pine trees, along with the rich soils, such wetlands were economically allur-ing but proved notoriously resistant to colonization and development. A mix of industries gathered at the outskirts of swamplands: turpentine stills, saw-mills, paper mills, and cotton plantations. But the swamp also accrued cul-tural and spiritual significance. In *Shadow and Shelter*, Anthony Wilson claims that for Harlem Renaissance writers such as Hurston, swamps provide a sort of "spiritual race-memory" (2006: 124). This mixing of spiritual, cul-tural, and material dimensions of the swamp plays out across several literary works of the early-twentieth century.

In the chapter "Of the Black Belt" in *The Souls of Black Folk*, Du Bois fig-ures the swamp in the larger context of the southern environment and the sharecropping economy. Foreshadowing *Darkwater*, Du Bois takes the seg-regated train to Georgia, continually reminding us that he sees the Georgia landscape from the Jim Crow car (described generously as "not so good as the other," but "fairly clean and comfortable") (1903: 84). For ecocritic Anne Raine, Du Bois's personal and geographical journey into the South signifies on nineteenth-century picturesque travel writings and evokes the romanti-cism of William Wordsworth, particularly in the swamp scene (2013: 324). After touring the "cotton kingdom," Du Bois continues his picturesque jour-ney to the "Land of the Unfenced" and to ever-intensifying degrees of wild-ness before finally arriving in the swamp:

> The shadow of an old plantation lies at its edge, forlorn and dark ... Then the swamp grows beautiful; a raised road, built by chained Negro convicts, dips down into it, and forms a way walled and almost covered in living green. Spreading trees spring from a prodigal luxuriance of undergrowth; great dark green shadows fade into the black background. (1903: 90)

This description of the swamp is a chronotope, where time and space entwine and thicken. The swamp lies somewhere between the past—the shadowed ruins of the old plantation—and the present, the return of slavery through forced convict labor. Du Bois deploys a trope that would appear across many twentieth-century representations of the swamp: that of slave-like, convict labor in the swamp. The "pendent gray moss" and hellish atmosphere (the burning wood, "smouldering in dull red anger") give way to the road, which seems to order the landscape, to show a direction out of—or at least a way for navigating within—the swamp. The trope of convict labor, the threat of snakes, and the eco-melancholia: all point to the swamp as a dangerous yet beautiful space in *The Souls of Black Folk*.

Published almost eight years after *The Souls of Black Folk*, Du Bois's novel *The Quest of the Silver Fleece* ambitiously interweaves multiple characters and storylines into a Marxian attempt to imagine the global cotton economic system in its totality. Even given the ensemble of characters, it is also a *bildungsroman* about Zora, a black southern girl who spent her childhood in an Alabama swamp. Zora, a "child of the swamp," is discovered by a young black man named Bles Alwyn in the opening of the novel (1911: 44). The chapter previews an ambivalence toward the swamp that runs through the novel. In one scene, Bles wanders through the claustrophobic night on his way to a backwoods schoolhouse set up by a white northern philanthropist. He hears a song—with "no tune nor melody ... just formless, boundless music"—that cuts through the darkness and, following it, stumbles upon Zora's cabin, where she lives with her mother, the alleged witch and folk healer, Elspeth. They hear Bles and, startled, he flees through the woods. In the novel's opening, the swamp appears as a mythical space, seemingly outside of history—formless and boundless like the music—even to the point that Bles recalls the event as "some witch-vision of the night" (1911: 16). The swamp is, in Zora's words, a "mysterious" place full of "dreams," and fairies and devils (1911: 19). In later chapters, she leads Bles through the "swamp-world" with its "great shadowy oaks and limpid pools" (1911: 45).

After attending the same school as Bles, Zora, a promising pupil, is recruited by Mrs. Vanderpool and taken to New York City. Upon her arrival at Manhattan's Fifth Avenue, Zora equates the urban setting to a swamp. Initially, Vanderpool laughs at the analogy, but Zora explains: "I mean, it is moving—always moving" (1911: 245). The image synthesis of city and swamp is unusual because the city is usually analogized to wilderness, the jungle, or an ecosystem rather than a swamp, whereas the swamp is typically figured as the antithesis of the urban because of its recalcitrant ecology, its resistance to settlement and development. Zora enthusiastically dives into her education, and the silver (not golden) fleece of the novel's title merges her knowledge of Greek mythology with cotton production. Thus, instead of two opposing spaces between the northern city and the southern swamp, we have three primary spaces represented in the novel: the mythical swamp, the plantation zone, and the urban environment.

In *The Quest of the Silver Fleece*, the swamp must be transformed into a synthesizing vision of pastoral reconciliation between the primitive swamp and modernity ([1911] 2015: 141). Using a check she received from Vanderpool, Zora has the swamp cleared so black farmers can grow cotton. Soon begins an aggressive pastoralization of the swamp space. Though she does not explicitly mention it, Zora is determined to follow the Tuskegee philosophy of racial uplift: "We must have land—our own farm with our own tenants—to be the beginning of a free community" (1911: 362). With the relatively small sum she has from Vanderpool, Zora resolves to buy the swamp. Through the mechanisms of formal education, travels in the north, and eventual return to Georgia, Zora's story is dialectical because she retains the spirit of the swamp (she says at one point, "We black folks is got the *spirit*") (1911: 46). Du Bois affirms an essence of black primitivism much like he does in *The Souls of Black Folk*.

In a preview of Hurston's ecological collectives, the black community unites to pastoralize the swamp and turn it into a black-owned, black-run agricultural cooperative. The workers throw themselves into action: the "ringing of axes and grating of saws and tugging of mules was heard ... until at last a wide black scar appeared in the thick south side of the swamp, which widened and widened to full twenty acres" (1911: 375).[1] The workers rest in the afternoon, cradled in an abundant pastoral scene: with "ravenous appetites the dark, half-famished throng fell upon the food, and then in utter weariness stretched themselves and slept: lying along the earth like huge bronze earth-spirits" (1911: 375). However, the swamp exists more in a dialectical relation to the external world rather than an object of pastoral assimilation. Zora must be formally educated, uplifted from the swamp, yet it is her continued connection to the swamp that preserves her affinity for the folk. Du Bois makes it clear that it is the swamp still inside Zora—a kind of spiritual essence—that motivates her leadership. She proposes to Bles Alwyn a "plan of wide scope—a bold regeneration of the land," calling the swamp her "university" (1911: 399–400). By the end of the novel, the swamp has "transformed" and is "now a swamp in name only" (426), yet it is still "living, vibrant, tremulous" (1911: 433).

In ways that envision the swamp as more dangerous than Du Bois imagined, a Harlem Renaissance-era short story brings together themes of race and labor within the setting of the southern swamp. Winner of a distinction award in the 1925 *Crisis* literary contest, N. B. Young Jr.'s "Swamp Judgment" begins *in media res* with a southern black sharecropper's flight from a lynch mob and into the "Big Swamp" and to the Little Cedar River, where he hopes to cross the Alabama border into Florida (1926: 65). Young imbues the swamp with menacing atmosphere: "voracious mosquitoes struck him with unrelenting force and frogs sprang under his feet" (1926: 65). While the swamp is figured here as a kind of refuge from the lynch mob, it still remains a dangerous space where water moccasins might strike at any moment. "Yet," the narrator says, "what he was fleeing from would out-torture both experiences" in the swamp and in the trenches of France during the Great War: "He had often thought the trenches overrun with vermin had been the very bottom of the earthly anguish, but now he knew the batter-like ooze in its dank surrounding was worse" (1926: 65). We know little of the sharecropper's background, other than his experiences in France's Argonne Forest, which left him a wounded leg that handicaps his flight through the swamp. The reason for this escape is revealed midway through the story: the greedy "overlord" of the cotton plantation had come to collect his "share" of cotton bales, which our protagonist had already turned in a week earlier. He initially hides from the overseer, but then shoots the overseer with his "old army automatic" when the overseer physically attacks his wife and children for not disclosing his hiding place (1926: 65).

The story's most distinctive mark—and its value for contextualizing *Their Eyes Were Watching God*—is its abundant descriptive passages of the swamp. The sharecropper is "ankle-deep in slush" (1926: 66); a "miasmal fog … hangs in the tops of the dense growth" of the cypress trees (1926: 65); the "ancient moss-draped cypress" (1926: 66); and a "kingfisher rattled its metallic cry as it darted above him" (1926: 66). After passing out from exhaustion, the sharecropper awakens to hear the bloodhounds on his trail and, in the story's ambiguous ending: he spots a water moccasin in a cesspool, having "rolled himself against a cypress sapling just off the edge of a stagnant pool of green-ish water and was ready to shut his eyes to it all when a slow vibration in the scum of water caught his attention" (1926: 67). The cypress trees, the water moccasin, the kingfisher, the fog, and the slush: all are anthropomorphized with intentionality and infused with agency. This portrayal is not as ambiva-lent as previous figurations of the swamp in slave narratives and in Du Bois's *The Quest of the Silver Fleece*: the swamp is clearly menacing and dangerous. Yet it also serves as an environmental correlative for unjust social systems. In terms of degrees of menace and danger, though, the swamp in Young's story seems preferable to the violence of the Jim Crow and sharecropping systems of the South. Indeed, the story ends with a kind of magical merger of human and nature.[2]

Hurston's contemporary, Arna Bontemps, likewise recognized the his-torical significance of the swamp in his 1936 novel, *Black Thunder: Gabriel's Revolt, Virginia 1800*. The novel dramatizes the failed slave revolt in Richmond in 1800, led by Gabriel Prosser, a figure similar to Denmark Vesey and John Brown. Unlike Hurston, Bontemps was immersed in the black radical politics of the Chicago Renaissance and Popular Front of the 1930s. While official accounts of Gabriel's failed revolt and subsequent hanging gave Bontemps a historical basis, he imagined the event from the perspective of history's silent others: the black men and women who planned the revolt without leaving behind a scrap of paper; the author uses the past to serve his own radical vision during the 1930s and thus turns Prosser into a proletarian hero and martyr (Rampersad 1992: xiv). Echoing the swamp versus city dichotomy in *The Quest of the Silver Fleece*, the stag-ing ground of the revolt against Richmond is the Brook Swamp, a place that provides the best cover for an attack and "where the creek broadens and the thicket is dense" (1936: 38). The novel dramatizes the failed rebel-lion; Prosser's capture, trial, and execution; and the newspapers' attempts to contain and narrativize the event as a product of French revolutionary agitators. Prosser's plan was to break the rebel slaves into groups so that they could overtake the town's supply of weapons and set one of the "big-gest fires these here white folks is ever seen" (1936: 60). During the revolt,

Bontemps evokes the connection between African-American identity and nature: "It was the earth that spoke" (1936: 61). But it thunderstorms the night of the revolt and the subsequent flooding makes it impossible for the slaves to coordinate their attack. In keeping with the historical events, Prosser is betrayed, captured, tried, and executed by the end of the novel. The swamp in *Black Thunder* holds spiritual as well as strategic signifi-cance, and returns us to Wilson's concept of race memory. This more pos-itive vision of the swamp continues in Hurston's *Mules and Men* and *Their Eyes Were Watching God*.

Hurston's Cultural Ecology and *Mules and Men*

Hurston's characters in *Mules and Men* embody the sort of primitivism rep-resented in *Quest of the Silver Fleece*, though she embraces such primitivism as an end in itself rather than a stage on the way to transcending the double environments imposed by segregation. Smith contends that "black intellec-tuals had a troubled (not to say tortured) relationship with primitivism and regionalism: they were drawn to the notion that black folk had something distinctive and valuable to contribute to American culture, but they struggled with the movement's conception of those folk" (2007: 137). The question of regionalism is important because it is tied up with notions of the black folk and southern culture in general.[3]

There is probably another influence on Hurston that reflected an emerg-ing new problematic in anthropology. Her approach to ethnography paral-lels ideas developed by a contemporaneous anthropologist: the theorist of "cultural ecology," Julian Steward. He introduced ecology into the disci-pline of anthropology through his notion of cultural ecology, elaborated in his watershed book, *Theory of Cultural Change*. Though published in 1955 (a decade after Hurston's active literary career had ended), it collects previ-ously published papers from the 1930s and 1940s, and collates a framework initially elaborated in those decades. Cultural ecology focuses on the interac-tion between culture and environment; it places greater emphasis on human and nonhuman environmental influences than Boasian anthropology did.

Hurston's methods in *Mules and Men* were no doubt similar to cultural ecology.

The research for *Mules and Men* began almost a decade earlier in two periods in 1927 and 1928. Writing *Mules and Men* took Hurston over six years and consumed a great deal of her energy, as opposed to *Their Eyes Were Watching God*, which she drafted in six weeks while in Haiti collecting material for *Tell My Horse* (1938). The process was multifaceted: it involved a lot of traveling, transcription of folktales, frequent consultations with Boas, and assembling the "lies" into a readable, coherent form.[4] Hurston biographer Valerie Boyd describes the book as "part folklore, part hoodoo chronicle, and part immersion journalism" (2003: 280). In 1927, after studying with Boas at Barnard College and approaching graduation, Hurston received a six-month-long fellowship to study black folklore in the South (Boyd 2003: 142). In *Dust Tracks on a Road*, Hurston gives a now well-known account of her research—what she defines as "formalized curiosity"—in Polk County, the setting for the middle section of the book (1942: 143). After purchasing a used car and a pistol (the Jim Crow cars on most trains were too dangerous for black women, as were the backroads of Florida, where Hurston risked lynching and sexual assault), Hurston moved from the cities of Jacksonville and St. Augustine southward to the small towns of Eatonville, Palatka, and Sanford—all located in lake-dense central Florida, just northeast of Orlando (Boyd 2003: 142–3). Hurston settled in Eatonville and took up residence at the Everglades Cypress Lumber Company, where Hurston ingratiated herself to a community of black working-class men (Boyd 2003: 162). Hurston describes the dynamic eyesore upon her arrival at the sawmill camp: the "asphalt curved deeply and when it straightened out we saw a huge smokestack blowing smut against the sky. A big sign said, 'Everglades Cypress Lumber Company, Loughman, Florida'" (1935: 59). This sawmill camp serves as the setting for the frame story of *Mules and Men*.

In Eatonville, the authorial Hurston records folktales told by the residents, while Hurston the narrator/character overhears the stories, she also engages them as an active participant, lending them a communal sense of authorial presence. Critics have noted both the communitarian spirit and the self-reflexivity of *Mules and Men*. D. A. Boxwell argues that Hurston's participation in the action is "not unique to the ethnological writing of her time, but the presentation of herself as a strong ordering force in the text is" (1992: 5). In her essay "Thresholds of Difference," Barbara Johnson points out that in works such as *Mules and Men*, Hurston undercuts the conventions of ethnographic writing with its "inside/outside oppositions," and in the process transforms the "plane of geometry of physical space into the complex transactions of discursive exchange" (1985: 318). According to Johnson, "Hurston's own introduction begins with a paraphrase of *Psalm* 122 which replaces the Biblical 'they' with an unnamed 'somebody,' and it ends by placing itself geographically just outside the town line of Eatonville" (1985: 324). Another way of thinking through these "complex transactions of discursive exchange" is community and the community-shaping work of the tales, the jook joints, and the worker solidarity. In *Mules and Men*, this undercutting begins with the book's initial framing, the preface by Boas, and the retroactive framing of the book's glossary and appendix (Johnson 1985: 324).

In the frame narrative, Hurston develops a covert critique of capitalism. Private property appears as a strange thing in Polk County: "signs all over that this was private property and that no one could enter without the consent of the company" (1935: 59–60). Published in 1931, Charlotte Todes's *Labor and Lumber* gives accounts of the lumber industry's influence on the southern environment: "smoke and fire from the sawmill burners are the sign posts of lumber towns built around the industry" (21). Todes reports that over 100,000 black workers were employed across Georgia, Florida, Mississippi, and other southern states (1931: 83).[5] In the twentieth-century South, the timber industry thrived on the exploitation of (mostly black) prison labor and the seemingly infinite supply of cypress trees.

Hurston's interest in the southern lumber industry and its dependence on black labor goes back to "Spunk," a short story published in *Opportunity* (1925). This David versus Goliath ghost story and folktale is often celebrated for its use of a southern African-American vernacular in the tradition of Charles Chesnutt, Paul Laurence Dunbar, and Jean Toomer (Boyd 2003: 97). "Spunk" tells the story of its brash title character, who, accustomed to getting whatever he wants, gets entangled in a tryst with Joe Kanty's wife. While the story's use of dialect and ethnographic authenticity previews *Mules and Men*, the southern environment also plays a prominent role. Spunk works in a saw mill, and his ability to excel on the job makes him reminiscent of other black folk heroes such as John Henry. Spunk's sexualized displays at work reflect his behavior in town: "[h]e rides that log down at saw-mill jus' like he struts round wid another man's wife" (1925: 26). Joe Kanty, the underdog in this story, is terrified to confront the physically intimidating Spunk Banks. One night, Spunk shoots Joe in the woods with a pistol, claiming a "clear case of self-defense" (1925: 29). Joe's ghost, however, returns to haunt Spunk in the form of a black bobcat, described by a witness as a "big black bob-cat, black all over, you hear me, *black*" (1925: 30). Once the bobcat—its blackness taking on a menacing, metaphysical quality—appears, the woods surrounding the town gain an eerie, southern gothic ambience: "Dusk crept in from the woods" (1925: 27). One day at the saw mill, Spunk falls (or Joe "pushes" Spunk – as Spunk claims with his dying breaths) into the mill's giant "singing, snarling, biting, circle-saw" (1925: 29). This gruesome maiming brings together themes of haunting with the parallel exploitation of black bodies (the workplace accident that Spunk dies in) and natural resources (the sawmill industry's deforestation). This parallel exploitation—its imagery and narrative elements—runs through the sawmill frame story of *Mules and Men*.

In *Dust Tracks on a Road*, Hurston describes her stay at the Polk County sawmills during the time of *Mules and Men*. In a passage similar to the descriptions of felling trees in "Swamp Moccasin," Hurston characterizes the black workers as artists:

> These poets of the swinging blade! The brief, but infinitely graceful, dance of body and axe-head as it lifts over the head in a fluid arc, dances in air and rushes down to bite into the tree, all in beauty. Where the logs march into the mill with its smokestacks disputing with the elements, its boiler room reddening the sky, and its great circular saw screaming arrogantly as it attacks the tree like a lion making its kill. The log on the carriage coming to the saw. A growling grumble. Then contact! Yeelld-u-u-ow! And a board is laid shining and new on a pile. All day, all night. Rumble, thunder and grumble. Yee-ee-ow! Sweating black bodies, muscled like gods, working to feed the hunger of the great tooth. Polk County! (1942: 147)

In this aestheticization of work and erotics of felling trees, Hurston celebrates the worker and lionizes the sawmill's machinery in a move typical of proletarian literature and the Marxian dialectic, in which the instruments of production are good but the modes are bad. This section undercuts itself, however, when it describes the smokestacks that "dispute" the air, the boiler room that reddens the sky, and the saw that screams "arrogantly" and "attacks" the tree.

In the Polk County section of *Mules and Men*, Hurston ventures into the swamp with the all-male workers. In her representation of the swamp, Hurston acknowledges the danger that we see in the stories by Young and Matheus. Whenever Hurston mentions sawmill and turpentine still jobs in *Dust Tracks on a Road*, she puts "jobs" in scare quotes, just as the law is the "law" in these areas. She portrays these camps as lawless and dangerous frontiers, where the mere perception of slight could get one killed: "since the law is lax on these big saw-mill, turpentine and railroad 'jobs,' there is a good chance that they [the murderer] never will be jailed for it" (1942: 146). The men "look out" for Hurston and "see to it that [she] didn't get snake-bit nor 'gator-swallowed" (1935: 66). The white watchman, Hurston learns, was killed by a panther two weeks before. She feels safe, though, for the men are like warriors as well as workers: "[t]hey can hurl their axes great distances and behead moccasins or sink the blade into an alligator's skull" (1935: 66). The danger is neutralized in this account and the swamp is treated with a sense of irreverence. Despite the all-male work camps, Hurston visited nearby phosphate mines and work gangs in the cypress swamps (Boyd 2003: 168). A group of workers undertake a journey to a sawmill in search of work. Along the way, they exchange stories like the travelers in Chaucer's *Canterbury Tales*.

Following the adage "God made de world and de white folks made work," the black migrants display various forms of resistance to the racialized capitalist system. They live in a community of work and play. An example of Leo Marx's machine in the garden, the intrusive whistle of the sawmill sonically marks the line between work and play: the "big whistle at the saw mill boomed and shrilled and pretty soon the log-train came racking along" (1935: 69). But the heat of the swamp makes work unbearable, and the workers just "naturally" take a siesta in the shade: "Phew! Sun and sawdust, sweat and sand. Nobody called a meeting and voted to sit in the shade. It just happened naturally" (1935: 84). When the "mill boss" refuses Hurston and the workers she is with, it shows that the mill depends on a surplus of reserve labor to keep wages down. In one incident, Eatonville local Jim Allen decides to go fishing when Mrs. Bertha Allen implores him to help clean up their living quarters. But Jim refuses to work the mill boss' property for free, finding a pocket of resistance in the constant give-and-take with the white mill owners: "You ain't de Everglades Cypress Lumber Comp'ny sho nuff. Youse just shacking in one of their shanties. Leave de weeds go" (1935: 92–3). This battle between the white boss and a collective of workers develops a few years later into an ecological collective in *Their Eyes Were Watching God*.

These "lying sessions," so called by Hurston in *Dust Tracks on the Road*, focus on a range of human and animal characters. The tales include such characters as John Henry the railroad worker who outworks the company's steam-driven machines (1935: 56–7; 248). Many of the tales reflect a nostalgia for a more agrarian way of life. One lying session involves bragging about who's "ole man" had the richest land, and the virtues of commercial versus natural fertilizer (1935: 101–2); Sack Daddy claims that "mosquito dust" makes the "finest fertilizer" (1935: 100), boasting that one year his father "raised pumpkins so big dat we et five miles up in one of 'em and five miles down and ten miles acrost one" (1935: 100). They then turn to bragging about who has seen the poorest land. One man saw land "so poor they had to wire up to Jacksonville for ten sacks of commercial-nal [commercial fertilizer] before dey could raise a tune on dat land" (1935: 102). Other tales revolve around anthropomorphized accounts of animals—lies of resistance, ironic reversals, and allegorical significance. Such tales relate comic accounts about snakes getting their poison (1935: 96); the "gator's" evolution (1935: 105–06); the boll weevil (1935: 99); and anthropomorphized, talking rabbits and mules (1935: 172).

The framing device and some of the tales bear a conscious/unconscious relationship, in which the tales are displacements and sublimations of the text's eco-unconscious—a repository of catastrophic events (e.g., floods and hurricanes) and fears of the wild. Hazel Carby argues for a form of historical, cultural, and mythical displacement that, I argue, coincides with the operations of displacement in the eco-unconscious: "Hurston's representation of the folk is not only a discursive displacement of the historical and cultural transformation of migration, but also is a creation of a folk outside of history" (1990: 77). In her introduction to *Mules and Men*, Hurston claims that migration is central to the collection, for Florida offers a "cross section of the Negro South" (1935: 1). Reasons for migration were environmental as well as social: natural disasters such as the Johnstown

Flood of 1899 and the Mississippi Flood of 1927; the 1926 and 1928 Florida hurricanes; the boll weevil's decimation of cotton monocultures; and the droughts of the 1930s.

These particular lies, usually comic in nature, sublimate and displace communal affects that can be found in the frame narrative's references to the southern environment of swamps, forests, sawmill camps, and turpentine stills. For example, the story of the Johnstown flood is separated spatially and typographically by the frame narrative. The tale undergoes a series of displacements: the tale, which takes place in western Pennsylvania (incidentally, near the setting of *Blood on the Forge*), is told in Eatonville, Florida. The Johnstown Flood of 1889 was, at the time, the most destructive flood in US history with a seventeen million dollar cost and over 2,000 dead. Located east of Pittsburgh, Johnstown was a steel mill town that could be found downriver from a dam, which burst during the flooding. Hurston sets up the tale: "So James told the story about the man who went to Heaven from Johnstown" (1935: 11). The tale itself is an outlandish retelling and resetting of the biblical flood in the American South. As James recounts and Hurston writes: "[i]n one place they call Johnstown they had a great flood. And so many folks got drownded that it looked jus' like Judgment day" (1935: 11). In the tale, a black southerner dies in the flood and goes the heaven. The joke on John is that once he arrives in heaven, he meets the angels Peter and Gabriel and tells them repeatedly about the flood, "jus' like [they] didn't know already" (1935: 12). Even though the angels give John a harp, he keeps "right on stoppin' every angel dat he could find to tell 'im about dat flood of water" (1935: 12). But John gets the cold shoulder from one very old angel, and he goes to Peter, who responds with the tale's punchline: "'Aw shucks,' Peter tol' im. 'Dat was Ole Nora. You can't tell *him* nothin' 'bout no flood" (1935: 13). The lie ends there, with Noah winning a bragging contest he never entered. The traumatic incident of the Johnstown flood is rendered comical. Also, given that much of this ethnographical material was gathered in 1928 and 1929, James's tale also invokes the Mississippi River flood of 1927—the most catastrophic flood in the region in recent history. The community Hurston studies, with its mesh of voices and affects, previews the workers in the Everglades in *Their Eyes Were Watching God*.

Ecological Collectives in *Their Eyes Were Watching God*

The last third of *Their Eyes Were Watching God* take Janie and Tea Cake
to the Florida Everglades, near Lake Okeechobee, with West Palm Beach
to the east and Belle Glade to the south. The geography is important here
because it contributes to the relative autonomy (as well as tragic outcome)
of Tea Cake and Janie's romance. The vernacular expression "on de muck"
substitutes the colonial name "Everglades" for a form of folk signification.
In this way, it is what Gates calls the "speakerly text," a text that is "oriented
toward imitating one of the numerous forms of oral narrative to be found in
classical Afro-American literature" (1988: 181). Gates argues that the swamp
functions in the opposite way that it does in Du Bois's *Quest of the Silver
Fleece*: "[w]hereas the swamp in Du Bois's text figures an uncontrolled chaos
that must be plowed under and controlled, for Hurston the swamp is the
trope of the freedom of erotic love" (1988: 193). My approach here is to treat
the swamp in its figurations, in Hurston and across early-twentieth-century
African-American texts, while also considering the swamp in the context
of its environmental history; moreover, the swamp is more than a "trope of
the freedom of erotic love"; it is also a space for an ecological, multiethnic
community.

The restless and whimsical Tea Cake spends his days roaming the muck,
where he enjoys a freedom of mobility rarely possessed by African-Americans
in the South. This freedom contrasts with Janie's relationship with her
deceased husband, Joe Stark—a relationship that is literally defined by immo-
bility, by sitting still. With reference particularly to *Dust Tracks on a Road*
and *Their Eyes Were Watching God*, Scott Hicks argues that Hurston's writings "embrace global consciousness, repudiating emplacement in and fealty
to a world order that denies her characters autonomy and equity" (2009: 64).
Thus, according to Hicks, Hurston refuses to yoke race and place together,
even as she focuses on a black South, she "envisions transformed black relationships to southern landscapes" (2009: 64). While mobility is certainly a
running motif throughout her work, I do want to emphasize her regional
specificity, or rather, her ability to synthesize the local with mobility.

Environmental historians remind us, however, that life in the swamp
is irreducible to tropes: it is the space of very real dangers, suffering, and

memory. Wilson argues that southerners saw the swamp as the "last pure vestige of undominated" southern environmental culture, and that the swamp "resisted, revised, or rejected" the southern nationalist project of white supremacy (2006: ix). Aarthi Vadde calls swamps (referring to the context of India) "backwaters spheres," a "third space of subjective formation" that goes beyond the public or private spheres (2009: 524). The backwaters sphere is a space of "cross-species solidarities" that form an "ecological collectivity" (2009: 524). This interspecies solidarity and collectivity that constitutes backwaters ecology are key notions that inform my reading of *Their Eyes Were Watching God.*

Like the real-life complexities of the swamps, Hurston's portrayal of African-Americans goes far beyond Richard Wright's infamous criticism that the novel stays in "that safe and narrow orbit in which America likes to see the Negro live: between laughter and tears" (1937: 22). Hurston introduces the Everglades/"muck" with a vision of the swamp sublime (to borrow a concept from Allewaert):

> Big Lake Okeechobee, big beans, big cane, big weeds, big everything. Weeds that did well to grow waist high up the state were eight and often ten feet tall down there. Ground so rich that everything went wild. Volunteer cane just taking the place. Dirt roads so rich and black that a half mile of it would have fertilized a Kansas wheat field. Wild cane on either side of the road hiding the rest of the world. People wild too. (1937: 123)

Hurston repeats the word "wild" several times with a sense of wonder similar to romantic writers of the nineteenth century—its positive valuation reinforced by the repetition of "w" sounds: wild, weeds, well, wheat, and world. The marshes are also a mix of wilderness and weeds with fertile ground "waiting" for agricultural development. Even the uncultivated roads easily trounce Kansas in agricultural potential. It is worth noting that for most of Florida's history, the Everglades were regarded as a useless bog, unsuited for agricultural and economic development (Wilson 2006: 4). For Hurston, the muck is a wondrous and wild space, bigger than human dominion.

The swamp also becomes a site that combines multiethnic solidarity with—albeit modest—forms of ecological agency. Janie and Tea Cake frequently mingle with Seminoles, Bahaman migrants, and poor white farmers.

The Seminoles, idealized by Hurston, enjoy a kind of ecological agency, "calmly winning their living in the trackless ways of the 'Glades" (1937: 124). Much of the intermingling among groups occurs in the recreational space of the jook joints, where the workers, after a full day in the bean fields, engage in "[d]ancing, fighting, singing, crying, laughing, winning and losing love" (1937: 125). At one point, Janie is intrigued by the rhythms of the Bahaman drummers, observing them accompany Tea Cake on guitar every night (1937: 133). Later, it is a large group of Seminoles that warn Janie about the impending hurricane (1937: 146). Even a "white doctor who had been around so long that he was part of the muck" provides further evidence for the diversity of this milieu (1937: 167).

Ecological community finds further expression in the forms of play and freedom of mobility that the swamp affords. The frequent fighting over loves lost and won, the gossip, and casual vices (e.g., alcohol and gambling) within this double environment contrasts with the systemic racism and exploitations of the official culture beyond the swamps: the forced labor, the sacrilegious mass graves, the refusal of healthcare to nonwhites, and the racist judicial system in Janie's trial by an all-white jury. Play becomes a form of defiance against the seriousness of the white regulatory gaze. When Tea Cake recruits Janie for work in the bean fields because he cannot stand to be separated from her all day, their "goofing off" on the job is infectious: "all day long the romping and playing they carried on behind the boss's back made her popular right away. It got the whole field to playing off and on" (1937: 127). Their house—full of guitar playing, drumming, dancing, and gambling—becomes the cultural center of the workers. They use forms of play against the "serious" white men and bosses.

For a moment existing as one part of a double environment, this ecological community in the Everglades is swept away by hurricane floodwaters in the novel's climax. The most likely historical referent for the hurricane in *Their Eyes Were Watching God* is the 1928 Okeechobee hurricane. But two other hurricanes, the 1926 hurricane and the 1929 hurricane that battered the Bahamas also serve as significant points of reference. Hurston was collecting material for *Tell My Horse* in the Bahamas at the time the 1929 hurricane struck (Boyd 2003: 187). This experience seemed to have left Hurston with an indelible impression of the destructive power of the Atlantic storm cycle. She describes the experience in *Dust Tracks on a Road*: "I lived through that terrible five-day hurricane of 1929. It was horrible in its intensity and duration. I saw dead people washing around on the streets when it was over. You could smell the stench from dead animals as well. More than three hundred houses were blown down in the city of Nassau alone" (1942: 159). The 1929 Bahamas hurricane, also known as the Great Andros Island Hurricane, did substantial damage to the Bahamas and claimed about fifty lives.

In many ways, the 1928 hurricane plays the farce to the tragedy of the 1926 hurricane. Both hurricanes were virtually identical in their wind power and landfall; both hurricanes flooded Lake Okeechobee and killed hundreds of black farmers, Seminoles, and migrant workers from Caribbean islands. Following the 1926 disaster, which killed 400 and displaced 40,000, a rivalry concerning how to manage the lake erupted between the Army Corps chief engineer and the *Everglades News* editor, Howard Sharp (Grunwald 2007: 186–8). The editor accused the Army Corps of refusing to drain the already high waters of the lake in the early summer of 1928. Tragic irony prevailed when Elliot defied his critics, refusing to clear drainage waterways and asserting that history would not repeat itself. The issue for Sharp was motivated by class: Elliot was protecting the interests of developments along the coast north of Miami in the West Palm Beach area. Elliot and the Florida governor eventually caved to pressure and passed a new property tax bill through the Florida legislature to fund a $20 million drainage project. But wealthy coastal landowners sued the government, blocking the execution of any such project by the time another hurricane season arrived (Grunwald 2007: 186–94).

The 1928 hurricane is the second deadliest in US history (second to the 1900 Galveston hurricane). The hurricane hit Lake Okeechobee and flooded the cities around the lake, drowning an estimated 2,500 people. About three quarters of these were migrant farm workers. Hurston personifies the hurricane as "Old Massa" and uses military metaphors to anthropomorphize its behavior. The clouds gather and "arm themselves with thunders and march forth against the world" (1937: 150). Old Massa presides over the world like it is a plantation, rearranging the furniture, as Motor Boat phrases it: "Big Massa draw him chair upstairs" (1937: 150). Critics have noticed Hurston's depiction of the inequality and exploitation of labor in the hurricane's aftermath. But the novel points out that environmental inequities exist alongside ecological collectives and prior to the hurricane. During the evacuation period, when the hurricane is still a mere ominous stillness, only the Seminoles and animals—rabbits, possums, rattlesnakes, deer, and panthers—flee the swamp for higher ground. Eventually others "hurried east like the Indians and rabbits and snakes and coons" (1937: 148). Thus, Hurston also dramatizes an ecological collective throughout the buildup to the storm.

This personification of the storm inadvertently underscores its tendency to amplify or exploit inequities already established by Jim Crow, segregation, and the legacy of slavery. Eventually Janie, Tea Cake, and Motor Boat have to leave their own house and find shelter in an abandoned house. But then they face their main threat: flooding. The levee breaks and Okeechobee's waters creep toward the house. The lake is a "monster" that "began to roll in his bed. Began to roll and complain like a peevish world on a grumble" (1937: 150). Tea Cake makes a quick calculation of the situation: "Lake Okeechobee is forty miles wide and sixty miles long. Dat's uh whole heap uh water. If dis wind is shovin' dat whole lake disa way, dis house ain't nothin' tuh swaller" (1937: 154). Janie and Tea Cake flee again, but Motor Boat decides to take his chances on the upper floors and the rooftop (he ends up surviving, and Tea Cake later says in hindsight that they should have stayed put).

Supposed divisions between human and animal, the living and the non-living, collapse into ecological collectives, before and throughout the storm, and temporarily replace carefully regulated racial and class dichotomies. Tea Cake reassures a man that a rattlesnake will not bite him—that "common danger made common friends. Nothing sought a conquest over the other" (1937: 156). The floodwaters are also "full of things living and dead," indifferent to the distinction (1937: 156). This ecological collectivity breaks down in the aftermath of the hurricane, when Tea Cake and Janie reach the so-called city of refuge (1937: 158). When Tea Cake and Janie seek a dry point on "the fill" (landfill), they find that the bridge—the highest point of elevation—is already too crowded: "[w]hite people had preempted that point of elevation and there was no more room" (1937: 156). This unraveling actually begins earlier, we find out, when Tea Cake is bitten by a rabid dog while in the process of intercepting the dog's attack on Janie. The infection does not affect Tea Cake until weeks later, when his rabies-induced paranoia and jealousy compel Janie to shoot him in self-defense.

Even as this accidental infection appears natural, Hurston undercuts this naturalization of Tea Cake's seemingly inevitable doom by emphasizing his lack of access to adequate healthcare, as well as his unwillingness to seek it out. As with the 1927 Mississippi Flood, the American Red Cross is on hand, but it is virtually absent in the novel, mentioned only in passing (1937: 161). Instead, the grip of white authority dominates the decimated landscape. The novel's focus turns to the grisly aftermath of corpses in the street. Tea Cake is spotted by two white men with guns, who then force him to join a group of laborers tasked with burying the dead. The men take Tea Cake as though he were a fugitive slave, assigning him a new name and ignoring his pleas that he is a "workin' man wid money" in his pocket (1937: 162). In this case, the commons, the public lands are spaces of regulation and coercive labor:

> Tea Cake found that he was part of a small army that had been pressed into service to clear the wreckage in public places and bury the dead. Bodies had to be searched out, carried to certain gathering places and buried. Corpses were not just found in wrecked houses. They were under houses, tangled in shrubbery, floating in water, hanging in trees, drifting under wreckage. (1937: 162)

The color line is administered even in the face of ambiguity. The white bodies are gathered and buried in coffins with marked graves, while the black bodies are thrown into an unmarked, "big ditch" (1937: 162). The workers, however, find it difficult to identify the color of the bodies because of their state of rapid decay in the Florida heat and humidity. "God have mussy! In de condition they's in got tuh examine 'em? Whut difference do it make 'bout de color? Dey all needs buryin' in uh hurry" (1937: 163). The white men with guns command the workers to divide the bodies based on hair if they cannot tell by skin color. Tea Cake remarks on how "mighty particular" these white men are about how these "folks goes tuh judgment" (1937: 163). When Tea Cake escapes and returns to Janie, it is the swamp where he suggests they seek refuge: "De quickest place is de 'Glades. Less make it on back down dere. Dis town is full uh trouble and compellment" (1937: 163). We learn later from the white doctor that during this period of forced labor, Tea Cake should have been seeking out care: some "shots right after it happened would have fixed him right up" (1937: 168). The simplicity of this fix underscores the tragic irony of Tea Cake's demise.

Conclusion

Hurston's politics are notoriously hard to pin down. She is individualist, rejecting the notion of "race achievement"—that is, both notions of the Washingtonian uplift and the Talented Tenth—and simultaneously a promoter of southern black folk culture (Boyd 2003: 25). Hurston notoriously claimed in 1934 that "the Jim Crow system works" because, despite segregation, it promotes equality (Boyd 2003: 365). But Hurston said her statements were taken out of context: her point was that while the South officially sanctioned segregation, the practice was supported de facto in the north. Thus, no such "equal" spaces are provided in the North; desegregation laws would be inconsequential (Boyd 2003: 366). This controversy shows Hurston's penchant for being contrarian, deliberately provocative and equivocal. Given this nonconformism, it is no surprise that her vision of ecological collectives does not align with Washington, Du Bois and *The Crisis*, or the black Marxism of William Attaway (discussed in Chapter 5).

Hurston's work exemplifies several swamp narrative tropes and figurations: struggles with poisonous snakes; the simultaneous danger and refuge of the swamp; the swamp's resistance to regulation and economic development; multiethnic, interspecies, and living/nonliving ecological collectives. In *Mules and Men*, the tales are framed by descriptions of black labor and white-owned spaces of sawmills, coal mines, and turpentine stills. These work spaces are juxtaposed with the small mostly black towns, jook joints, swamps, and evenings spent telling "lies" on the porch. These two opposing southern spaces are intimately linked through the tales themselves, for the tales render into comic form not only the traumatic experiences of slavery and racism, but also the southern environment itself with its floods, boll weevil attacks, and unpredictable wilderness spaces. In Hurston's account of the southern environment, she sets up a contrast between communal folk and corporate–capitalist practices. The spaces populated by African-American, Bahaman migrant laborers, and Seminoles cannot be resolved with the white-capitalist order. This irresolvability or mere coexistence, which takes its own forms in the writings of Washington and Newsome, is not coequal either, but it does provide a space for agency alongside a public domain ordered by white supremacy. In Hurston, the ontological blurring of interspecies solidarities, and of the living and nonliving contrasts rather than correlates with the separations imposed by anthropocentric and white supremacist biopolitical regulation. Though the tales in *Mules and Men* rely so heavily on anthropomorphism, Hurston seems more concerned (especially in *Their Eyes Were Watching God*) with the effects of human activity on animals than other writers studied in this book (with the exception of Newsome).

In this chapter, I have tried to treat the swamp in its literary figurations in the context of environmental history and pull out the racial, political, and ontological implications. In the opening of her autobiography *Dust Tracks on the Road*, Hurston reflects on the mystical interfusion of memory and the material environment: "[l]ike the dead-seeming, cold rocks, I have memories within that came out of the material that went to make me" (1942: 1). Just as Booker T. Washington's writings reflect environmental and human time, Hurston's words juxtapose the geologic time of the animistic rocks and the human time of memory. By 1941, William Attaway would develop this concern with race and environment into a black Marxist "land ethic" in his Great Migration proletarian novel *Blood on the Forge*.

From Black Marxism to Industrial Ecosystem

Racial and Ecological Crisis in William Attaway's Blood on the Forge

Introduction

Remarkable for its apocalyptic view of industrial capitalism, William Attaway's 1941 novel *Blood on the Forge* follows in the naturalist and black Marxist tradition of Richard Wright's *Native Son* (1940). One of the novel's central conflicts is the clash between southern pastoral and northern industrial–urban ways of living. Employing both naturalism and pastoralism to dramatize this clash, Attaway breaks out of these two representational modes through his use of a relatively minor secondary character named Smothers, a prophetic spokesman for the earth's pain: "[o]ne of the men whispered that Smothers was off his nut. Yet they listened and heard a different sort of tale: 'It's wrong to tear up the ground and melt it up in the furnace. Ground don't like it. It's the hell-and-devil kind of work" (1941: 52–3). His legs dismembered in a brutal steel mill accident, Smothers's shrill prophecies are the product of wisdom gained through suffering, of a heightened sense of what the "ground" feels as it is mined, smelted, and made into steel. Because he brings an ecological perspective to the ethical and ontological relations among worker, machine, and earth, this character appears on the literary scene as an enigma. Building on previous themes of urban nature in Du Bois's *Darkwater* and *The Crisis*, this chapter explores this strange anomaly of Smothers and the confluence of ecological themes and intersectionality in *Blood on the Forge*.

As with most of the literary texts examined in *Civil Rights and the Environment*, no critic has explored the ecological themes in *Blood on the Forge*, nor asked why a novel published in 1941 and set in 1919 should so strongly engage the conservation movement.[1] Perhaps this marginalization is due partly to the novel's critical reception and classification as African-American fiction, a genre typically associated with social injustices rather than environmental causes. Lawrence R. Rodgers, for example, categorizes *Blood on the Forge* as a "fugitive migrant novel," a special variant of the Great Migration novel that challenges narratives about black migrants' socioeconomic ascent in northern cities (1997: 98). Alan Wald reads the novel within the political context of the late 1930s, calling Attaway a black Marxist "whose exertions were aimed in part at educating the white labor movement about the corrosive costs of continued racial chauvinism" (2002: 282). Wald cites Attaway's involvement with the Communist Party as evidence for his strong political commitments, though *Blood on the Forge* reveals more an analyst of race and capitalism than a propagandist supplying cultural weapons for an American October Revolution.

We never see in *Blood on the Forge* the triumph of racial accommodation and assimilation, or the awakening of class consciousness. Set in 1919, when the First World War had cut off migratory flows from Europe and thus depleted the pool of cheap immigrant labor in northern industrial cities, *Blood on the Forge* follows the three Moss brothers—Big Mat, Chinatown, and Melody—as they migrate from the Jim Crow South to the industrial wasteland of western Pennsylvania. Northern steel mill employers saw that if they could maintain the influx of racially diverse labor, then they could rely on perpetual conflict to undermine organized labor (Marks 1989: 15). The narrative ends tragically with one brother dead, another blinded by a mill explosion, and the third with an injured hand that prevents him from "slicking away" his blues on the guitar. The two surviving brothers catch a train ride farther north to the Pittsburgh city limits, each feeling uncertain about his future. Attaway's protest is bleak, even nihilistic, but it does testify to the singular experience of workers who might otherwise be lost in a Chicago School sociologist's or proletarian novelist's progressive narrative of racial assimilation: the Moss brothers do not pass through stages on life's way toward unionization.

Great Migration narrative, naturalism, ghetto pastoral, and black Marxism: all of these frames, of course, help to illuminate the novel, but they also tend to downplay its central figuration of ecological degradation— a degradation comparable to the representations in the work of Booker T. Washington, whose writing is similar to Attaway's in its scientific orientation. Building on these critical frameworks, this chapter argues that *Blood on the Forge* both complicates and radicalizes the Great Migration narrative and black Marxism by engaging in the same problematic as the 1930s ecological discourses. This 1930s problematic consists of questions concerning the short-term and long-term effects of human activity on local and global ecosystems; thus, it focuses on the interaction between social and environmental history. Such an analysis of the novel requires an eco-historical method that folds together its setting—the Pittsburgh area during the Red Summer of 1919—with its late Great Depression publication in 1941. The first half of this article, then, situates *Blood on the Forge* alongside a paradigm shift within the scientific ecology of the 1930s—a shift partly demanded by humanmade ecological catastrophes such as the Dust Bowl. In 1935, botanist Arthur Tansley defined the "ecosystem" concept, which signified ecology's turn away from an organic model of environments and toward what historian Donald Worster calls a more materialist "energy-based economics of nature" (1977: 306). As I show, the shared materialist ontology of Marx's philosophy and Tansley's ecosystem ecology enfolds *Blood on the Forge*'s black Marxist with its ecological vision; its ecology is internal to and inseparable from its radical politics.

My subsequent reading of the novel examines how it refracts the industrialized and polluted Pittsburgh of 1919 through this materialist ontology, in the process participating in the 1930s ecological discourses by linking ecological degradation to racial conflict and exploitative labor policies. The last section of this chapter focuses on how *Blood on the Forge* develops an ecological ethic that anticipates conservationist Aldo Leopold's "land ethic" (1949). For Leopold, the land ethic encapsulates conservationist values, for it "changes the role of *Homo sapiens* from conqueror of the land-community to plain member and citizen of it" (1939: 240). Attaway's ecological ethic, on the other hand, focuses more on the intersection of race, labor, and industrial capitalism than conservation per se; his ethic comes packaged in the form of Smothers, who gives voice to what he calls the earth's "feelin'" (1941: 53).

Ecology of the 1930s: A. G. Tansley and the Ecosystem Concept

The 1930s natural disasters and large-scale industrial pollution conspired with urban infrastructure problems and economic inequality to amplify the havoc, prompting ecologists such as Tansley to consider the blurred distinctions between economics and ecology, between human-made and natural disaster. For instance, the Dust Bowl made the Great Depression as much an ecological as an economic catastrophe. Beginning on April 4, 1934, a large cloud of dust—nicknamed the "black blizzard"—swarmed out of Texas and dumped millions of tons of dirt on major cities ranging from Chicago to Washington, DC (Worster 1979: 221). Partly the product of drought, more the bad karma of decades of poor farming practices that depleted the soil, the Dust Bowl was, according to Worster, the "inevitable outcome of a [capitalist] culture that deliberately, self-consciously, set itself the task of dominating and exploiting the land for all it was worth" (1979: 4). Like the Joads in John Steinbeck's *The Grapes of Wrath* (1939), Dust Bowl refugees were forced to travel west for work (Merchant 2007: 106). The Dust Bowl's impact, like its origins, was as social as it was environmental; some ecologists were inspired by this confluence. For example, Paul Sears, author of the Dust Bowl history *Deserts on the March* (1935), later wrote about the crucial social function of ecology as a method for shaping human and natural environments in his 1939 *Life and Environment* (129).

Closer to the setting of Attaway's novel, this social–environmental confluence also spills over into Pittsburgh's 1936 St. Patrick's Day Flood, which exposed the consequences of poor urban planning. Over the course of two days in March 1936, heavy downpours added to rapidly melting snow and raised the city's water levels to forty-six feet—nearly twice the height of flood stage levels. Trolleys, cars, and many homes were completely submerged or uninhabitable; five thousand people were marooned throughout the city (Lorant 1964: 359). When the waters receded, approximately 135,000 people had lost their homes, sixty were dead, and hundreds injured; the city suffered $150 to $200 million in property damage (Lorant 1964: 370). This disaster revealed how regional planning and natural forces are especially intertwined in the unique geography of the Pittsburgh region. Situated where the Allegheny

River from the north and the Monongahela River from the south converge to form the Ohio River, Pittsburgh had always left itself exposed to flood dangers. In fact, the city saw eleven major floods between 1832 and 1907 (R. Smith 1975: 8). In 1908, the city's Chamber of Commerce appointed a Flood Commission to assess the danger and develop a mitigation plan that would call for multiple protective measures, most notably the construction of nine flood control dams north of the city in the Upper Ohio River Valley. But on attempting to implement the plan in 1912, a conflict arose between the United States Congress and the city's local Corps of Engineers, who were wary of federal involvement in regional affairs (Kleppner 1989: 171). In an unpublished 1928 report, the Corps of Engineers secretly concluded that it would be more profitable to sustain flood losses than to build the dams (R. Smith 1975: 17). Moreover, the US Congress stated that it would provide federal funding for the dam project only if it aided river navigation (R. Smith 1975: 14). After thirty years of gridlock and cost–benefit analyses, the Congress passed the federal Flood Control Act of 1936 and finally approved the plan in June of that same year, three months after the disastrous Saint Patrick's Day flood (Lorant 1964: 370).

Disasters such as the Dust Bowl and the 1936 Pittsburgh Flood accelerated scientific ecology's rise to prominence in the popular mind throughout the 1930s. By the start of the 1930s, and spurred along partly by the Tuskegee Institutes innovations in agricultural science, ecology was already an established academic discipline in the United States, centered in the Midwestern universities of Nebraska, Chicago, and Illinois at Urbana-Champaign, where William Attaway studied creative writing and earned his degree in 1936 (Wald 2002: 281). Most of these schools borrowed their vocabulary from Frederick Clements, whose ideas are significant because they represent the paradigm from which fellow ecologist Arthur Tansley broke in 1935. A botanist at the University of Nebraska, Clements published the highly influential study *Plant Succession: An Analysis of the Development of Vegetation* (1916). Clementsian discourse reflected an ontology grounded in late-nineteenth-century philosophical holism and organicism; he conceived of plant formations as organs within a "super-organism," as productive citizens functioning on behalf of a "community." These communities follow developmental stages known as "successions," which move toward a "climax state" or a final point of balance and stability (Worster 1977: 209–20). All the individual members seem to work harmoniously for the community, ushering it toward its highest evolutionary stage. As Worster summarizes, Clements "insisted stubbornly and vigorously on the notion that the natural landscape must eventually reach a vaguely final climax stage" (1977: 210).

In his pivotal 1935 essay, "The Use and Abuse of Vegetational Concepts and Terms," British botanist Arthur G. Tansley directly challenged the ontological roots of this Clementsian paradigm. Published in *Ecology*, the leading American journal in the field, Tansley's essay sought to replace the organicist premises of Clementsian ecology with a more rigorous scientific materialism that drew from thermodynamics and systems theory (Kingsland 2005: 184). After critiquing, fine-tuning, and cordially dismissing a number of Clementsian concepts (succession, climax, organism), Tansley goes on to attack the organicist philosophy of holism that underpins these concepts. He argues that holism implies a closed system, a unified whole—the community or the superorganism—that acts on the parts; the concept of wholeness is at worst a nonscientific transcendent vital principle, at best an analytic category that is purely heuristic (Tansley 1935: 298–9). Tansley's goal, as environmental historian Sharon E. Kingsland claims, was not to discard a sense of the whole, but rather "to express the concept of wholeness without falling into the circumlocutions of organicism" (2005: 184). To do this, Tansley borrowed the term "systems" from physics and substituted it for "community" and "organism" in order to designate "highly integrated wholes" that, crucially, included inorganic factors (Tansley 1935: 297). In other words, he both expands and limits the "whole" of Clementsian holism: he expands it to include nonliving factors, while limiting it to the material parts of the various micro- and macro-systems that produce it.

Tansley was implicitly replacing an organicist with a materialist ontology, for he extended the field of the living to the nonliving while dropping the organicist principle. A fusion of ecology and physics, this materialist ontology led Tansley to a neologism, "ecosystem," that did not assume ontological distinctions among the organic, inorganic, natural, and human components of a given region or formation (1935: 299). Ecosystems form the "basic units of nature on the face of the earth," and include such factors within the physical environment as climate and soil. He asserts the reliance of organic life on inorganic factors: "there could be no systems without them, and there is constant interchange of the most various kinds within each system, not only between the organisms but between the organic and the inorganic" (1935: 299). Most importantly, Tansley recognized that nature could not be studied apart from human interference, particularly with the advent of industrialization: "[i]t is obvious that modern civilised man upsets the 'natural' ecosystems or 'biotic communities' on a very large scale" (1935: 303). Perhaps while thinking of the Depression-era and the human-made ecological catastrophes, Tansley bluntly states: "[r]egarded as an exceptionally powerful biotic factor which increasingly upsets the equilibrium of preexisting ecosystems and eventually destroys them, at the same time forming new ones of very different nature, human activity finds its proper place in ecology" (1935: 303). Ecology, in short, must apply itself to environments produced or manipulated by human activity (1935: 304). Worster further explains the concept's materialist edge: "all relations among organisms can be described in terms of the purely material exchange of energy and of such chemical substances as water, phosphorus, nitrogen, and other nutrients" (1977: 302). This turn toward what Worster calls an "energy-based economics of nature" would eventually take hold as orthodox ecology by the 1940s (1977: 306).

Although Tansley was himself politically conservative and a supporter of Herbert Spencer's social Darwinism early in his career, the ontology of the ecosystem concept shares striking parallels with the premises of the Marxist politics informing Attaway's novel. To understand these political implications, one must consider how the Clementsian paradigm is derived from Spencer's philosophy. In a political reading, Worster locates the origins of Clements's ontology in the Spenserian ideology of social Darwinism that naturalized the capitalist mode of production (1977: 212). For Spencer, profit could be analogized to the healthy growth of the organism, driving the progress and evolution of society toward a "more perfect state of complex organismic interdependence" (Worster 1977: 213). This vision of progressive evolution, of course, justifies the capitalist exploitation of more "primitive" social formations; it provided a convenient ideology for Europe's late-nineteenth-century Scramble for Africa. It also underpins Clements's theory of developmental stages toward a climax community.

Just as Clements and Spencer shared the same organicist ontology, so did Tansley and Marx share the same materialist ontology. In *Capital*, Marx defines labor as the metabolic exchange between humans and nature, a "process by which man, through his own actions, mediates, regulates and controls the metabolism between himself and nature" ([1867] 1976: 283). Just as the human laborer confronts the world as a resistant "force," so too must he mobilize the "natural forces" that belong to his body, through which he acts "upon external nature and changes it, and in this way he simultaneously changes his own nature" (Marx [1867] 1976: 283). Humans are an active part of nature, continually shaping and being shaped by natural, material forces.

This connection between ecology and Marxism was not lost on Attaway's contemporary, Kenneth Burke, a leftist literary critic. In his 1937 *Attitudes toward History*, Burke saw a latent politics in 1930s scientific ecology that was more Tansleyian than Clementsian. He found there a concealed Marxist critique of profit and exploitation: "[ecology] teaches us that the *total* economy of this planet cannot be guided by an efficient rationale of exploitation alone, but that the exploiting part must itself eventually suffer if it too greatly disturbs the *balance* of the whole" (1937: 192). While the notion of "balance" evokes Clementsian ecology, "total economy" suggests the human–nature material exchange found in Tansley and Marx. Speaking of the 1930s ecological catastrophes, Burke continues in a more distinctly Tansleyian vein: "laws of ecology have begun avenging themselves against restricted human concepts of profit by countering deforestation and deep plowing with floods, droughts, dust storms, and aggravated soil erosion" (1937: 192). Rather than encouraging natural growth, profit destroys the ecosystem, which then avenges itself on humans. The Tansley–Burke parallelism forms a sort of discursive chiasmus: Burke saw the need to bring ecology into historical materialism, while Tansley saw the need to bring human (and by extension, social and economic) history into ecology. Attaway's novel is a narrative and theoretical extension of this chiasmus: it conceives of the relation between human and environmental history, and pushes this relation through the Tansley–Burke crucible.

Carnegie Steel, Labor Policy, and Ecological Degradation

By the twentieth century, Allegheny County, or the Pittsburgh region, had grown into the world's leading iron and steel producer, owing much of its rise to Andrew Carnegie's entrepreneurial skill and the ready abundance of coke—fuel used for smelting iron and steel—in nearby Connellsville (Lubove 1969: 4). It also became a leading polluter. Pittsburgh historian Roy Lubove quips that "[f]ew communities were so frequently compared to hell" (1969: 1). With its air pollution, disease-ridden slums, and rivers full of sewage and industrial waste, the region lived perpetually on the cusp of an ecological catastrophe, turning extreme environmental conditions into an everyday way of life for its poor black migrants and Eastern European immigrants.

The ecologically destructive and racist labor policies of Carnegie Steel (later US Steel under J. P. Morgan), the leading steel manufacturer of the Industrial Era, typifies Pittsburgh-area business practices. Andrew Carnegie was the most well known of Pittsburgh's entrepreneurs and a figure difficult to caricature as a one-dimensional, top-hatted capitalist. His intuition for business put him in the vanguard of the industry shift from iron to steel manufacturing in the 1870s. He made millions from his Carnegie Steel, and by the time he sold it to J. P. Morgan in 1901, he was possibly the richest man in the world (Nasaw 2006: xii). Carnegie's love for philanthropy and profit made him a paradoxical figure: the more he gave to the public the more he took from his workers. In order to finance his philanthropic enterprises, Carnegie "pushed his partners and his employees relentlessly forward in the pursuit of larger and larger profits, crushed the workingmen's unions he had once praised, increased the steelworkers' workday from eight to twelve hours, and drove down wages" (Nasaw 2006: xi). Publicly, Carnegie cultivated the image of a reconciler between the contradictory demands of "Capital" and "Labor"; in practice, he implemented antilabor policies and delegated their execution to his subordinates. These antilabor policies were most notoriously represented in his handling of the 1892 Homestead Strike, which resulted in the long-term dissolution of the Amalgamated Association of Iron and Steel Workers (Rees 1997: 518). Facing increased competition from rival companies, Carnegie decided to destroy the union at Homestead, hiring Pinkertons and entrusting union-buster Henry Clay Frick with the task. Frick refused to recognize the union, locked out the workers, and brought in scabs, which led to a violent clash between Pinkertons and strikers that left ten dead (Rees 1997: 526–7). After Homestead, the steelworkers' union took decades to reemerge.

Carnegie's attitudes toward race followed a similar tension between philosophy and policy, between public statements and managerial actions. His racism took the indirect form of white paternalism, sins of omission, and condescension toward workers. To be sure, Carnegie donated money to the Tuskegee Institute and publicly praised Washington; yet he exemplifies the same white paternalism lampooned by Ralph Ellison in the figure of Mr. Norton in *Invisible Man* (1952). He reserves his explicit prejudices mainly for immigrants rather than African- Americans. In his autobiography, Carnegie extols the manliness of the native-born "working man," while brushing off the "queer" and effeminate "foreigner": "[t]here is one great difference between the American working-man and the foreigner. The American is a man" (1920: 237). Presumably he means eastern European immigrants from countries such as the Poland, Lithuania, and Ukraine. He conceives of American racial identity as primarily a mix of British and German ancestry—a notion, of course, with no basis in reality. Carnegie himself was Scottish and an avid Scottish cultural nationalist: he idolized and frequently quoted poet Robert Burns. But Carnegie failed to see a connection between his exploitative labor policies and his racial views. The industry shift from iron to steel allowed him to hire cheaper, lesser-skilled laborers, namely immigrants and, later, black migrants: "[w]hile iron had to be puddled by hand, technological innovations in steel mills made it increasingly easy to train immigrants and other less-skilled workers to replace skilled union men" (Rees 1997: 520). Inevitably, his contempt for labor unions would go hand-in-hand with his contempt for the lesser-skilled immigrant workforce.

Typified by Carnegie, the racial contempt of local elites for foreign laborers buffered the progress of urban planning, resulting in the formation of chaotic communities that resembled mycelia. First-generation European immigrants and black migrants made up a combined 71 percent of the workforce in 1910 (Dickerson 1986: 25); this number dropped to 60 percent overall by 1920, though with a 10 percent increase in black workers (98). Because zoning laws were not passed until 1923, working-class communities were somewhat of a macabre experiment in "natural" living as they were left to sprout "organi-cally," free from the human intervention of rational planning. In his contem-poraneous 1928 sociological study of northern city slums, T. J. Woofter Jr. posits the formula "death by density" to characterize the proportion of death rate to population density (1928: 78). He blames land-exploitation and the profit motive for these death-by-density conditions:

> Spaces that should have been occupied by single-family houses have been built up thickly with flats. In other places single-family houses have been built with a common wall, the effect of which is to eliminate side yards and to reduce the amount of light and of air-space to less than is necessary for health. Front yards have been eliminated by building flush on the sidewalk, and the rear yards have then been cut in two by alleys and secondary streets on which rows of houses have been built. (1928: 88)

In Pittsburgh, a combination of hilly topography and greedy slumlords look-ing to reap high profits from small plots of land led to the construction of sardine-packed, vertical housing that allowed for little sunlight or open space (Lorant 1964: 369). Overcrowding was so rampant in many mill towns that workers often shared the same bunks, alternating according to shifts (Dickerson 1986: 56). Because they typically lived in areas four times denser than whites (Woofter 1928: 78), African-Americans were more adversely affected by slum conditions, enduring death rates almost twice as high as whites between 1915 and 1930 (Dickerson 1986: 58). Most homes lacked run-ning water and sewage systems. In one neighborhood, Skunk Hollow, steel employees lived in dilapidated shacks built on steep slopes; inadequate toilet facilities sent human waste flowing downhill into the valley below (Lubove 1969: 14). Diseases thrived under these conditions, with frequent outbreaks of tuberculosis, typhoid, influenza, pneumonia, syphilis, and gonorrhea (Dickerson 1986: 59).

Companies such as Carnegie Steel treated the region's air, rivers, and land as a dumping ground for industrial wastes, further contributing to this slum-generated ecological degradation. Pittsburgh's transformation from a primar-ily iron-producing to steel-producing hub lead to an increase in coal burning, reinforcing the Steel City's second nickname: the Smoky City. Locals grew accustomed to blackened skies, even going so far as to equate Pittsburgh's high smoke levels with thriving industry, the visual measure of economic prosperity: a "smoky Pittsburgh is a healthy Pittsburgh," many would say (Lorant 1964: 364). In a 1912 article, "The Smoky City," John T. Holdsworth attributed the "smoke nuisance" to the profit motive and the low cost of coal, the burning of which was a "scourge to vegetation, a defilement of buildings and merchandise, and a positive check upon civic and industrial progress— all because it is cheap!" (1976: 86). Historian Dennis C. Dickerson describes western Pennsylvanian mill towns as so polluted that "street lamps glowed in midafternoon to chase away the darkness created by the smoke-filled skies" (1986: 55). A 1936 photograph for *Life* magazine, taken by Margaret Bourke-White, shows a sweeping bird's-eye-view of the city: murky and smoke-choked, more an industrial trash heap than a human dwelling, the city resembles a modern Gehenna (Lorant 1964: 364–5). The need for smoke control had been a long-debated urban planning and public health issue since the early nineteenth century, but the city government and local elites avoided action for decades; it finally passed the Smoke Control Ordinance in 1941, although demands for increased wartime production would delay its enforcement (Lorant 1964: 370).

These same factories that pumped smoke into the air dumped waste into the Ohio, Allegheny, and Monongahela rivers (Lubove 1969: 15). The process of mining the coal necessary to produce steel released a steady stream of sulfuric acid into the rivers; in 1920, 2.5 million tons of acid flowed into the Ohio River, destroying riverbanks and causing massive fish kills (Casner 2003: 89–92). The impact of acid drainage was extra-regional too, extending as far as 170 miles downriver (Casner 2003: 93). Company towns such as Homestead beaded the three rivers as far as thirty miles from Pittsburgh's downtown; residents relied on the rivers for their water supply (Muller 2003: 54). This dependence on polluted water won the region the dubious distinction for the highest mortality rate in the nation for waterborne diseases (Casner 2003: 93). Because of the lack of water treatment facilities, frequent typhoid outbreaks in the early 1900s killed working-class immigrant and black migrants at nearly twice the rate of native whites (Tarr and Yosie 2003: 70). Produced by and intertwined with labor and regional planning policies, these environmental conditions shape the historical backdrop to *Blood on the Forge*.

South to North: Soil Depletion to Industrial Pollution in *Blood on the Forge*

Attaway represents the subjective experience of this social and environmental history, forming an integrated vision of the Great Migration, industrial landscapes, slum life, and labor struggle. In its scope and concern with ecological degradation, this integrated vision engages, on the aesthetic level, the same problematic as Tansley's ecosystem concept. The novel follows the four stages of the Great Migration narrative as schematized by Farah Jasmine Griffin in *Who Set You Flowin'? The African-American Migration Narrative*: migration out of the South, initial contact with the northern urban environment, an attempt to adjust to northern life, and finally a "vision of the possibilities or limitations of the Northern, Western, or Midwestern city and the South" (1995: 3). Each of these stages, which center on the migrants' changing consciousness, is given a particular ecological inflection in the novel, thus expanding the purview of both the migration narrative and the ecosystem concept. *Blood on the Forge* also contributes to black Marxism in its emphasis on steel production's intertwined, ecosystemic byproducts: a wounded earth, injured workers, and slum living conditions.

In the novel's opening section, Attaway emphasizes the slow, "natural" tempo of southern life, which later serves as a striking contrast with the jarring industrial rapidity of northern life. Unlike the later parts of the novel, the opening section follows a dream-like flashback structure, as narrative form imitates the natural cycles of the Moss brothers' environment: the changing seasons, weather cycles, harvest time, and birth and death for both humans and nature. This premigration scene is set in 1919 Kentucky as the Moss family struggles to survive as sharecroppers. Richard Wright describes the sharecropping system's injustice in his 1941 photographic essay, *Twelve Million Black Voices*: "[t]he Lords of the Land [white landowners] assign us ten or fifteen acres of soil already bled of its fertility through generations of abuse. They advance us one mule, one plow, seed, tools, fertilizer, clothing and food" (38). Black sharecroppers, Wright protests, are forced into debt peonage, always bound more to their white creditors than to the land.

Racial and economic oppression in the South follows a predictable, though tragic, routine that allows the Moss family to cope by means of a blues stylization of life—one that "slicks away" hardship and cauterizes emotional wounds. Melody, the emotional glue that holds the family together, embodies this blues ethos in the novel's opening sentences: "[h]e never had a craving in him that he couldn't slick away on his guitar. You have to be native to the red-clay hills of Kentucky to understand that" (Attaway [1941] 2005: 1). Melody laments the family's wretched condition in a song called "Hungry Blues":

> Done scratched at the hills,
>> But the 'taters refuse to grow . . .
> Done scratched at the hills,
>> But the 'taters refuse to grow . . .
> Mister Bossman, Mister Bossman,
>> Lemme mark in the book once mo'. (3)

Attaway's vision of labor as non-redemptive toil is a striking contrast to the optimist, Tuskegee georgic discussed in Chapter 1.[2] The first four lines characterize failed agricultural labor as futile "scratching," a practice that becomes even more futile in the final lines when the black sharecroppers fall into deeper debt to the white "bossman." The hint of sarcasm in the final lines reveals Melody's awareness of the white creditor and black debtor economic relation that determines the farmer's relation to the land. Two forms of inscription—scratching the land and marking the book—racialize the land as white, shaping the ecosystem into an extension of a hostile creditor.

Despite this failure at laboring the land, the blues offer a form of resistance—if only at an intuitive, sensory level—to the endless white creditor–black debtor cycle that dominates the family's relation to the land. Through Melody, the blues are articulated to the land, offering a black vernacular counter-racialization of a land systematically racialized by white property owners. Melody cuts through this property relation and holds onto an affective bond to the earth: "[r]ight then Melody was feeling the earth like a good thing in his heart" (1941: 22). This affective bond suggests an immediate link between laboring the earth—between the black sharecropper's literal propinquity to the soil—and the vernacular tradition of country blues that Melody embodies. Because of his blues sensibility, Melody intuits that no one owns the earth: "I got a big feelin' like the ground don't belong to the white boss—not to nobody," he proclaims to Big Mat (1941: 22). This sublime moment even escapes the codifying force of the blues: "[e]very once in a while he would get filled up like this with a feeling that was too big to turn into any kind of music" (1941: 23). He says this while trekking across Vagermound Common, which borders the Moss farm plot, representing for the brothers a geographic and metaphoric horizon that offers a model and promise of common land. Unlike Booker T. Washington's emphasis on private property acquisition, Attaway places value on common ownership and the subjective experience of the land. These two factors—Melody's blues and close proximity to unenclosed, public land—allow the brothers access to some sense of nature unmediated by racism and capitalism.

Attaway further racializes the land through a counter-pastoralist mode of representation. The Kentucky landscape is neither a pastoral ideal nor an anti-pastoral reality; it is marked by both natural beauty and racial violence, doubling as safe haven and potential lynching site. Crab-apple trees are analogous to African-Americans; they populate and racialize the landscape: "[m]ost of the country beyond Vagermound Common was bunched with crab-apple trees, posing crookedly, like tired old Negroes against the sky" (7–8). They seem to follow Big Mat like ancestral guardians: "[a]gainst the dark sky the darker crab-apple trees kept pace with him as he walked" (16). The nighttime landscape resembles a color-blind society, an insight suggested by Melody: "[a] t night the hills ain't red no more. There ain't no crab-apple trees squat in the hills, no more land to hoe in the red-hot sun—white the same as black" (11). That in daytime the crab apple trees "squat in the hills" is significant: it suggests that they are hiding from a lynch mob: "[h]iding in the red-clay hills was something always in the backs of their heads. It was something to be thought of along with bloodhound dogs and lynching" (35). Nature at night offers refuge and cover from racial antagonisms that appear naturally embedded in the daytime landscape. This scene, then, reveals the brothers'—and by extension, all black sharecroppers'—fraught relation to the pastoral.

This ambiguous pastoral scene is disrupted by a series of traumas that eventually render the pastoral condition unlivable for African-Americans. For example, Big Mat's wife Hattie, a human analog to the barren and eroded land, has miscarried six children six springs in a row, leaving the couple childless. While Hattie's miscarriages appear "natural," Attaway hints that they most likely have an economic origin: the constant references to the family's chronic hunger and diet of white pork, molasses, and saltwater cornbread imply that Hattie suffers from malnutrition. This suggests an ontological link between human and nonhuman forms of failed reproduction (i.e., childbirth and land cultivation). Also, the novel ties infertility to a naturalized masculine as well as feminine identity, portraying Big Mat as a Job-like figure suffering from a double "castration": his simultaneous inability to escape an emasculating economic system and to "harvest" children. When Big Mat travels north, Hattie stays behind with the land, as though she were permanently rooted to it, forgotten by the brothers as they struggle to adjust to northern life.

Through a flashback, the narrative recounts the novel's primal, traumatic scene: the mother's death at the plow:

> She had dropped dead between the gaping handles of the plow. The lines had been double looped under her arms, so she was dragged through the damp, rocky clay by a mule trained never to balk in the middle of a row. The mule dragged her in. The rocks in the red hills are sharp. She didn't look like their maw anymore. (7)

The sharecropping system, which forces the mother to help labor the fields, and soil erosion, which leaves the ground hard and rocky, conspire to amplify the trauma of her death. Dragged across this eroded, rocky terrain, her body is mutilated beyond recognition.

Although the mother's bodily mutilation may seem an unfortunate "natural" accident, soil erosion itself is a byproduct of an economy that exploits and destroys the ecosystem. In *Twelve Million Black Voices*, Wright attributes soil erosion to rampant deforestation:

> We ... watch the men with axes come through ... and whack down the pine, oak, ash, elm, and hickory trees, leaving the land denuded as far as the eye can see. And then rain comes in leaden sheets to slat and sour at the earth until it washes away rich layers of top soil, until it leaves the land defenseless, until all vegetation is gone and nothing remains to absorb the moisture and hinder the violent spreading floods of early spring. (1941: 78)

Poor farming methods were also a culprit in soil erosion; the widely practiced one-crop (usually cotton or tobacco) system, as opposed to the crop rotation system advocated by agricultural scientist George Washington Carver at the

Tuskegee Institute (discussed in Chapter 1), quickly depleted soil nutrients. Environmental historian Albert E. Cowdrey states: "Any system which covers too many fields with the same plant falls afoul of the ecological principle which states that the simplest systems are apt to be the most unstable" (1996: 79). Big Mat complains about this erosion to Mr. Johnston, the white landlord: "[w]ind and rain comin' outen the heavens ever' season, takin' the good dirt down to the bottoms. Last season over the big hill the plow don't go six inches in the dirt afore it strike hard rock" (14). Johnston faults nature rather than the system from which he profits, but, fearing his tenants will migrate north for better work, he decides to replace the mule Mat killed in an angry outburst after his mother's death (15). When he goes to retrieve the promised mule, Big Mat lashes out at Johnston's "poor white" riding boss for insulting his dead mother. A recruiting agent or "jackleg" from the north offers the Moss brothers a convenient escape from the lynch mob that will inevitably come after Big Mat; the jackleg arranges for them a free train ride to the steel mills of western Pennsylvania (31). Originating in racism and poor environmental conditions, trauma and its aftermath catalyzes the brothers' move to the north.

Attaway focalizes the subsequent descriptions of Allegheny County's polluted industrial landscape—everywhere marked by human traces—through the agrarian eyes of the Moss brothers. It is in these northern scenes that parallels to Tansley's ecosystem concept become more apparent. Immediately upon their arrival, the brothers wander about their new home, an unnamed steel mill town along the Monongahela River that reminds them of an *"ugly, smoking hell out of a backwoods preacher's sermon"* (45; emphasis in original). They see the land as the victim of a giant agricultural machine:

> A giant might have planted his foot on the heel of a great shovel and split the bare hills. Half buried in the earth where the great shovel had trenched were the mills. The mills were as big as creation when the new men had ridden by on the freight. From the bunkhouse they were just so much scrap iron, scattered carelessly, smoking lazily … None of this was good to the eyes of men accustomed to the pattern of fields. (43)

Mixing shock and awe, the lyrically beautiful and the industrially damned, this passage draws parallels and differences between micro-agricultural and macro-industrial modes of production. The image of the giant's "great shovel" conflates a farming tool that would be familiar to the Moss brothers with the awesome power of dynamite to "split" the hills as a farmer would furrow a field. When seen from up close, the mills appear to be steel-producing monsters; from a distance, they shrink to mere bits of litter or "scrap iron," suggesting that their power and size are not so great compared with the vaster landscape. This image of a wounded earth also echoes a poetic conceit used by John Milton in his description of Pandemonium in *Paradise Lost*: "Soon had his [Mammon's] crew / Opened into the hill a spacious wound / And digged out ribs of gold" (1674: 1833). By linking the industrial environment with the Christian hell, Attaway suggests that torment of the material landscape is also a kind of spiritual torment. This objective–subjective, material–spiritual dialectic is mediated by aesthetics: the eyesore landscape assaults the brothers' sense of what nature is, and thus disturbs their own inner nature or *habitus*. Veteran steelworkers use the slang term "green men" to designate these fresh-eyed proletarians, easily spotted because they are not yet habituated to their surroundings.

Like the land, the rivers are also polluted. Attaway describes the Monongahela River where it converges with the Allegheny River to form the Ohio: "[i]n back of [the Moss brothers] ran a dirty-as-a-catfish-hole river with a beautiful name: the Monongahela. Its banks were lined with mountains of red ore, yellow limestone and black coke" (43). Echoing T. S. Eliot's lament for the trashy Thames River in *The Waste Land* (1922), Attaway envisions the Monongahela under the strain of industrial waste; its beautiful, iambic Native American name serves as a distant reminder of its preindustrial past. To amplify and anthropomorphize the river's horrors, Attaway sets the riverbank as the scene of a violent sexual assault. A gang of boys, as if playing a game, rape a ten-year-old girl they call "ol' Betty": "[t]wisting and turning, a furious little figure [Betty] was dragged away to the tall weeds up the riverbank. The weeds tossed violently and then trembled for a little time" (99). While this scene typifies the naturalist novel (with people reduced to animal-like behavior by their brutal environment), it also connects ecological damage to sexual violence. Like most of the working-class immigrants in the area, Betty is probably Slavic. Her image condenses the simultaneous exploitation of a feminized immigrant workforce and a feminized nature.

It also places her on a sort of assembly line that mechanizes the sexual act itself.

Just as steel production requires violence to the landscape and rivers, so too does it maim and terrorize the steelworkers. Even though the workers operate the machines, they are still, like the land, tormented by their violence. After the brothers' initial contact with the landscape, Attaway proceeds to connect their aesthetic experience with the labor experience. Still absorbing their new environment, the brothers listen to the testimony of mill workers. Attaway structures these accounts according to the verse-chorus pattern of a work song, as the workers' attitudes collectively speak in a refrain: *"[w]hat men in their right minds would leave off tending green growing things to tend iron monsters?"* (44; emphasis in original). Individual accounts of violence on the job separate these refrains. A worker recounts how one non-English-speaking Slavic immigrant could not understand shouted warnings of an impending accident, leaving him with a "chest like a scrambled egg" (44). Another calls one machine a "skull buster," because it involves dropping an eight-ton steel ball on scrap metal, sending shrapnel flying everywhere and often wounding or even killing workers unfortunate enough to stand in its deadly path (45). One black worker, Bo, warns the brothers to be careful because the employers like to put green men on the "hot jobs before they know enough to keep alive" (52). "Hot jobs" refers to those working the Bessemer furnaces, the most dangerous jobs in the mill. These tales of machinic violence and terror reinforce the literal meaning of the novel's title: steel cannot be made without the crucial ingredient of human blood.

For the brothers, life off the job proves as potentially violent and disabling as life on the job. The division between work and home is blurred, not just because of the close proximity between housing and the mills, but also because of the seepage of industrial pollutants into the living space that this proximity enables. The accounts of polluted slums imply the interconnectedness of ecosystemic processes. The air is polluted by the massive amounts of burning coal; Chinatown complains, "[a]ll this smoke and stuff in the air! How a man gonna breathe?" (46). The workers do not care whether they work the night or day shift, for the dense smoke blocks the sunlight: "[t]hey did not like the taste of sooty air. They missed the sun" (54). The town's infrastructure is almost nonexistent: in one enclave there is only one water pump for fifty families (47); people urinate in the streets because the outhouses smell too bad (51); feral dogs and rats scurry around "Mex Town" (69); and kids toss around "kerosene-soaked balls of waste" for sport (152).

Garbage heaps are one of the novel's strongest ecological motifs: they block the makeshift dirt roads, forcing pedestrians to scramble over them; they segregate Slavic from black enclaves by imposing physical barriers. There is no system for domestic waste removal. The brothers have two significant encounters with a garbage heap, notable for their place in the narrative. The first encounter occurs when Chinatown and Melody get lost while exploring their new neighborhood. Hoping to pinpoint their position, Chinatown climbs the heap and attracts the attention of some Slavic immigrants: an "old Slav bent like a burned weed out of the window . . ."

With eyes a snow-washed blue, he looked contempt at Chinatown. Then he wrinkled his nose and spat" (49). This contempt turns to hatred near the end of the novel when the all-white union prepares to combat black strikebreakers. As Melody passes from an increasingly hostile Slavic enclave to his home, he encounters the heap again:

> He had known that the big pile of ashes and garbage would be in his path, but now it seemed to hop suddenly in front of him. He was too tired to change direction and walk around it ... He stepped into the soft stuff around the edges of the mound and struggled to the top. The brittle ashes broke under his feet ... A tin can left a burning streak across one of his ankles. (211–12)

Melody climbs the heap under the gaze of the Slavs. It is as though the boiling racial hostility is embodied in the uncanny agency of the trash heap as it "hops" in his path; the tin can that cuts his ankle appears as a weapon-like extension of the Slavic gaze. If the heap symbolizes the "waste" that Melody's life is becoming, it is a symbol that also literally embodies the racial barriers that prevent the brothers from assimilating to the union and joining the strikers.

As suggested in the Mosses' initial encounter with the industrial landscape, each brother's response to his new environment dramatizes the lived subjectivity of the steel mill ecosystem. Sickened and tormented by the relentless heat on the "hot jobs," Melody no longer feels the strength, let alone the inspiration, to play the blues: he is worn down by the strange new "rhythms of the machinery play[ing] through his body" (80). When he does have the time and energy to play, he strums "quick chords" and adopts a "strange kind of playing for him, but it was right for that new place" (62). While he does occasionally succeed in translating the rhythms of his new environment into music, this "new music" is "nothing like the blues that spread fanwise from the banks of the Mississippi" (63). While the rhythms of the steel mill work to undermine the slower tempo of country blues, twelve-hour shifts eventually leave him too tired to even play; thus Melody loses his ability to emotionally heal himself and those around him with music. Out of a subconscious impulse, Melody smashes his right hand, his " 'picking' hand," in one of the machines (127). Attaway suggests that this "accident" is intentional, as Melody is tormented by his failing blues: "[h]e had been thinking of the guitar, knowing it could never pluck away the craving that was in him ... The last three days of picking at his guitar had wearied him. Yet he knew he would not be able to let the music box alone" (128). Melody's brother Chinatown is similarly affected by work in the mills. After he is blinded by a major blast furnace explosion, Chinatown is, like Melody, emotionally defeated. Reduced to a state of helplessness, he depends on Melody and a Mexican prostitute, Anna, for constant emotional and physical consolation.

While Melody and Chinatown are physically and emotionally destroyed by their encounter with the machines, Big Mat thrives in his new environment. The classic Marxist contest of worker versus machine runs aground in Mat's perfect functioning as a steel worker. The other workers' attitudes toward the Bessemers reflect Marx's dictum about mechanized labor: "the instrument of labor, when it takes the form of a machine, immediately becomes a competitor of the worker himself" (1867: 557). When the typical new migrant first encounters the large-scale machines, his attitude is one of despair at the impossibility of his ever matching the labor-power of the machines. By contrast, Big Mat identifies more with the machines than with his fellow white workers, for they allow him to flourish in a way denied him by Jim Crow: "[i]n competition with white men, he would prove himself." While many workers faint from the heat, Big Mat "proved to be a natural hot-job man," finding his "natural" rhythm in a world of machines and performing at twice the speed of any other worker (Attaway 1941: 78). In direct contrast to Melody, Big Mat's muscles and body achieve a rhythmic coordination with the machines, expressed in metaphors of musical and natural growth: "[h]is muscles were glad to feel the growing weight of the steel. The work was nothing. Without labor his body would shrivel and be a weed. His body was happy. This was a good place for a big black man to be . . ."

Mat's muscles sang" (80). This musical metaphor, which indicates Mat's success—expressing the harmony with machines—inverts the parallel narrative of Melody's failed blues. This inversion sets the destructive potential contained within Mat's identification with the machines against the creative potential of the blues in Melody's identification with the southern soil. On this level, one can read Attaway's novel as a *bildungsroman* of a mechanized subject, of a man becoming machine and thus becoming a destroyer of the ecosystem and, eventually, himself.

As embodied in Big Mat, this link between machinic and racial violence becomes more pronounced in the novel's climactic strike scene. As the all-white union plans to strike and picket against the mill owners' brutal policies, Big Mat is deputized and hired to help suppress the white workers. In the historical 1919 strike, black deputies served a particularly useful function for the mill owners as strikebreakers and promoters of racial discord. According to the testimony of an organizer for United Mine Workers, black deputies "started a reign of terror in the town . . . Men were jostled along the street at the points of pistols, and men were struck down and shot down" (qtd. in Dickerson 1986: 91). Through Big Mat and free indirect discourse, Attaway imagines the subjective state of these black deputies. While assisting some other deputies to corner a group of strikers, Big Mat relishes the terror he inspires: "[t]he absolute terror in these people made him feel like flinging himself on their backs and dragging them to the ground with his teeth" (215). The authority that comes with being a deputy heals Big Mat's "ruptured ego," for it gives him a "sense of becoming whole again" and completes the self-realization that began with his superior performance on the hot-jobs (212). The thought of being an authority figure also fuels Big Mat's fantasies of avenging himself on whites: "[a]ll of his old hatreds came back and added flame to his feeling . . . He was the law. After all, what did right or wrong matter in the case? . . . He was a boss, a boss over whites" (196–7). With scathing irony, Big Mat's anger and resentment toward whites makes him the perfect instrument of terror, played by the very powers that oppress him. Once the strike begins and the furnaces start to cool down because there are not enough workers to keep them burning, Big Mat single-handedly tries to keep the machines functioning, as he "rush[es] madly about the yards, knowing that only his will would keep a fatal crack from their big, brittle insides" (213). This impossible effort shows the extent to which Big Mat has himself become a machine. Only as he dies, after a Slavic striker delivers a blow to his head with a pickax, does Big Mat glimpse the reality that in siding with the mill owners and in becoming a machine, he has become an agent of oppression.

Smothers and Aldo Leopold: Toward an Ecological Ethic

While Big Mat lacks the critical awareness to evaluate and challenge his immediate environment, Smothers, a relatively minor character, opens a space for ecological and ideological critique. Because of Smothers, *Blood on the Forge* in many ways exceeds the scope of essayist and environmentalist Aldo Leopold's more well-known articulation of a land ethic. The main tenets of Leopold's land ethic evolved throughout the course of the 1930s, particularly in three key published lectures, "The Conservation Ethic" (1933), "Land Pathology" (1935), and "A Biotic View of the Land" (1939). These lectures were substantially revised and sutured into "The Land Ethic," his most influential work and the final essay of his 1949 book *A Sand County Almanac*. Worster claims that the book's famous concluding essay would become "the single most concise expression of the new environmental philosophy" that emerged in the 1960s and 1970s (1977: 284). Ultimately, Smothers is a sort of Tiresian black environmentalist who anticipates the trajectory of Leopold's thought by arguing for the ethical relation between human and nonhuman. But they differ in three crucial ways. First, Attaway approaches such an ethic from the perspective of anticapitalist critique rather than conservationism, which leads to a more human-centered focus that strongly correlates worker and public health with land health. Second, the novel criticizes an entire network of productive relations that are more global in scope than is Leopold's preoccupation with certain regions in the United States. Third, Attaway's ethic is based on "feeling" or affective relations to the earth, rather than the more legalistic basis for Leopold's ethic.

Along with Thoreau and Muir, Aldo Leopold occupies a central place in ecocriticism's canon of American environmentalist writers. He worked as a forester for the United States Forest Service in New Mexico from 1909 to 1928, founded the preservationist Wilderness Society in 1924, and developed the game management profession, for which he received its first professorship at the University of Wisconsin at Madison in 1933. A theory wrung from practical experience, Leopold's land ethic received its first test run over a decade earlier in "The Conservation Ethic," a lecture delivered in 1933 and later published in the *Journal of Forestry* (Meine 1988: 302). Leopold's purpose was to seize the vanguard of the conservation movement and add philosophical teeth to its calls for land-use reform measures (Meine 1988: 303). Drawing attention to the interdependency of human and environmental history, Leopold finds it strange that "[t]here is yet no ethic dealing with man's relationships to land and to the non-human animals and plants which grow upon it. Land, like Odysseus' slave-girls, is still property" (1933: 182). He cites numerous inefficient uses of land across the American Midwest and Southwest, all showing how "unforeseen ecological reactions" can "condition, circumscribe, delimit, and warp all enterprises, both economic and cultural, that pertain to land" (1933: 185). The ethic he then proposes amounts to the extension of rational planning to nature in order to realize a vision of "controlled wild culture" (1933: 190–1). Using musical metaphors later echoed by Attaway, he calls for the "harmonious integration" of economics and aesthetics, business and culture, in a new orientation toward land that treats it as "not only a food-factory but an instrument for self-expression, on which each can play music of his own choosing" (1933: 191). By advocating a conservation ethic, Leopold aims to change minds first; politics and economics will follow.

Leopold's 1935 lecture "Land Pathology" again argues for an integrated economic–aesthetic land-use facilitated by public–private partnerships, with higher education serving as intermediary (213). Though in this essay he uses the phrase "land ethic" for the first time, "land pathology" is the central concept: "[r]egarding society and land collectively as an organism, that organism has suddenly developed pathological symptoms, i.e. self-accelerating rather than self-compensating departures from normal functioning" (1935: 217). The "machine age" is to blame for launching the "self-accelerating" destruction of the land—accelerating because temporality of the ecosystem's self-replenishing cycles is thrown out of joint. A later address delivered in 1939, "A Biotic View of the Land" shows Leopold taking up Tansley's ecosystem concept for the first time (Flader and Calicott 1991: 7). He considers organic and inorganic parts of an environment systemically organized into a "biotic pyramid" that facilitates the flow and conversion of energy. The biotic pyramid is a visualization of the ecosystem's metabolism, a structure in which land is "not merely soil; it is a fountain of energy flowing through a circuit of soils, plants, and animals" (Leopold 1939: 268). Leopold characterizes the technological interruption of this flow as "biotic violence," against which conservationists must promote a "nonviolent land use" (1939: 270).

In his final mature formulation of the land ethic in 1949, Leopold challenges profit-driven conservation, the kind promoted in Washington's *Working with the Hands* which advocates conservation on economic rather than ethical grounds. Leopold's argument depends on the premise that "the individual is a member of a community of interdependent parts" that must cooperate in order to survive (1949: 239). Human beings must participate in the "biotic community" as citizens rather than conquerors, and take individual responsibility for the "health" of the land (1949: 240). Reflecting scientific ecology's 1930s and 1940s turn toward systems theory, thermodynamics, and physics, Leopold argues that the biotic community forms an intricate and delicate "energy circuit," and human violence to this circuit has "effects more comprehensive than is intended or foreseen" (1949: 255). Though not a philosopher, Leopold basically extends a Kantian ethic to the entire field of the living, arguing that the "land"—soil, water, plants, and animals—should be treated as an end-in-itself. In ecocritical parlance, the land ethic is now understood as a form of ecocentric rather than anthropocentric thinking, one that places environmental concerns on par with human ones.

As articulated via Smothers, the ecological worldview of *Blood on the Forge* anticipates and further develops Leopold's ethical vision. Smothers gives voice to the earth's suffering, speaking as though the earth were itself an organic, living entity:

> It's wrong to tear up the ground and melt it up in the furnace. Ground don't like it. It's the hell-and-devil kind of work. Guy ain't satisfied with usin' the stuff that was put here for him to use—stuff of top of the earth. Now he got to git busy and melt up the ground itself. Ground don't like it, I tells you.

Now they'll be folks laugh when I say the ground got feelin'. But I knows
what it is I'm talkin' about. (53–4)

Sounding like a fire-and-brimstone preacher, Smothers ascribes a kind of
uncanny agency and affectivity to the "ground," suggesting that it will eventually avenge itself against humans. His protest registers a radical shift in
intensity from agricultural cultivation of the earth to the outright violence of
industrial exploitation.[3] Smothers's poetic raptures about nature could also
be an instance of the organic trope, but in this case the trope serves a purpose
beyond asserting a black nationalist identity.

Part prophecies, part philosophical meditations, Smothers's rants are,
however, neither simply romantic nor pastoral anachronisms. Smothers's
reference to the earth's "feeling" actually adds to the novel's overall, distinctly materialist understanding of the relations among worker, earth, and
machine. "Feeling" in this context cannot simply be explained as an anthropomorphism, for Smothers refrains from projecting human emotions onto
the earth. Rather, Smothers's use of the word in this context resembles Brian
Massumi's notion of "affect" (2002). Massumi draws a distinction between
emotion and affect, defining the former as a reification and humanization of
the later. "Emotions," such as anger or jealousy, can be named and brought
within the bounds of language and human experience; they are, as he says, a
"subjective content, the sociolinguistic fixing of the quality of an experience
which is from that point onward defined as personal" (2002: 28). By contrast,
"affect" refers to a pre-personal intensity, felt but never entering consciousness or getting caught in linguistic shackles (2002: 36). This means that affect
as intensity exceeds the domain of strictly human experience and arises out
of the interface between bodies, human or nonhuman (2002: 25). Because
"affect" applies to all beings, it forces us to reconceptualize the categories of
the human and the nonhuman as forming an ontological continuum, much
like Tansley's ecosystem concept.

Smothers's sense for the earth's feeling reveals his heightened, almost scientific sensitivity to the material process of steel production, a multistep process of mining, melting, and manipulating iron to produce an alloy. When
asked how he knows what the ground feels, Smothers responds: "[s]ame way
I hears bridges talk in the wind" (64). Attuned to the slightest changes in the

affectivity of steel-making, Smothers repeatedly warns his coworkers about the destructive power of the machines and is able to anticipate a blast furnace explosion. Though his coworkers think that Smothers's prophecies are only half-mad, shrill rants, Attaway goes out of his way to invest him with a "strange dignity" and characterize him as a Tiresian speaker of truth. For example, one morning Smothers warns a group of Irish and Italian workers before they start the day's work on the blast furnaces: "[e]ver'body better be on the lookout. Steel liable to git somebody today. I got a deep feelin' in my bones" (145). Initially, the workers tease Smothers, but when he recounts his own tale of getting struck by a hot steel bar, leaving him permanently disabled, laughter fades to shocked silence. Smothers's prophecy does prove true when the blast furnace explodes, leaving fourteen men dead, including himself, and Chinatown blind. His feelings prove superior to the mill's "experts," none of whom could predict the accident. As the narrator comments: "[b]ut steel workers also felt the truth of Smothers' last words: steel just had to get somebody that day. There was no conflict between what Smothers had said and the facts" (160). By granting agency to the ground, Smothers sees that biotic violence leads to violence against the worker: ecological degradation can lead to industrial accidents, understood as the land avenging itself against humans.

This ethic differs from Leopold's in that it also serves as a form of ideology critique. To use the Marxist definition operative during Attaway's lifetime, ideology consists of the structure of human experience and practices as they are refracted through the actual, material conditions of the capitalist mode of production. Ideology is the social and psychic fragmentation that structures the Moss brothers' experience; this is a level of ideology that is not even beginning to become aware of itself as a way of experiencing. In the world of *Blood on the Forge*, these actually existing material conditions can extend to the interdependent relations within the ecosystem itself. Above all, Smothers's insight into these conditions grows out of a change in his material relation to his physical environment: the steel plant where he suffered a crippling injury years before. Through the enhanced perception acquired with his disabled body, Smothers unveils the dependence of all human bodies on the external, inorganic environment—an axiom of both Marx's materialist ontology and ecosystem ecology. The disabled body, in other words, shows forth the real relation of all human bodies to what Marx calls the "second body" of nature: "[n]ature is man's *inorganic* body—nature, that is, in so far as it is not itself the human body. Man *lives* on nature—means that nature is his *body*, with which he must remain in continuous intercourse if he is not to die" (1844: 74). Smothers is able to reveal the layers of mediation that conceal the real conditions of the steel worker's existence. To suggest this mediation, he uses the terms "ground" and "steel" interchangeably, which not only establish the material consistency between the two substances, but also suggest that a land ethic is inseparable from the circulation of commodities made from the land. Steel is the ground given commodity form: mined iron is melted in the Bessemer converters, and then shaped for (in most cases) railroad tracks or structural components for skyscrapers or bridges. Stripped of mediation, steel—and the living the workers make from its manufacture—is intimately bound to the "heart of the earth": "[a]ll the time I listen real hard and git scared when the iron blast holler to git loose, an' them big redhead blooms screamin' like the very heart o' the earth caught between them rollers. It jest ain't right" (53). Smothers's intuitive "rightness," then, condemns this par-ticularly violent disruption of the material relations among interdependent parts of the ecosystem on which the capitalist mode of production, in reality, depends.

As suggested previously, the novel's ecological ethic also takes the problem of commodity fetishism in an ecological direction. Again substituting spiri-tual metaphors for a material process, Smothers speaks of a "cuss o' steel" or cursed steel (64). This "curse" suggests the material consistency obscured by the ground's transformation into the commodity form: the steel is haunted by and infused with the ground, its true origin, which now appears to take on its own agency. This agency or "curse" is distinct from the imaginary agency that commodities in the marketplace seem to have; it is literally the volatility introduced by the ground's chemical alteration, its being-toward-commodity. It refers to the ground's surplus yet substantive counter-agency produced simultaneously alongside steel's illusory agency as an exchangeable commodity used for railroad tracks, structural components, armaments, and the like. It is as though the commodity form is haunted by an earthly residue that makes itself felt unpredictably and in the future: the earth threatens to blast apart the commodity at any moment. In fact, the blast furnace explosion is itself caused by a surplus byproduct, a residue left over from the production process: "[a] shelf of hot metal had built itself high up in the faulty furnace. When that shelf had broken the force of its fall had been explosive" (160). Just as the worker's blood goes into the forge, so too does the earth's: an industrial accident is here reframed as an ecological one. More precisely, the industrial accident is an unpredictable future event that has its origin in the past violence done to the land. To memorialize Smothers, his coworkers ritually turn the steel scraps from the accident into watch fobs, which they wear around their necks for luck (168). In so doing, the workers give the steel a ritual value that escapes the logic of exchange value; these scraps open up a space for resistance, insofar as they signify the workers' communal bonding.

After the accident and Smothers's death, this critique of steel-making is extended to a critique of biotic and racial violence on a more global scale. Perhaps so as to register a shift in the workers' consciousness—with the watch fobs serving as material signifiers of that shift—the narration itself gains a heightened awareness of the connection between steel and the ground. On the narrative level, it seems that Smothers is ritually sacrificed for the sake of more direct commentary on steel production as a globally interdependent process:

> The nearness of a farmer to his farm was easily understood. But no man was close to steel. It was shipped across endless tracks to all the world. On the consignment slips were Chicago, Los Angeles, New York, rails for South America, tin for Africa, tool steel for Europe. This hard metal held up the new world ... Steel is born in the flames and sent out to live and grow old. It comes back to the flames and has a new birth. But no one man could calculate its beginning or end. It was old as the earth. It would end when the earth ended. It seemed deathless. (179–80)

This passage places steel within both the global economy and the global ecosystem. As an export, it moves from national—the three major US cities—to intercontinental distribution. Used primarily for railroad tracks and large buildings, steel literally serves as the material base for the "new" modern world. The apparent contradiction between steel's "birth" in flames and its immortality is reconciled through its analogy to the earth. Insofar as steel is converted earth, the two substances are coterminous but not the same. Steel appears to the workers as part of the earth's natural cycles, although it is the product of a historically situated mode of production. That steel only "seemed deathless" becomes clear when the strike proves effective at halting production (213).

While steel goes out into the world, the world migrates to Allegheny Valley: European immigrants and southern black migrants turn the steel mills into a miniaturized global space, a space that combines moments of misrecognition and mutual recognition. Labor flows where raw materials are extracted from the earth, producing rifts among the various races and nationalities that make workers' lives as volatile as the hot Bessemer furnaces. The collision of cultures, races, and subjectivities lead to violence analogous to biotic violence. Big Mat's slaying of a Ukrainian immigrant during the labor strike is framed as a tragically ironic, global event: "[h]e had never been in the South. He was from across the sea. His village was in the Ukraine, nestling the Carpathian mountains. From that great distance he had come to be crushed by hands that had learned hate in a place that did not exist in his experience" (231). This discontinuity between the origin of anger and its release is contrasted by the novel's final scene of mutual recognition between a blind Chinatown and a blind First World War veteran. Aboard a Pittsburgh-bound train, Melody and Chinatown sit across from the veteran: "Melody looked from the soldier to Chinatown. Two blind men facing one another, not knowing" (235). After bumming a cigarette from Chinatown, the veteran informs the brothers that before the war he was a steel worker. He claims to hear guns in the distance, "maybe a hundred miles" away, "cannon guns, bigger 'n a smokestack" (237). Whether or not the sound is actually real, to the soldier "it was like a big drum somewhere in the valley" (236). The imaginary sound seems to originate from both the steel mills and the distant European battlefields of the First World War. Again, steel manufactured for war armaments places it in a global context that also suggests a link between armed soldier and steel worker, between casualties of war and casualties of industrial accidents.

Conclusion

Attaway's narrative ultimately suggests that, under industrial capitalism, the biotic violence done to the earth is reproduced at the ideological level as racial discord, with labor serving as the mediating factor. Whether performed by animals, humans, or machines, labor is a material process that, in *Blood on the Forge*, divides the earth through the appropriation of natural resources; likewise, race divides labor through management's (e.g., Carnegie Steel's) divide-and-conquer policies of exploiting racial differences and resentments. In one of Smothers's speeches, steel appears to have the ability to affect worker subjectivity and amplify interracial conflict:

> Steel want to git you. Onliest thing—it ain't gittin' you fast enough. So there trouble in the mills. Guys wants to fight each other—callin' folks scabs and wants to knock somebody in the head. Don't no body know why. I knows why. It's 'cause steel got to git more men than it been gittin'. (53)

On one level, this passage mystifies the true causes behind worker conflict. The violence Smothers speaks of is racial violence, not the mystical power of steel on workers' emotions. Scabs are black migrants shipped in by management to break strikes, for management's policy preys on white animosity toward African-Americans. On another level, however, it suggests that biotic and racial violence are linked through acceleration—"gittin' you fast enough." If negligence contributes to the blast furnace explosion, it is a negligence that accelerates production levels at the expense of worker safety. The more production accelerates the more resources must be extracted from the ecosystem, interrupting its self-replenishing cycles, and thus contributing to the destabilization of the system. The destructive logic of the profit motive eventually unhinges the whole production process, including its material substratum (the earth).

Of all the African-American environmental writing examined in this book, Attaway's novel is by some measure the darkest and most despairing in its depiction of how overwhelming systemic forces crush the worker and the land. Yet unlike Washington's *Up from Slavery* and *Working with the Hands*, in which ecological agencies and capitalism coexist alongside each other, *Blood on the Forge* advances an ethical orientation toward the earth that critiques industrial capitalism and demands an alternative to the system itself. *Blood on the Forge* shows that ecological crisis has already occurred along the color line in places such as Allegheny County.

Conclusion

Lynched Earth: Resilience, Solidarity, and the Uses of Eco-historicism

Near the end of *Between the World and Me* (2015), Ta-Nehisi Coates links the problem of climate change to the problem of the color line. The technological revolutions of white Europeans—those whom Coates calls with cynical irony "Dreamers"—has "freed the Dreamers to plunder not just the bodies of humans but the body of the Earth itself" (2015: 150). Echoing the prophetic mode of Smothers in *Blood on the Forge*, Coates incants:

> The Earth is not our creation. It has no respect for us. It has no use for us. And its vengeance is not the fire in the cities but the fire in the sky. Something more fierce than Marcus Garvey is riding on the whirlwind. Something more awful than all our African Ancestors is rising with the seas. The two phenomena are known to each other. It was the cotton that passed through our chained hands that inaugurated this age. It is the flight from us that sent them sprawling into subdivided woods. And the methods of transport through these new subdivisions, across the sprawl, is the automobile, the noose around the neck of the earth, and ultimately, the Dreamers themselves. (2015: 150–1)

The Atlantic slave trade, cotton monocultures, the sharecropping economy, the lynching industry, and white flight from the cities to the suburbs: this history of the color line is also the history of global warming and planetary crisis. The ancient dead Africans haunt the present; it is as though the dead give rise to sea levels, returning the dredged and developed wetlands of Florida and Louisiana to the wild swamps they once were.

Coates reminds us that we cannot escape from seeing the past as a history of the present, from the perspective of our own time and place. The eco-historical vantage forces us to also consider our embeddedness in the geologic time of environmental history. The scholar cannot escape from seeing the past filtered through her own historical moment, her situatedness in time and place, geology and geography. History has utility, whether the scholar accepts this or not. We always live "in" history—history is immanent and existential, *a posteriori* and not *a priori*—and the concerns of the "now" condition the possible interpretations of the past.

In *On the Uses and Disadvantages of History for Life*, Nietzsche advances a notion of an active, critical history that calls for the scholar to "break up and dissolve a part of the past" ([1874] 1997: 76). Such a critical history is needed only by she who is "oppressed by a present need, and who wants to throw off this burden at any cost" (72). Critical history is a history for the oppressed. In *The Fire Next Time*, James Baldwin discusses the acceptance paradox of African- American history: to "accept one's past—one's history—is not the same thing as drowning in it; it is learning how to use it" (1963: 103). In a Nietzschean spirit, the paradox here is that the act of accepting the past—of affirming it and taking possession of it—is, in one and the same movement, an act of overcoming (*aufheben*, in Hegel's terms). Baldwin raises the question of this overcoming when he then asks: "how can the American Negro past be used?" (1963: 103).

It is one contention of this book that eco-historicism is a method for breaking up the past and reinventing it for the present, which is a central task for the interdisciplinary field of the environmental humanities. Those in the environmental humanities should integrate into their analyses the dual temporalities of environmental (deep time and the *longue durée*) and anthropocentric (human, social, cultural, and economic) histories. Make history plastic. Force the past to self-avail itself for the future. In breaking up the past produced by anthropocentric historicisms, I have sought a history for the present—a life-serving, politically exigent history—by assembling an archive of African-American and race-conscious environmental writing that engage, directly or indirectly, the rhetoric and politics of conservation, the natural sciences, scientific ecology, and other emergent forms of early-twentieth-century environmentalism. This project has also recontextualized African-American writing in light of environmental history, breaking up, and reinventing more anthropocentric histories. In such a way, eco-historicism provides a model on which to build for future scholarship in the environmental humanities.

In *Civil Rights and the Environment*, I have argued that problems of ecology, nature, and environments play a significant role in the development of early-twentieth-century African-American writing, including the racial uplift debates, in black periodicals such as *The Crisis*, the Harlem Renaissance, and the Great Migration narrative. Ecology, nature, and conservation were appropriated, refashioned, or discarded for the political aims of civil rights and black radicalism. This interest in nature also shows that African-American writers are more pluralist—politically and aesthetically—than most scholars indicate. In rereading modern African-American literature, I argue that writers such as Du Bois and Hurston grappled with questions about the relation of civil rights and racial uplift to nature, environment, and ecological events. The history of civil rights and environmental history are interfused, and should not be isolated from one another. There are usable histories here that can add to the intellectual and political diversity of movements for environmental, climate, and interspecies justice.

My own interpretive strategies have included rhetorical and comparative forms of textual analysis, placing African-American history in the context of environmental history, and reading for the textual eco-unconscious. At the same time, I have not confined myself to a single approach, instead adopting a number of heuristics and methods as multivariate as the writers, texts, and environments studied in this book. My goal has not been to downplay the 1980s emergence of environmental justice, but rather to expand its scope by predating the movement's issues well before the 1980s; the literature and politics of the early civil rights movement already encompassed and responded to the issues that the contemporary environmental justice movement raises.

If conservation, scientific ecology, and a general politicization of nature were already there in the work of Washington, Du Bois, and other black writers and intellectuals, then race is already also interconnected with environmental politics in the early twentieth century and even before. Though their methods and views differ, African-American writers and black intellectuals approach ecological events such as the 1927 flood disaster or the slow violence of industrialization through the prism of social exclusion and disparate impacts. Their rhetorical and interpretive strategies include setting up counter-discourses, as in the case of Du Bois and Newsome; or narrating the intersection of class, gender, race, and ecology, as in the cases of Hurston and Attaway; or revealing the workings of environmental history and ecological agencies in debates about racial advancement, as in the case of Washington.

What new visions of an eco-politics of color and a justice-oriented conservationism might come into view in the twenty-first century? An ecological perspective on civil rights can connect in newly productive ways to urgent political and scholarly problems today. Look at the variegated models in *Civil Rights and the Environment* for a black eco-politics or a civil rights-based approach to conservation and climate change that is grounded in the concepts of social, economic, climate, and interspecies justice. The civil rights and the environmental movements of today can draw on the history of this difficult marriage. An eco-historicism of twentieth-century America shows that concepts of civil rights, social justice, and environmentalism have been intertwined at least since Washington's autobiographies and possibly as far back as the abolitionist movement.[1]

With Booker T. Washington, for example, we find a layered textual engagement with southern environmental history, and the histories of the plantation form and sharecropping system. Washington's writings unconsciously give voice to ecological agencies, including a proto-sustainability that activists employ today, such as Majora Carter with her praxis of "Greening the Ghetto" (Pope et al., 2011: 516–17). The unconscious advocacy of ecological agencies in Washington's autobiographies finds echoes in the sustainable communities guided by a "New Work" philosophy in rust belt "waste places" such as Detroit.[2] The New Work movement focuses on local efforts to build sustainable communities in such "waste places" as Flint and Detroit, Michigan. What is most crucial in Washington's writings for today is the easy synthesis between economic justice and sustainability. Recall that sustainable farming or gardening practices are just one form of ecological agency: other agencies include setting up local economies that acquire some level of relative autonomy vis-à-vis global capitalism, or the assertion of dignified labor by partially withdrawing from an alienated labor market. Tapping into ecological agencies also goes much further than the neoliberal focus on consumer habits (recycling, buying eco-friendly products, etc.), without relying on an overarching twentieth-century vision of communist revolution. There is also the integrated history of sustainable practices and racial uplift discussed with regard to the Tuskegee Institute. The current ideology of sustainability, which attaches "green" and "eco" to more and more consumer products, means nothing other than the continuation of consumerism with a slightly better conscience; sustainability can regain some of its subversive power to the existing order of corporate, big agribusiness capitalism when coupled with the Tuskegee program for economic empowerment of the poor and people of color. Ecological agencies cannot be fully controlled by state apparatuses, and they can be used for either capitalist or collectivist ends.

Du Bois develops an aesthetic and political project of parallel racial integration and integrated access to the "nature" of modern spaces such as national parks and urban natural spaces. Du Bois's notion of double environments marks both the physical separation of black and white neighborhoods, and the psychological difference between white and black experiences of human-made and natural environments. Taking his notion of "second sight" into account will always already racialize any environment. Newsome promoted the coexistence of human and natural worlds; she strengthened the connection between civil rights and natural environments through an—albeit flawed—analogy between biodiversity and integrationism.[3] The histories of conservation and environmentalism remain incomplete if *The Crisis* is not included along with *Forest and Stream*, *Ecology*, and other traditionally "white" publications. In the pages of *The Crisis*, conservation has indeed been a concern of black intellectuals and writers, especially Newsome, Du Bois, and Charles Young. Hurston envisioned multiethnic ecological collectives, in which distinctions between human and nonhuman break down, suggesting solidarity not just across racial and class groups—southern black folk, migrant Bahaman laborers, and the like—but also across species. Attaway narrated a Marxian and ecosystemic analysis of the Great Migration and industrialization in the Pittsburgh region. *Blood on the Forge* implies that environmental justice and climate justice alone may not solve the global warming crisis. In *Blood on the Forge*, when Smothers affectively registers the gathering intensity of the steel, the narrator waxes sublime on its creative and destructive possibilities on a global scale: steel "was shipped across endless tracks to all the world. On the consignment slips were Chicago, Los Angeles, New York, rails for South America, tin for Africa, tool steel for Europe" (1941: 179–80). It may take a more radical and global transformation of the capitalist mode of production. That novel implies that saving the planet, saving the "ground," cannot be done without also fighting the class war and the way the class war pits races against each other. Solidarity across race, class, and gender is necessary to combat planetary destruction.

The concerns of Anne Spencer's "White Things" and Du Bois's "The Souls of White Folk," which opened this book, come full circle in 2017. The historic path of death and domination left by this modern invention of personal whiteness continues to soldier onward with the seeming force of destiny. Despair freezes the moment when decisive action against climate change is necessary but seems impossible. Stoked by anti-immigrant *ressentiment*, these anti-globalization, authoritarian nationalists in Europe (e.g., Turkey's Erdoğan) and in the United States seem to personify the death drive. It is telling that so many Trump "survival" books and websites have become available only weeks after the November 2016 election. See, for instance, Gene Stone's *The Trump Survival Guide: Everything You Need to Know About Living through What You Hoped Would Never Happen* (2017).

But survivalism, to invoke Spencer again, is a white thing. Survivalism is an individualistic persistence through despair, while resilience is a collective persistence through despair that—through the support of the group—can potentially overcome despair. Resilience depends on solidarity and thus has more potential for a leftist model of civil rights advancement and antiauthoritarian resistance. This book provides a usable past, an integrated history of civil rights and the environment, a critical history of the oppressed: it is in many ways a history of resilience and solidarity. Instead of making the connections today across the fragmented left—the Sierra Club over here, Black Lives Matter over there—we can *recover* an integrated history that can allow us to reconfigure these fragments into some kind of solidarity—a kind of historically grounded solidarity that grows out of shared oppression (to invoke the Combahee River Collective statement). The literature and politics of the early civil rights and environmentalist movements—combined with the spirit of those movements' ethos of resilience—can illuminate the darkness of our current political and existential moment. The problems of the color line and the destruction of our common home are more soldered and burning than ever.

Notes

Introduction

1   Around 1917–18, local organizers in Lynchburg, Virginia began to institutionalize a NAACP chapter, and Anne Spencer, mentored by James Weldon Johnson, helped lead the way (Greene 48). Though a NAACP activist, she was not as politically militant as some of her male contemporaries such as McKay and Hughes. The Spencers hosted a number of black intellectual and Harlem Renaissance luminaries at their 1313 Pierce Street home, using the Spencer home served as a stopover from New York and Washington DC to southern cities such as Atlanta or Nashville (Greene 66). The guest list included Paul Robeson, Roland Hayes, Walter White, Charles S. Johnson, George Washington Carver, Adam Clayton Powell, Du Bois, Hughes, Gwendolyn Brooks, and Georgia Douglas Johnson (Greene 68; Salmon 3; Frischkorn and Rainey 16).

    Though she wrote hundreds of poems, Spencer only published twenty during her lifetime, most of them during the Harlem Renaissance. She devoted her time to gardening and working as a librarian at Lynchburg's only black school, Dunbar High School (Frischkorn and Rainey 16). The twenty published poems, however, were placed in some of the most prestigious and well-known periodicals of the day, among them the widely read *The Crisis*, the National Urban League's *Opportunity*, and the sociological *Survey Graphic* (Greene 63). She also published in anthologies that came to define the Harlem Renaissance, most notably Johnson's 1922 *Book of American Negro Poetry*, Alain Locke's 1925 *The New Negro*, and Countee Cullen's 1927 *Caroling Dusk*. Her poetry could be seen as genteel and sentimental in a modernist era that rejected Victorianism and realism. But some of her poems, such as "White Things," are among the most modernist of Harlem Renaissance poets.

2   Its use of imagery and symbolism to depict the horrors of whiteness echo "The Whiteness of the Whale" chapter in Herman Melville's *Moby Dick*.

3   Jeffrey Myers's pathbreaking work *Converging Stories: Race, Ecology, and Environmental Justice in American Literature* is arguably the first book-length study to claim forcefully that black writers "drew strong connections between racial oppression and destructive attitudes toward the land" (2005: 4). Moving from Thomas Jefferson, to Hendry David Thoreau, and then to Charles Chesnutt, Myers covers a number of American writers who make connections between the

physical environment and racial struggle. While conceptually groundbreaking, the broad scope of Myers's book exemplifies the first problem; it needs more theoretical rigor and historical specificity in exploring the race-nature connection.

4 Two more recent studies continue to develop threads spooled by Outka's work. Ian Finseth's *Shades of Green: Visions of Nature in the Literature of American Slavery, 1770–1886* (2009) surveys a century of African-American nature-oriented literature, ranging from Ralph Waldo Emerson and Harriet Beecher Stowe to Martin Delaney and Frederick Douglass. He detects links between slavery and abolitionism and the advance of the natural sciences into mainstream discourse, contending that "nature" is an evolving concept in antebellum views of race and slavery. Antislavery philosophy and rhetoric, he argues, engaged natural science and developed "shifting imagistic patterns" that humanized African-descended peoples (2009: 5). This angle into discourses about nature both "liberated and constrained" antislavery thought and representation by associating nonwhites positively with nature and yet naturalizing race at the same time (2009: 7).

5 Chris Williams's *Ecology and Socialism* convincingly argues for the urgency and continued relevance of Marxist critique when capitalism's seemingly unstoppable ability to revolutionize itself batters against the material and thus ecological limits of the earth's resources. Williams portends a "global ecocide" for the twenty-first century, in which "thousands of species sit on Extinction Death Row" (2010: 1).

6 Speaking to the influence of Marxism during the interwar period of modern African-American literature, William J. Maxwell argues that the "history of African-American letters cannot be unraveled from the history of American Communism without damage to both" (1999: 2).

7 As Garrard puts it, "[o]ne of the major forms ecofeminism now takes is 'intersectional analysis,' which claims that justice for oppressed groups— originally women in ecofeminism, but now many other human identity groups are included—coincides both theoretically and in practice with environmentalist objectives" (2014: 5). Patricia Hill Collins highlights the problems surrounding the definition of intersectionality (2015). She does, however, define the term according to the "general consensus" that it refers to "critical insight that race, class, gender, sexuality, ethnicity, nation, ability, and age operate not as unitary, mutually exclusive entities, but as reciprocally constructing phenomena that in turn shape complex social inequalities" (2015: 2).

8 In some ways, I prefer the term "integrated analysis" because the rhetoric of integration was so prominent in the age of Du Bois; it has a more distinctive civil rights ring to it than "intersectional" does.

9 Applied to the context of climate change, intersectional analysis should, as prescribed by Anna Kaijser and Annica Kronsell, be concerned with "how individuals relate to climate change," which "depends on their positions in context-specific power structures based on social categorisations" (2014: 421).

Chapter 1

1 Washington biographer Louis Harlan says that Roosevelt's "amalgam of Darwinism and traditional racism allowed him … to believe that racial inferiority rather than economics, technology, politics, and culture explained the difficulties of Haiti and Liberia" (1972: 312).

2 The first autobiography, *The Story of My Life and Work* (1900), ghostwritten by the black journalist Edgar Webber, was so inadequate that Washington hired Thrasher to revise and republish it in 1901 (Norrell 2009: 216). The resulting *Up from Slavery*, then, became a revised version of Max Thrasher's revision of Webber's narrative (Norrell 2009: 217). Later, the travelogue *The Man Farthest Down* (1913) and the fourth autobiography *My Larger Education* (1911) were written in collaboration with Robert Ezra Park, who went on to head the Chicago School of Sociology.

3 This minstrel game strategy was also not lost on Du Bois. When Andrew Carnegie donated $600,000 in US Steel bonds to Tuskegee's endowment after reading *Up from Slavery*, Du Bois commented that Washington "had no faith in white people, not the slightest, and he was most popular among them, because if he was talking with a white man he sat there and found out what the white man wanted him to say, and then as soon as possible he said it" (qtd. in Harlan 1983: 134).

4 In contrast to Du Bois, Harold Cruse, who emerged from the 1960s Black Arts Movement, reframes the debates and argues that many black intellectuals, including those in the militant Black Power movement, fail to give Washington due credit. In his 1967 seminal study *The Crisis of the Negro Intellectual*, he casts Washington as an economic nationalist and Du Bois as an integrationist, although he notes that their philosophies were never as polarizing as they were later made out to be. Cruse argues that starting around 1940, Du Bois gravitated toward Washington's position: he began to focus on economic self-sufficiency as the road to full citizenship and racial integration ([1967] 2005: 176). If Du Bois's long intellectual arc bent toward the Tuskegee philosophy, then he did so "[w]ithout ever admitting that Booker T. Washington had indeed been closer to the truth in 1900" (Cruse [1967] 2005: 177). As Cruse sees it, the "problem of Afro-American nationalism is as American as are its historical roots. Its origins

are to be found in the nationalist vs. integrationist Frederick Douglass—Martin R. Delaney—Booker T. Washington—W. E. B. Du Bois conflicts down through the 1920s" ([1967] 2005: 344). Ultimately, Cruse's terms avoid the reductive binary of Washington the conservationist and Du Bois the radical by adopting the more value-neutral terms of economic nationalism versus integrationism.

In his 2009 biography *Up from History: The Life of Booker T. Washington*, Robert J. Norrell argues that Washington's diminished status as a heroic figure is the result of historical forgetting and "lost truths" (13). Norrell criticizes Harlan's earlier two-volume biography for comparing Washington "not just to Uncle Tom but also to a minotaur, an amoral and manipulative wizard, and a bargainer with the devil for momentary earthly power" (15). Focused too much on Washington's white sympathizers, critics forget just how violently southern whites were opposed to his tactics. To counter this anachronistic wisdom of hindsight, Norrell contends that Washington's "emphasis on educational, moral, and economic development became a lost artifact for most American thinking about how to integrate minorities and any other disadvantaged group in the modern world" (16).

5   In "Booker T. Washington as Pastoralist: Authenticating the Man at Century's End," Jones argues for the political and economic efficacy of Washington's valorization of pastoral life. Jones sees Washington's pastoral politics as a strategy for reconciling social antagonism by championing simplicity over complexity, or rustic southern life over northern urban life. His pastoral politics led Washington to seek racial harmony over racial equality—politics consistent with his five fingers-one hand metaphor from his Atlanta address (Jones 1999: 42). This pastoral ideal of harmony translates into a two-pronged approach to education that integrates mind and body, "head" and "hand" (Jones 1999: 43), or what Theodore Lewis calls Washington's "audacious vocationalist philosophy" (2014: 189). Though I interpret Washington through the georgic mode rather than pastoral, Jones's conclusions do offer an early ecocritical example of how Washington's value can be reassessed from this perspective.

6   Bontemps's historical novel *Black Thunder* (1936) dramatizes the failed Gabriel Prosser slave revolt in Virginia in 1800. In this case, the swamp functions much as it does in Bartram's *Travels*, as a space of resistance to the plantation zone. When the slaves launch an assault on Richmond, they do it from Brook Swamp, using a thunderstorm as cover (84–5). See the end of Chapter 4 for further discussion.

7   Walter Benjamin's statement on engaged literary activity also works as a fitting description of Washington's approach to genre: "[s]ignificant literary work can only come into being in a strict alternation between action and writing; it must nurture the inconspicuous forms that better fit its influence in active

communities than does the pretentious, universal gesture of the book—in leaflets, brochures, articles, and placards" ([1955] 1978: 61).

8 For more on blood-and-soil ideology in modern African-American political thought, see Foley (2003) and M. C. Thompson, *Black Fascisms: African American Literature and Culture between the Wars* (2007), Charlottesville: University of Virginia Press.

9 Margaret Ronda interprets the poetry of Paul Laurence Dunbar through a pessimistic georgic lens, in which labor is necessarily fruitless toil because of the sharecropping system. In contrast to my view of Washington, Ronda argues that "Dunbar's georgics reveal the material effects of the uneven modernization of racialized labor in the post-Reconstruction era" (2012: 864). She argues that Washington's 1895 Atlanta speech presents a vision in which "African American labor, in his argument, remains labor for another, the undertaking of marginal drudge work that whites refuse" (867). Washington's vision lacks the pessimism and "negative modernity" of Dunbar's. Dunbar "presents a philosophical alternative to Washington's optimistic rhetoric of capitalist progress" (870). The ambiguity of pessimism versus optimism goes back to the original Latin text of the *Georgics* and how classicists have long disputed Virgil's vision of dignified labor versus cursed toil. In his reading of the georgic mode in Sterling Brown's poetry, David Anderson argues that Brown "made the georgic central to the African-American literary tradition in his scholarship and criticism" (2015: 86). Michael Collins emphasizes how Brown's depictions of agrarian labor become occasions for a larger critique of the sharecropping system and paradoxical condition of black labor—neither free nor slave—in the post–Reconstruction South.

10 Scott Hicks likewise protests Washington's attitudes toward nature, drawing on a few passages from *Up from Slavery* and the Atlanta address: "[i]n recreation and in industry, Washington posits nature as something that must be conquered and exploited" (2006: 205). Because he advocates the domination of nature for the sake of racial uplift by economic gain, Washington "celebrates environmental degradation and exploitation past and future" (Hicks 2006: 205).

Chapter 2

1 Like *The Souls of Black Folk*, many of the essays in *Darkwater* are retooled versions of earlier publications, such as "The Souls of White Folk," originally published in a 1910 issue of *The Independent* (Lewis 2004: v).

2 Ecocritics such as Scott Hicks have already explored the numerous instances of the complex pastoral and other nature themes in *The Souls of Black Folk*. In an

extension of the complex pastoral, Anne Raine reads the book's environmental aesthetic as an "ambient poetics"—or what Du Bois himself calls an "atmosphere of the land"—of the racialized southern landscape (2013: 322–41; 1904: 129).

3   Outka describes Muir's racist rhetoric in his encounter with an African-American woman and boy while hiking through the woods: "Muir's racism comes in the way he looks, in how his language and his eye collapses dark-skinned humans into the natural landscape" (2008: 160).

4   Ecocritic Lawrence J. Oliver is wrong, then, to claim that "[t]here is no social or political subtext to the description of the Grand Canyon" (2015: 466).

5   Neither Du Bois's later autobiographies nor Lewis's biography mention such an actual trip, though it seems likely that Du Bois found time to visit these places in his life before 1919.

6   Washington had spoken to Young's soldiers while they were stationed in San Francisco prior to their work at Sequoia Park (Kilroy 2003: 54).

7   For more on urban nature writing, see *The Nature of Cities: Ecocriticism and Urban Environments* (1999), edited by M. Bennett and D. W. Teague.

Chapter 3

1   From "Life without Principle" (1863). Thoreau continues: "What is the value of any political freedom, but as a means to moral freedom? Is it a freedom to be slaves, or a freedom to be free, of which we boast?" (369). In context, Thoreau targets wage slavery more than the institution of slavery itself, though he would certainly include slavery as part of his critique of the busy-ness of "business" and its reductive work-ethic ideology.

2   Yolande is Du Bois's daughter, who was briefly married to Countee Cullen.

3   Throughout her work, Newsome mentions three nature writers, all men: John Burroughs, Dallas Lore Sharp, and Walter Prichard Eaton.

4   As Harlem Renaissance scholars have observed over the years, many of the movement's luminaries spent most of the 1920s away from Harlem: McKay split his time living in Harlem, London, Marseille, Tangiers, and other cities; Georgia Douglas Johnson lived in Washington, DC; Toomer was a perpetual wanderer as a proselytizer for the Gurdjieff movement; Spencer lived in Lynchburg, Virginia; and Wallace Thurman did not move to Harlem until 1925. Though she cites no sources, Mary B. Zeigler paints a portrait of Newsome as a mover-and-shaker: children's librarian, elementary teacher, and organizer of the Boys of Birmingham Club (1988: 128). Zeigler notes that not much can be

determined about Newsome's life because a tornado destroyed her estate in 1974 (1988: 129).

5   Scholars usually periodize the Harlem Renaissance into two distinct phases, of which Locke's change to the title of McKay's militant sonnet "The White House"—a title that could be construed as a direct threat against the president—to the less incendiary "White Houses." For Foley, the militant, masculine, and radical New Negro forged out of the Red Summer of 1919 gave way to the feminized, sanitized, cultural nationalism of Locke's *The New Negro* of 1925. Indeed, 1930s proletarian portrayals of the "failed" Harlem Renaissance depict an effete, bourgeois Talented Tenth blind to the concerns of black masses. However, Newsome's work does not seem to reflect this periodization.

6   Merchant traces a genealogy of this association in her classic study *The Death of Nature: Women, Ecology, and the Scientific Revolution* (1980).

7   Wright divides bird citizens into three groups according to migration patterns: Summer Citizens, Winter Visitors, and Citizens who stay at home (1897: 69–70).

8   "Negro Spirituals," an undated poem removed from *Gladiola Garden*, compares the singing of sparrows to slave music:

> A race was bound in chains as slaves.
>
> With freedom gone, there seemed all night.
>
> And yet it made a song and sang.
>
> In spite of all, it gave earth LIGHT.
>
> Who sang so sweetly in the night? (K. C. Smith 2004: 220)

Dunbar wrote a poem called "The Sparrow" that also offers a positive valuation of the maligned bird: "A little bird, with plumage brown, / Beside my window flutters down" (1913: ll. 1–2), and "So birds of peace and hope and love / Come fluttering earthward from above" (ll. 9–10).

9   Newsome captures the pedagogical "message" of her "springtime friends" in her "book on the out-of-doors" (1915: 90). At this time, I cannot find this book, if copies of it even exist. Newsome's "Bird Romance" continues many of the themes and style of "Birds and Manuscripts."

10 By "damoiselles," Newsome probably means damselflies, which are similar to dragonflies.

11 The caged animal trope is reminiscent of English and German romanticism. William Blake's "Auguries of Innocence" contains the lines: "A robin redbreast in a cage / Puts all heaven in a rage. / A dove-house filled with doves and pigeons / Shudders hell through all its regions" (1803: ll. 5–8). In the late German romanticism of Rainer Maria Rilke's "Der Panther," the speaker

observes a panther trapped in a zoo with a "mighty Will" that "stands paralyzed" (1907: l. 8).

Chapter 4

1 The image of the scarred earth is a trope with negative connotations that goes back to John Milton's *Paradise Lost*; it is also used in Attaway's critique of industrialization in *Blood on the Forge*.

2 Similar to Young's short story, John F. Matheus's "Swamp Moccasin" revolves around the menace of the swamp and particularly the titular snake. It brings us closer to themes in *Mules and Men* and *Their Eyes Were Watching God* with its focus on a group of twenty-three black prison laborers rather than a single fugitive. Appearing in *The Crisis* in 1926, the story takes place somewhere on Florida's Gulf Coast in the early morning. Matheus fills the story with descriptive passages of the swamp: "[t]hey saw only swamp tangles, labyrinth of long-leaved pines" (1926: 67). The prisoners are encamped in the swamp: the white "swamp boss" and guards can leave when their shift is over, but the convicts must stay. They work for an unnamed turpentine production company. Again, the swamp is menacing, but this menace is more closely aligned with the constant controlling gaze of the white guards: "Circe of the Swamp was metamorphosing them into beasts—hogs, possums, skunks, wolves. The Camp Boss, whose footsteps struck terror, whose glance petrified, who wielded force and power unchecked, was her visible agent" (1926: 68). This passage displays the fear of the swamp as a space where human/nature and human/animal boundaries break down. A water moccasin appears: "far above all in terror the pitiless, ferocious viper snake of the morasses, the swamp moccasin" (1926: 68). This time the water-moccasin is ambiguously identified with the black convict who captures the snake when it attacks one of the white guard's dogs. The convict tries to gain control of the writhing, poisonous snake. But the snake bites him quickly in the face, and the white guard panics and shoots the convict in the face, mirroring the snake's violence. The story ends ambiguously: the convict "fell heavily and as the dogs licked his blood, the Camp guards heard their boss muttering, while his face was turning purple and swelling as big as three: 'God—must be—a nigger! He looks so black'" (1926: 69). The ending is ambiguous as the snake and the black convict seem to become interchangeable both from the narrator's perspective and the white guards'.

3 Hurston's views on the southern environment were informed directly by the cultural anthropology of Franz Boas. Since the personal and intellectual influence of Boas on Hurston has been mapped out in the scholarly research,

I do not go into a detailed account here. What's notable here is that Hurston inherited a nature-culture problematic from Boas. This problematic develops out of methodological concerns, asking how nature and culture interact without confusing what is really a cultural phenomenon with a natural one. Boas famously applied this method when he conducted studies to prove that there were no biological/natural differences between races, but rather cultural differences.

4 *Mules and Men* met praise from anthropologists and mainstream book critics, particularly for its view, in Du Boisian terms, behind the Veil of black life without white presence. Sterling Brown, who covered similar ground in poetic form in his 1932 *Southern Road*, criticized the book's apparent apolitical portrayal of southern black life (Boyd 2003: 281). He took issue with the book's incompleteness, its refusal to portray head on the exploitation of black labor and the despair of poverty and deprivation in the South: "[t]hese people live in a land shadowed by squalor, poverty, disease, violence, enforced ignorance and exploitation. Even if browbeaten, they do know a smouldering resentment ... *Mules and Men* should be more bitter; it would be nearer the total truth" (qtd. in Boyd 2003: 281).

5 Tode continues: "Mexican and Negro workers only are employed in the insect ridden cypress swamps, often up to their hips in water, and must live with their families in house boats built over the swamps. Living quarters for Negro workers are 'match-box' shacks or box cars, segregated from white workers in the towns and in the camps. Negro lumber workers share the lot of all other Negro workers in the South, in that they are discriminated against in the types of jobs given them, are paid lower wages and provided inferior housing conditions and poorer schools for their children" (1931: 83–4).

Chapter 5

A version of this chapter was previously published in *Modern Fiction Studies* 55 (3) (Fall 2009): 566–95.

1 In "Work and Culture: The Evolution of Consciousness in Urban Industrial Society in the Fiction of William Attaway and Peter Abrahams," Cynthia Hamilton focuses on the novel's seeming antiurbanism, but she is primarily concerned with its lament for the decaying cultural forms that once sustained black life in the South (1987). In "Migration, Material Culture, and Identity in William Attaway's *Blood on the Forge*," Stacy I. Morgan works within a migration narrative frame when she argues that the novel shows us how "material culture serves not only to *reflect* but to *shape* the lives of poor and

working-class Americans" (2001: 715). Edward Margolies goes the furthest when he conflates Smothers's worldview with Attaway's, arguing that the novel condemns "a kind of greed that manifests itself as a violence to the land, a transgression of Nature" (1970: xiv).

2 Because of this ambiguity in the georgic mode (optimism versus pessimism), I use the terminology of pastoralism in this section to convey Attaway's generally pessimistic attitude toward country living.

3 Edward Margolies ties this view to an early-nineteenth-century romanticism, one that condemns the capitalist "greed that manifests itself as a violence to the land, a transgression of Nature" (1970: xiv). He goes on to caution that "[f]rom one point of view [Attaway's] feelings about the sanctity of nature now seem almost quaint in an age of cybernetics," though, he adds, this critique does not devalue the novel's relevance to the global environmental crisis (1970: xviii).

Conclusion

1 As Joni Adamson and Scott Slovic observe, the "roots of the environmental movement can be traced back to the abolition movement" and "many of the most successful strategies of early environmentalism were borrowed from the abolition, civil rights, and women's movements and American Indian Land Claims lawsuits" (2009: 6).

2 See http://newworknewculture.org/. See also the writings of American philosopher, Frithjof Bergmann.

3 For a discussion of the problems involved in analogizing biodiversity with cultural diversity, see Schaffner (2008).

Bibliography

Adamson, J. and S. Slovic (2009), "The Shoulders We Stand On: An Introduction to Ethnicity and Ecocriticism." *MELUS*, 34 (2): 5–24.

Aiken, C. S. (1998), *The Cotton Plantation South since the Civil War*. Baltimore: Johns Hopkins University Press.

Alaimo, S. (2010), *Bodily Natures: Science, Environment, and the Material Self.* Bloomington: Indiana University Press.

Alexander, M. (2010), *The New Jim Crow: Mass Incarceration in the Age of Colorblindness*. New York: New Press.

Allewaert, M. (2013), *Ariel's Ecology: Plantations, Personhood, and Colonialism in the American Tropics*. Minneapolis: University of Minnesota Press.

Allin, C. W. (1982), *The Politics of Wilderness Preservation*. Westport, CT: Greenwood Press.

Anderson, D. R. (2016), "Sterling Brown and the Georgic Tradition in African-American Literature." *Green Letters: Studies in Ecocriticism*, 20 (1): 86–96.

Attaway, W. ([1941] 2005), *Blood on the Forge*. New York: New York Review of Books.

Baker, H. A., Jr. (1987), *Modernism and the Harlem Renaissance*. Chicago: University of Chicago Press.

Baker, H. A., Jr. (2001), *Turning South Again: Re-Thinking Modernism / Re-Reading Booker T.* Durham: Duke University Press.

Baldwin, J. (1963), *The Fire Next Time*. New York: Random House.

Barry, J. M. (1997), *Rising Tide: The Great Mississippi Flood of 1927 and How It Changed America*. New York: Simon & Schuster.

Bartram, W. ([1791] 1928), *Travels of William Bartram*, edited by M. V. Doren. New York: Dover Publications.

Benjamin, W. ([1955] 1978), "One-Way Street," in P. Demetz (ed.), E. Jephcott (trans.), *Reflections*. New York: Schocken Books, 61–94.

Bennett, J. (2010), *Vibrant Matter: A Political Ecology of Things*. Durham: Duke University Press.

Bennett, M. and D. W. Teague (1999), "Urban Ecocriticism: An Introduction," in M. Bennett and D. W. Teague (eds.), *The Nature of Cities: Ecocriticism and Urban Environments*. Tucson: University of Arizona Press, 3–14.

Bergthaller, H., R. Emmett, A. Johns-Putra, A. Kneitz, S. Lidström, S. McCorristine, I. Pérez Ramos, D. Phillips, K. Rigby, and L. Robin (2014), "Mapping Common Ground: Ecocriticism, Environmental History, and the Environmental Humanities." *Environmental Humanities* 5: 261-76.

Bieze, M. (2008), *Booker T. Washington and the Art of Self-Representation.* New York: Peter Lang.

Bishop, R. S. (2007), *Free within Ourselves: The Development of African American Children's Literature.* Westport, CT: Greenwood Press.

Blake, W. (1803), "Auguries of Innocence." *Poets.org*, Academy of American Poets. Available online: https://www.poets.org/poetsorg/poem/auguries-innocence (accessed July 28, 2016).

Bontemps, A. (1927), "Tree." *The Crisis*, 34 (2): 48.

Bontemps, A. ([1936] 1992), *Black Thunder.* Boston: Beacon.

Boxwell, D. A. (1992), "'Sis cat' as Ethnographer: Self-Presentation and Self-Inscription in Zora Neale Hurston's *Mules and Men*." *African American Review*, 26 (4): 605–18.

Boyd, V. (2003), *Wrapped in Rainbows: The Life of Zora Neale Hurston.* New York: Scribner.

Braithwaite, W. S. (1919), "Some Contemporary Poets of the Negro Race." *The Crisis*, 17 (6): 275–80.

Braithwaite, W. S. ([1925] 1992), "The Negro in American Literature," in A. Locke (ed.), *The New Negro: Voices of the Harlem Renaissance.* New York: Simon & Schuster, 29–44.

Brinkley, D. (2009), *The Wilderness Warrior: Theodore Roosevelt and the Crusade for America.* New York: HarperCollins.

Buell, L. (2001), *Writing for an Endangered World: Literature, Culture, and Environment in the U.S. and Beyond.* Cambridge: Harvard University Press.

Buell, L. (2007), "Ecoglobalist Affects: The Emergence of U.S. Environmental Imagination on a Planetary Scale," in L. Buell and W. C. Dimock (eds.), *Shades of the Planet: American Literature as World Literature.* Princeton: Princeton University Press, 227–48.

Bullard, R. D. ([1990] 2000), *Dumping in Dixie: Race, Class, and Environmental Quality.* 3rd ed. Boulder: Westview.

Burke, K. (1937), *Attitudes toward History.* New York: New Republic.

Burroughs, J. ([1871] 1880), *Wake-Robin.* 2nd ed. Boston: Houghton, Osgood.

Carby, H. (1990), "The Politics of Fiction, Anthropology, and the Folk: Zora Neale Hurston," in M. Awkward (ed.), *New Essays on Their Eyes Were Watching God.* Cambridge: Cambridge University Press, 71–93.

Carnegie, A. ([1920] 1948), *Autobiography of Andrew Carnegie*. Boston: Houghton Mifflin.

Carson, R. ([1962] 2002), *Silent Spring*. Boston: Mariner Books.

Carver, G. W. (1987), *George Washington Carver: In His Own Words*, edited by Gary R. Kremer. Columbia: University of Missouri Press.

Casner, N. (2003), "Acid Mine Drainage and Pittsburgh's Water Quality," in J. A. Tarr (ed.), *Devastation and Renewal: An Environmental History of Pittsburgh and Its Region*. Pittsburgh: University of Pittsburgh Press, 89–109.

Coates, T. (2015), *Between the World and Me*. New York: Spiegel & Grau.

Collins, M. (1998), "Risk, Envy and Fear in Sterling Brown's 'Georgics.'" *Callaloo*, 21 (4): 950–67.

Collins, P. H. (2015), "Intersectionality's Definitional Dilemmas." *Annual Review of Sociology*, 41: 1–20.

Combahee River Collective ([1977] 1978), "A Black Feminist Statement," in Z. Eisenstein (ed.), *Capitalist Patriarchy and the Case for Socialist Feminism*. New York: Monthly Review Press, 210–18.

Commission for Racial Justice (1987), *Toxic Wastes and Race in the United States: A National Report on the Racial and Socio-economic Characteristics of Communities with Hazardous Waste Sites*. New York: United Church of Christ.

Cowdrey, A. E. (1996), *This Land, This South: An Environmental History*. Lexington: Kentucky University Press.

Crenshaw, K. (1989), "Demarginalizing the Intersection of Race and Sex: A Black Feminist Critique of Antidiscrimination Doctrine, Feminist Theory and Antiracist Politics." *The University of Chicago Legal Forum*, 140: 139–67.

Cripps, T. R. (1969), "Introduction," in T. R. Cripps (ed.), *Working with the Hands*. New York: Arno Press, i–xv.

Cruse, H. ([1967] 2005), *The Crisis of the Negro Intellectual: A Historical Analysis of the Failure of Black Leadership*. New York: New York Review of Books.

Cullen, C. (1926), "Thoughts in a Zoo." *The Crisis*, 33 (2): 78.

Cullen, C. (ed) (1927), *Caroling Dusk: An Anthology of Verse by Negro Poets*. New York: Harper & Brothers.

Cutright, P. R. (1985), *Theodore Roosevelt: The Making of a Conservationist*. Urbana: University of Illinois Press.

Dickerson, D. C. (1986), *Out of the Crucible: Black Steelworkers in Western Pennsylvania, 1875–1980*. Albany: State University of New York Press.

Dixon, M. (1987), *Ride Out the Wilderness: Geography and Identity in Afro-American Literature*. Urbana: University of Illinois Press.

Douglass, F. ([1855] 2005), *My Bondage and My Freedom*, edited by B. H. Edwards. New York: Barnes & Noble Classics.

Dorman, R. L. (2004), "Introduction," in R. L. Dorman (ed.), *The Wilderness Hunter* by Theodore Roosevelt. New York: Barnes and Noble, xiii–xx.

Du Bois, W. E. B. ([1903] 2003), *The Souls of Black Folk*. New York: Barnes & Noble Classics.

Du Bois, W. E. B. (1904), "Credo." *The Independent* (July): 787.

Du Bois, W. E. B. (1911), *The Quest of the Silver Fleece*. Chicago: A. C. McClurg, Ebook. University of Illinois Library. Accessed January 2, 2015.

Du Bois, W. E. B. (ed.) (1915a), Cover. *The Crisis*, 9 (4).

Du Bois, W. E. B. (1915b), "The Late Booker T. Washington." *The Crisis*, 11 (December): 82.

Du Bois, W. E. B. ([1920] 2004), *Darkwater: Voices from within the Veil*. New York: Washington Square Press.

Du Bois, W. E. B. ([1924] 2009), *The Gift of Black Folk: The Negroes in the Making of America*. Garden City Park, NY: Square One Publishers.

Du Bois, W. E. B. ([1925] 1997), "Worlds of Color: The Negro Mind Reaches Out," in A. Locke (ed.), *The New Negro: Voices of the Harlem Renaissance*. New York: Simon & Schuster, 385–414.

Du Bois, W. E. B. (1926), "Criteria of Negro Art," in H. L. Gates Jr. and N. Y. McKay (eds.), *The Norton Anthology of African American Literature*. 2nd ed. New York: W. W. Norton, 777–84.

Du Bois, W. E. B. (1927), "The Flood." *The Crisis*, 34 (5): 168.

Du Bois, W. E. B. ([1940] 1975), *Dusk of Dawn*. New York: Harcourt Brace.

Du Bois, W. E. B. ([1946] 2015), *The World and Africa: An Inquiry into the Part Which Africa Has Played in World History*. New York: International Publishers.

Dunbar, P. L. ([1899] 2000), "Sympathy," in Cary Nelson (ed.), *Anthology of Modern American Poetry*. New York: Oxford University Press, 39–40.

Dunbar, P. L. ([1913] 1993), *The Collected Poetry of Paul Laurence Dunbar*, edited by Joanne M. Braxton, Charlottesville: University Press of Virginia.

Eliot, T. S. ([1922] 1930), *Selected Poems*. New York: Harcourt, Brace.

Evans, M. M. (2002), "'Nature' and Environmental Justice," in J. Adamson, M. M. Evans, and R. Stein (eds.), *The Environmental Justice Reader: Politics, Poetics, and Pedagogy*. Tucson: University of Arizona Press, 181–93.

Fine, G. A. and L. Christoforides (1991), "Dirty Birds, Filthy Immigrants, and the English Sparrow War: Metaphorical Linkage in Constructing Social Problems." *Symbolic Interaction*, 14 (4): 375–93.

Finney, C. (2014), *Black Faces, White Spaces: Reimagining the Relationship of African Americans to the Great Outdoors*. Chapel Hill: University of North Carolina Press.

Finseth, I. F. (2009), *Shades of Green: Visions of Nature in the Literature of American Slavery, 1770–1860*. Athens: University of Georgia Press.

Fisher, C. (2006), "African Americans, Outdoor Recreation, and the 1919 Chicago Race Riot," in D. Glave and M. Stoll (eds.), *"To Love the Wind and Rain": African Americans and Environmental History*. Pittsburgh: University of Pittsburgh Press, 63–76.

Fisher, L. R. (2015), "Head and Hands Together: Booker T. Washington's Vocational Realism." *American Literature*, 87 (4): 709–35.

Fisher, R. ([1925] 1992), "The City of Refuge," in A. Locke (ed.), *The New Negro: Voices of the Harlem Renaissance*. New York: Simon & Schuster, 57–74.

Fiskio, J. (2012), "Unsettling Ecocriticism: Rethinking Agrarianism, Place, and Citizenship." *American Literature*, 84 (2): 301-25.

Foley, B. (2003), *Spectres of 1919: Class and Nation in the Making of the New Negro*. Urbana: University of Illinois Press.

Foster, J.B. (2000), *Marx's Ecology: Materialism and Nature*. New York: Monthly Review Press.

Freud, S. ([1920] 1961), *Beyond the Pleasure Principle*, translated by J. Strachey. New York: W. W. Norton.

Garrard, G. (2014), "Introduction," in G. Garrard (ed.), *The Oxford Handbook of Ecocriticism*. New York: Oxford University Press, 1–24.

Gates, H. L., Jr. (1988), *The Signifying Monkey: A Theory of African-American Literary Criticism*. New York: Oxford University Press.

Gifford, T. (2006), *Reconnecting with John Muir: Essays in Post-Pastoral Practice*, Athens: University of Georgia Press.

Grandison, K. I. (1996), "Landscapes of Terror: A Reading of Tuskegee's Historic Campus," in Patricia Yaeger (ed.), *The Geography of Identity*. Ann Arbor: University of Michigan Press, 334–67.

Griffin, F. J. (1995), *"Who Set You Flowin'"? The African-American Great Migration Narrative*. New York: Oxford University Press.

Grimké, A. W. ([1923] 2000), "The Black Finger," in Cary Nelson (ed.), *Anthology of Modern American Poetry*. New York: Oxford University Press, 145.

Grunwald, M. (2007), *The Swamp: The Everglades, Florida, and the Politics of Paradise*. New York: Simon & Schuster.

Grusin, R. (2004), *Culture, Technology, and the Creation of America's National Parks*. New York: Cambridge University Press.

Hamilton, C. (1987), "Work and Culture: The Evolution of Consciousness in Urban Industrial Society in the Fiction of William Attaway and Peter Abrahams." *Black American Literature Forum*, 21 (1/2): 147–63.

Harlan, L. R. (1972), *Booker T. Washington: The Making of a Black Leader, 1856–1901*. New York: Oxford University Press.

Harlan, L. R. (1983), *Booker T. Washington: The Wizard of Tuskegee, 1901–1915*. New York: Oxford University Press.

Harriot, T. ([1590] 1972), *A Briefe and True Report of the New Found Land of Virginia*. New York: Dover Publications.

Heise, U. K. (2008), *Sense of Place and Sense of Planet: The Environmental Imagination of the Global*. New York, Oxford University Press.

Heise, U. K. (2013), "Globality, Difference, and the International Turn in Ecocriticism." *PMLA*, 128 (3): 636–42.

Hicks, S. (2006), "W. E. B. Du Bois, Booker T. Washington, and Richard Wright: Toward an Ecocriticism of Color." *Callaloo*, 29 (1): 202–22.

Hicks, S. (2009), "Rethinking King Cotton: George W. Lee, Zora Neale Hurston, and Global/Local Revisions of the South and the Nation." *Arizona Quarterly*, 65 (4): 63–91.

Holdsworth, J. T. ([1912] 1976), "The Smoky City," in R. Lubove (ed.), *Pittsburgh*. New York: New Viewpoints, 83–6.

Honey, M. (ed.) (1989), *Shadowed Dreams: Women's Poetry of the Harlem Renaissance*. New Brunswick: Rutgers University Press.

Horkheimer, M. and T. W. Adorno (1944), *Dialectic of Enlightenment: Philosophical Fragments*, edited by G. S. Noerr, translated by E. Jephcott. Stanford: Stanford University Press.

Hughes, L. ([1921] 1994), "The Negro Speaks of Rivers," in A. Rampersad and David Roesell (eds.), *The Collected Poems of Langston Hughes*. New York: Vintage Books, 23.

Hughes, L. ([1925] 1992), "Earth Song," in A. Locke (ed.), *The New Negro: Voices of the Harlem Renaissance*. New York: Simon & Schuster, 142.

Hughes, L. ([1927] 1994), "Mulatto," in A. Rampersad and David Roesell (eds.), *The Collected Poems of Langston Hughes*. New York: Vintage Books, 100.

Hughes, L. and A. Bontemps (eds.) (1949), *The Poetry of the Negro 1746–1949*. Garden City: Doubleday.

Hurston, Z. N. ([1925] 1995), "Spunk," in *The Complete Stories of Zora Neale Hurston*. New York: HarperCollins, 26-32.

Hurston, Z. N. ([1934] 2008), *Jonah's Gourd Vine*. New York: HarperCollins.

Hurston, Z. N. ([1935] 2008), *Mules and Men*. New York: HarperCollins.

Hurston, Z. N. ([1937] 1990), *Their Eyes Were Watching God*.
New York: Harper & Row.

Hurston, Z. N. ([1942] 2006), *Dust Tracks on a Road: An Autobiography*.
New York: HarperCollins.

Hurt, R. D. (2003), *American Agriculture: A Brief History*. West Lafayette: Purdue
University Press.

Iovino, S. (2012), "Steps to a Material Ecocriticism: The Recent Literature about
the 'New Materialisms' and Its Implications for Ecocritical Theory." *Ecozon@*,
3 (1): 134–45.

Jacoby, K. (2001), *Crimes against Nature: Squatters, Poachers, Thieves, and
the Hidden History of American Conservation*. Berkeley: University of
California Press.

James, C. L. R. ([1938] 1963), *The Black Jacobins: Toussaint L'Ouverture and the San
Domingo Revolution*. 2nd ed. New York: Random House.

Jameson, F. (1981), *The Political Unconscious: Narrative as a Socially Symbolic Act*.
Ithaca: Cornell University Press.

Johnson, B. (1985), "Thresholds of Difference: Structures of Address in Zora
Neale Hurston," in Henry Louis Gates Jr. (ed.), *"Race," Writing, and Difference*.
Chicago: University of Chicago Press, 317–28.

Johnson, G. D. (1922), "Motherhood." *The Crisis*, 24 (6): 264.

Jones, E. W. (1999), "Booker T. Washington as Pastoralist: Authenticating the Man
at Century's End." *CLA Journal*, 43 (1): 38–53.

Kaijser, A. and A. Kronsell (2014), "Climate Change through the Lens of
Intersectionality." *Environmental Politics*, 23 (3): 417–33.

Kant, I. ([1764] 2011), *Observations on the Feeling of the Beautiful and Sublime
and Other Writings*, edited and translated by P. Frierson and P. Guyer.
Cambridge: Cambridge University Press.

Kant, I. ([1793] 2001), *Critique of Judgment*, edited by A. W. Wood, translated by
J. C. Meredith, *Basic Writings of Kant*. New York: Random House, 273–366.

Kilroy, D. P. (2003), *For Race and Country: The Life and Career of Colonel Charles
Young*. Westport, CT: Praeger.

Kingsland, S. E. (2005), *The Evolution of American Ecology, 1890–2000*.
Baltimore: Johns Hopkins University Press.

Kleppner, P. (1989), "Government, Parties, and Voters in Pittsburgh," in
S. P. Hays (ed.), *City at the Point: Essays on the Social History of Pittsburgh*.
Pittsburgh: University of Pittsburgh Press, 151–80.

Latour, B. (2004), *Politics of Nature: How to Bring the Sciences into Democracy*,
translated by Catherine Porter. Cambridge: Harvard University Press.

Leopold, A. ([1933] 1991), "A Conservation Ethic," in S. L. Flader and J. Baird (eds.), *The River of the Mother of God and Other Essays*. Callicott. Madison: University of Wisconsin Press, 181–92.

Leopold, A. ([1935] 1991), "Land Pathology," in S. L. Flader and J. Baird Callicott (eds.), *The River of the Mother of God and Other Essays*. Madison: University of Wisconsin Press, 212–17.

Leopold, A. ([1939] 1991), "A Biotic View of the Land," in S. L. Flader and J. Baird Callicott (eds.), *The River of the Mother of God and Other Essays*. Madison: University of Wisconsin Press, 266–73.

Leopold, A. ([1949/1953] 1966), *A Sand County Almanac with Essays on Conservation from Round River*. New York: Random House

Lewis, D. L. (1981), *When Harlem Was in Vogue*. New York: Oxford University Press.

Lewis, D. L. (1993), *W. E. B. Du Bois: Biography of a Race 1868–1919*. New York: Henry Holt.

Lewis, D. L. (2000), *W. E. B. Du Bois: The Fight for Equality and the American Century, 1919–1963*. New York: Henry Holt.

Lewis, D. L. (2004), "Introduction." Du Bois, *Darkwater*. 1920: v–xix.

Lewis, T. (2014), "Booker T. Washington's Audacious Vocationalist Philosophy." *Oxford Review of Education*, 40 (2): 189–205.

Linebaugh, P. and M. Rediker (2000), *The Many-Headed Hydra: Sailors, Slaves, Commoners, and the Hidden History of the Revolutionary Atlantic*. Boston: Beacon Press.

Lloyd, S. (2005), "Du Bois and the Production of the Racial Picturesque." *Public Culture*, 17 (2): 277–98.

Lorant, S. (1964), *Pittsburgh: The Story of an American City*. New York: Doubleday.

Lubove, R. (1969), *Twentieth-Century Pittsburgh: Government, Business, and Environmental Change*. New York: John Wiley.

MacCann, D. (1988), "Effie Lee Newsome: African American Poet of the 1920s." *Children's Literature Association Quarterly* (Summer): 60–5.

McDougald, E. J. ([1925] 1992), "The Task of Negro Womanhood," in A. Locke (ed.), *The New Negro: Voices of the Harlem Renaissance*. New York: Simon & Schuster, 369–82.

McGurty, E. M. (1997), "From NIMBY to Civil Rights: The Origins of the Environmental Justice Movement." *Environmental History*, 2 (3): 301–23.

Macherey, P. ([1966] 2006), *A Theory of Literary Production*, translated by G. Wall. New York: Routledge.

McKay, C. ([1916] 2004), "In Memoriam: Booker T. Washington," in W. J. Maxwell (ed.), *Complete Poems: Claude McKay*. Urbana: University of Illinois Press, 130.

McKay, C. ([1919] 2004), "If We Must Die," in W. J. Maxwell (ed.), *Complete Poems: Claude McKay*. Urbana: University of Illinois Press, 177–8.

McKay, C. (1920), *Spring in New Hampshire and Other Poems*. London: Grant Richards.

McKay, C. ([1922] 2004), "The White House," in W. J. Maxwell (ed.), *Complete Poems: Claude McKay*. Urbana: University of Illinois Press, 148–9.

McKay, C. ([1928] 1987), *Home to Harlem*. Boston: Northeastern University Press.

McKay, C. ([1934] 2004), "Cities," in W. J. Maxwell (ed.), *Complete Poems: Claude McKay*. Urbana: University of Illinois Press, 223–40.

McKay C. ([1937] 1970), *A Long Way from Home*. New York: Harcourt, Brace, & World.

Margolies, E. (1970), "Introduction," in *Blood on the Forge*. 1941. New York: Collier Books, vii–xviii.

Marks, C. (1989), *Farewell—We're Good and Gone: The Great Black Migration*. Bloomington: Indiana University Press.

Marx, K. ([1844] 2007), *Economic and Philosophic Manuscripts of 1844*, translated by Martin Milligan. Mineola: Dover Publications.

Marx, K. ([1867] 1976), *Capital*, translated by Ben Fowkes. Vol. 1. New York: Penguin.

Marx, L. ([1964] 2000), *The Machine in the Garden: Technology and the Pastoral Ideal in America*. New York: Oxford University Press.

Massumi, B. (2002), *Parables for the Virtual: Movement, Affect, Sensation*. Durham: Duke University Press.

Matheus, J. F. (1926), "Swamp Moccasin." *The Crisis*, 33 (2): 67–9.

Maxwell, William J. (1999), *New Negro, Old Left: African-American Writing and Communism between the Wars*. New York: Columbia University Press.

Mayer, Sylvia (ed) (2003), *Restoring the Connection to the Natural World: Essays on the African American Environmental Imagination*. FORECAAST (Forum for European Contributions to African American Studies), 10. Münster: LIT.

Medovoi, L. (2010), "The Biopolitical Unconscious: Toward an Eco-Marxist Literary Theory." *Mediations*, 24 (2): 122–39.

Meine, C. (1988), *Aldo Leopold: His Life and Work*. Madison: University of Wisconsin Press.

Melville, H. ([1855] 1986), *Benito Cereno*. New York: Penguin.

Merchant, C. (1980), *The Death of Nature: Women, Ecology, and the Scientific Revolution*. New York: Harper & Row.

Merchant, C. (2003), "Shades of Darkness: Race and Environmental History." *Environmental History*, 8 (3): 380–94.

Merchant, C. (2007), *American Environmental History: An Introduction*.
    New York: Columbia University Press.

Merriam, F. A. (1889), *Birds through an Opera Glass*. Cambridge: Riverside Press.

Miller, Kelly. (1903), "A Tuskegee Visit." *Tuskegee Student* 15 (August 29): 3–4.

Milton, John. ([1674] 2000), *Paradise Lost. The Norton Anthology of English
    Literature*. Gen. Ed. M. H. Abrams. Vol. 1. 7th ed. New York: W. W. Norton.
    1771–2044.

Mizelle, R. M., Jr. (2014), *Backwater Blues: The Mississippi Flood of 1927 in the
    African American Imagination*, Minneapolis: University of Minnesota Press.

Morgan, S. I. (2001), "Migration, Material Culture, and Identity in William
    Attaway's *Blood on the Forge* and Harriette Arnow's *The Dollmaker*." *College
    English*, 63 (6): 712–40.

Morton, T. (2007), *Ecology without Nature: Rethinking Environmental Aesthetics*.
    Cambridge: Harvard University Press.

Morton, T. (2013), *Hyperobjects: Philosophy and Ecology after the End of the World*.
    Minneapolis: University of Minnesota Press.

Muir, J. (1901), *Our National Parks*. New York: Houghton Mifflin.

Muir, J. (1916), *A Thousand-Mile Walk to the Gulf*, edited by William Frederic Badè.
    New York: Houghton Mifflin.

Muller, E. K. (2003), "River City," in J. A. Tarr (ed.), *Devastation and Renewal: An
    Environmental History of Pittsburgh and Its Region*. Pittsburgh: University of
    Pittsburgh Press, 41–63.

Myers, J. (2005), *Converging Stories: Race, Ecology, and Environmental Justice in
    American Literature*. Athens: University of Georgia Press.

Nasaw, D. (2006), *Andrew Carnegie*. New York: Penguin.

Nash, R. F. ([1967] 2001), *Wilderness and the American Mind*, 4th ed., New
    Haven: Yale University Press.

Newman, L. (2002), "Marxism and Ecocriticism." *ISLE: Interdisciplinary Studies in
    Literature and Environment*, 9 (2): 1–25.

Newsome, E. L. (1915), "Birds and Manuscripts." *The Crisis* (June): 89–91.

Newsome, E. L. (1918), "Morning Light: The Dew-drier." *The Crisis* 17 (1)
    (November): 17.

Newsome, E. L. (1920), "Bird Romance." *The Crisis* 19 (6) (April): 308–9.

Newsome, E. L. (1922), "The Bronze Legacy (To a Brown Boy)." *The Crisis* 24 (6)
    (October): 265.

Newsome, E. L. (1925), "March Hare." *The Crisis* 29 (5) (March): 214.

Newsome, E. L. (1926a), "A Great Prelate: Bishop Lee at Home." *The Crisis* 32 (2)
    (June): 69–71.

Newsome, E. L. (1926b), "The Little Page: Something about Birds." *The Crisis* 33 (1) (November): 25.

Newsome, E. L. (1926c), "Mariposita." *The Crisis* 32 (4) (August): 195.

Newsome, E. L. (1926d), "The Satisfied Swifts." *The Crisis* 31 (6) (April): 292.

Newsome, E. L. (1927a), "At the Pool." *The Crisis*, 33 (4) (February): 318–19.

Newsome, E. L. (1927b), "The Bird in the Cage." *The Crisis*, 33 (4) (February): 190.

Newsome, E. L. (1927c), "Bluebird." *The Crisis* 34 (2) (April): 48.

Newsome, E. L. (1927d), "The Bluebirds Are Coming." *The Crisis* 36 (2) (February): 56.

Newsome, E. L. (1927e), "Child Literature and Negro Childhood." *The Crisis* 34.8 (October): 260–82.

Newsome, E. L. (1927f), "Mattinata." *The Crisis* 34 (5) (July): 158.

Newsome, E. L. (1928), "The Little Page." *The Crisis* 35 (6) (June): 195.

Newsome, E. L. (1940), *Gladiola Garden: Poems of Outdoors and Indoors for Second Grade Readers*. Washington: Associated Publishers.

Nietzsche, F. ([1874] 1997), "On the Uses and Disadvantages of History for Life," in D. Breazeale (ed.), R. J. Hollingdale (trans.), *Untimely Meditations*. Cambridge: Cambridge University Press, 57–123.

Nixon, R. (2011), *Slow Violence and the Environmentalism of the Poor*, Cambridge: Harvard University Press.

Norrell, R. J. (2009), *Up from History: The Life of Booker T. Washington*. Cambridge: Harvard University Press.

Norwood, V. (1993), *Made from This Earth: American Women and Nature*. Chapel Hill: University of North Carolina Press.

O'Connell, J. (2003), "Charles Young and the Road through Sequoia." *The Kaweah Commonwealth Online*. August 15, 2003. http://www.kaweahcommonwealth. com/08-03/8-1features.htm

Oliver, L. J (2015), "Apocalyptic and Slow Violence: The Environmental Vision of W. E. B. Du Bois's *Darkwater*." *ISLE: Interdisciplinary Studies in Literature and Environment*, 22 (3): 466–84.

Outka, P. (2008), *Race and Nature: From Transcendentalism to the Harlem Renaissance*. New York: Palgrave Macmillan.

Park, R. E. and B. T. Washington, ([1913] 1984), *The Man Farthest Down: A Record of Observation and Study in Europe*. New York: Doubleday, Page.

Payne, J. B. (1929), *The Mississippi Valley Flood Disaster of 1927: Official Report of Relief Operations*. Washington, DC: American National Red Cross.

Phillips, D. (2003), *The Truth of Ecology: Nature, Culture, and Literature in America*. Oxford University Press.

Pinchot, G. ([1910] 1967), *The Fight for Conservation*. Seattle: University of Washington Press.

Pope, B. D., E. A. Smith, S. J. Shacks, and J. K. Hargrove (2011), "Booker T. and the New Green Collar Workforce: An Earth-Based Reassessment of the Philosophy of Booker T. Washington." *Journal of Black Studies*, 42 (4): 507–29.

Price, J. (1999), *Flight Maps: Adventures with Nature in Modern America*. New York: Basic Books.

Raine, A. (2013), "Du Bois's Ambient Poetics: Rethinking Environmental Imagination in *The Souls of Black Folk*." *Callaloo*, 36 (2): 322–41.

Rampersad, A. (1992), "Introduction," in Arna Bontemps, *Black Thunder*. (Originally published in 1936). Boston: Beacon, vii–xx.

Reed, T. V. (2002), "Toward an Environmental Justice Ecocriticism," in J. Adamson, M. M. Evans, and R. Stein (eds.), *The Environmental Justice Reader: Politics, Poetics, and Pedagogy*. Tucson: University of Arizona Press.

Rees, J. (1997), "Homestead in Context: Andrew Carnegie and the Decline of the Amalgamated Association of Iron and Steel Workers." *Pennsylvania History* 64 (3): 509–33.

Rilke, R. M. ([1907] 1980), "Der Panther," in S. Mitchell (ed. and trans.), *The Selected Poetry of Rainer Maria Rilke*. New York: Random House.

Robinson, C. J. ([1983] 2000), *Black Marxism: The Making of the Black Radical Tradition*. Chapel Hill: University of North Carolina Press.

Rodgers, L. R. (1997), *Canaan Bound: The African-American Great Migration Novel*. Urbana: University of Illinois Press.

Rogers, J. A. (1952), *Nature Knows No Color-Line: Research into the Negro Ancestry in the White Race*. 3rd ed. New York: Helga M. Rogers.

Ronda, M. (2012), "'Work and Wait Unwearying': Dunbar's Georgics." *PMLA*, 127 (4): 863–78.

Roosevelt, T. ([1893] 2004), *The Wilderness Hunter*. New York: Barnes & Noble.

Ruffin, K. N. (2010), *Black on Earth: African American Ecoliterary Traditions*. Athens: University of Georgia Press.

Schaffner, S. (2008), "A Response to Ursula Heise's 'Ecocriticism and the Transnational Turn in American Studies,'" *American Literary History*, 20 (1/2): 405–9

Schaffner, S. (2011), *Binocular Vision: The Politics of Representation in Birdwatching Field Guides*, Amherst: University of Massachusetts Press.

Sears, P. B. (1935), *Deserts on the March*. Norman: University of Oklahoma Press.

Sears, P. B. (1939), *Life and Environment: The Interrelations of Living Things*. Camden: Haddon Craftsmen.

Seymour, N. (2013), *Strange Natures: Futurity, Empathy, and the Queer Ecological Imagination*, Urbana: University of Illinois Press.

Smith, K. C. (1999), "From Bank Street to Harlem: A Conversation with Ellen Tarry." *The Lion and the Unicorn*, 23 (2): 271–85.

Smith, K. C. (2004), *Children's Literature of the Harlem Renaissance*. Bloomington: Indiana University Press.

Smith, K. K. (2005), "'What Is Africa to Me?' Wilderness in Black Thought, 1860–1930." *Environmental Ethics*, 27 (Fall): 279–97.

Smith, K. K. (2007), *African American Environmental Thought: Foundations*. Lawrence: University Press of Kansas.

Smith, R. M. (1975), "The Politics of Pittsburgh Flood Control, 1908–1936." *Pennsylvania History*, 42: 5–24.

Spivak, G. C. (1999), *A Critique of Postcolonial Reason: Toward a History of the Vanishing Present*. Cambridge: Harvard University Press.

Steward, J. H. ([1955] 1990), *Theory of Cultural Change*. Urbana: University of Illinois Press.

Stoff, M. (1972), "Claude McKay and the Cult of Primitivism," in A. Bontemps (ed.), *The Harlem Renaissance Remembered*. New York: Dodd.

Stone, G. (2017), *The Trump Survival Guide*. New York: HarperCollins.

Sundquist, E. J. (1992), *The Hammers of Creation: Folk Culture in Modern African American Fiction*. Athens: University of Georgia Press.

Sweet, T. (2002), *American Georgics: Economy and Environment in Early American Literature*, Philadelphia: University of Pennsylvania Press.

Tansley, A. G. (1935), "The Use and Abuse of Vegetational Concepts and Terms," *Ecology*, 16 (3): 318–41.

Tarr, J. A. and T. F. Yosie (2003), "Critical Decisions in Pittsburgh Water and Wastewater Treatment," in J. A. Tarr (ed.), *Devastation and Renewal: An Environmental History of Pittsburgh and Its Region*. Pittsburgh: University of Pittsburgh Press, 64–88.

Thompson, M. C. (2007), *Black Fascisms: African American Literature and Culture between the Wars*. Charlottesville: University of Virginia Press.

Thoreau, H. D. ([1863] 1962), "Life without Principle," in J. W. Krutch (ed.), *Thoreau: Walden and Other Writings*. New York: Bantam Books.

Todes, C. (1931), *Labor and Lumber*. New York: International.

Toomer, J. (1923), *Cane*. New York: Boni and Liveright.

Vadde, A. (2009), "The Backwaters Sphere: Ecological Collectivity, Cosmopolitanism, and Arundhati Roy," *MFS: Modern Fiction Studies*,

55 (3), Spec. Issue. "Modern Fiction and the Ecological: the Futures of Ecocriticism": 522–44.

Vaughan, P. H. (1975), "From Pastoralism to Industrial Antipathy in William Attaway's *Blood on the Forge*," *Phylon*, 36 (12): 422–5.

Villard, O. G. (1920), "Review of *Darkwater*." *The Nation* 110 (2865): 726–7.

Vogel, S. (1996), *Against Nature: The Concept of Nature in Critical Theory*. Albany: State University of New York Press.

Wald, A. M. (2002), *Exiles from a Future Time: The Forging of the Mid-Twentieth-Century Literary Left*. Chapel Hill: University of North Carolina Press.

Washington, B. T. ([1900] 1901), *An Autobiography of Booker T. Washington: The Story of My Life and Work*. Toronto: J. L. Nichols.

Washington, B. T. ([1901] 2003), *Up from Slavery: An Autobiography*, New York: Barnes & Noble.

Washington, B. T. ([1902] 2008), "Getting Down to Mother Earth," in *Character Building*, in *The Booker T. Washington Reader*. Radford, VA: Wilder Publications, 342–4.

Washington, B. T. ([1903] 2008), "Industrial Education for the Negro," in *Character Building*, in *The Booker T. Washington Reader*. Radford, VA: Wilder Publications, 355–60.

Washington, B. T. ([1904] 1969), *Working with the Hands*, New York: Arno Press.

Washington, B. T. ([1909] 2009), *The Story of the Negro: The Rise of the Race from Slavery*, New York: Barnes & Noble.

Washington, B. T. ([1911] 2008), *My Larger Education*, in *The Booker T. Washington Reader*. Radford, VA: Wilder Publications. 131–246.

White, W. (1927), "The Negro and the Flood," *The Nation* 22 June: 688–9.

Williams, C. (2010), *Ecology and Socialism: Solutions to Capitalist Ecological Crisis*. Chicago: Haymarket Books.

Williams, R. ([1976] 1985), *Keywords: A Vocabulary of Culture and Society*. New York: Oxford University Press.

Wilson, A. (2006), *Shadow and Shelter: The Swamp in Southern Culture*. Oxford: University of Mississippi Press.

Wirth, L. (1938), "Urbanism as a Way of Life." *American Journal of Sociology*, 44: 1–24.

Wood, G. D. (2008), "Introduction: Eco-historicism." *The Journal for Early Modern Cultural Studies*, 8 (2): 1–7.

Wood, G. D. (2011), "Leigh Hunt's New Suburbia: An Eco-historical Study in Climate Poetics and Public Health." *ISLE: Interdisciplinary Studies in Literature and Environment*, 18 (3): 527–49.

Woofter, T. J., Jr. (1928), *Negro Problems in Cities*. New York: Doubleday, Doran.

Worster, D. (1977), *Nature's Economy: The Roots of Ecology*. San Francisco: Sierra Club Books.

Worster, D. ([1979] 2004), *Dust Bowl: The Southern Plains in the 1930s*. New York: Oxford University Press.

Wright, M. O. (1895), *Birdcraft: A Field Book of Two Hundred Song, Game, and Water Birds*. New York: Macmillan.

Wright, M. O. and E. Coues ([1897] 1907), *Citizen Bird: Scenes from Bird-Life in Plain English for Beginners*. New York: Macmillan.

Wright, R. (1937), "Between Tears and Laughter," *New Masses*, 5 October: 22–3.

Wright, R. ([1941] 1988), *Twelve Million Black Voices*. New York: Thunder's Mouth Press.

Wright, R. ([1954] 2008), *Black Power: A Record of Reactions in a Land of Pathos*, in *Black Power: Three Books from Exile:* Black Power; The Color Curtain; and White Man, Listen! New York: HarperCollins, 1–427.

Young, C. (1903), "Report of the Acting Superintendent of Sequoia and General Grant National Parks, California." United States Dept. of Interior: 15 October: 3–18.

Young, N. B., Jr. (1926), "Swamp Judgment." *The Crisis*, 32 (2): 65–7.

Zeigler, M. B. (1988), "Effie Lee Newsome," in T. Harris and T. M. Davis (eds.), *Dictionary of Literary Biography*, Vol. 76: *Afro-American Writers, 1940–1955*. Detroit: Gale Research, Inc. 126–9.

Zimmerman, A. (2010), *Alabama in Africa: Booker T. Washington, the German Empire, and the Globalization of the New South*. Princeton: Princeton University Press.

Index